Tübinger Beiträge zur Anglistik   5

Herausgegeben von Joerg O. Fichte
und Hans-Werner Ludwig

Piero Boitani / Anna Torti (eds.)

Literature in Fourteenth-Century England

The J. A. W. Bennett Memorial Lectures
Perugia, 1981–1982

gn⩔ Gunter Narr Verlag Tübingen
D. S. Brewer Cambridge

Published in Great Britain by D. S. Brewer,
240 Hills Road, Cambridge
an imprint of Boydell & Brewer Ltd,
P.O. Box 9, Woodbridge, Suffolk IP 12 3DF.

Druck: Gulde-Druck GmbH, Tübingen
Printed in Germany

ISBN 3 87808 509 7 (Narr)
ISBN 0 85991 151 9 (Brewer)

Contents

Contributors

Piero Boitani	Professor of English, University of Perugia
Derek Brewer	Reader in English, University of Cambridge
Peter Dronke	Reader in Medieval Latin, University of Cambridge
Jörg O. Fichte	Professor of English, University of Tübingen
Enrico Giaccherini	Lecturer in English, University of Pisa
Douglas Gray	Professor of Medieval English Literature, University of Oxford
Bruce Harbert	English College, Rome
Agostino Lombardo	Professor of English, University of Rome
Jill Mann	Lecturer in English, University of Cambridge
John Norton-Smith	Professor of English, University of Dundee
Anthony C. Spearing	Lecturer in English, University of Cambridge
Anna Torti	Lecturer in English, University of Perugia

Of these twelve contributors, eight have been either pupils or colleagues of J.A.W. Bennett.

Preface

The idea of holding a series of lectures on Medieval and other topics in Perugia had occurred to us before Jack Bennett's death, and precisely in the spring of 1980. Our original plan was to invite eminent medievalists, in the first place from Britain, and then from other European countries, to join the staff in Perugia in a series of lectures that would cover several aspects of fourteenth-century English literature. Gradually, if the lectures were to be held over a number of years, the initial focus would be extended to include as much of European literature as possible, but references or whole papers devoted to this wider context were welcome right from the start. Here already, Peter Dronke's paper considers Latin as well as English drama, and John Norton-Smith's essay, faithful to Jack Bennett's wider interests, goes well beyond the fourteenth century.

The first person we invited as guest lecturer was Jack Bennett himself, a man to whom fourteenth-century studies owe much, who had taught one of the Editors much of what he knows in the field, with whom he had worked for years in close contact and who was one of his best friends. Much as he would have liked to come, Jack Bennett declined the invitation because he wanted to go 'home', to return to New Zealand for a period of a few months for what he thought would be the last time. It was on his way to New Zealand that he died. And the Perugia lectures became the J.A.W. Bennett Memorial Lectures.

The first series, in the winter and spring of 1981, was made possible by a collaboration — financial as well as organizational — of various bodies. The British Council in Rome, and particularly Miss Elizabeth Rylance, have been foremost in helping us not only in 1981, but in 1982 as well, and we hope they will continue to help. The Regional Council of Umbria, with Professor Roberto Abbondanza as Assessore alla Cultura, were — and are — extremely cooperative. The City of Perugia, and Professor Enzo Coli as Assessore alla Cultura, accepted our proposal with enthusiasm. The University of Perugia, and the Rector, Professor Giancarlo Dozza, sponsored our initiative. The organization of the lectures, however, would have been impossible if the staff of the English Department in our University had not worked very hard to translate into practice what was only an idea. Stefania Piccinato and Sergio Rufini, Marinella Salari, Francesca Montesperelli, Yvette Marchand, Clara Bartocci and Marina Gradoli have all made their contributions, equally important for the success of our programme.

The first series proved to be a success. So we organized a second, if shorter one, in 1982. It was while organizing this second series that the idea of publishing the J.A.W. Bennett Memorial Lectures occurred to us. Once more, we were helped by fortune and good will. The University of Perugia gave us a grant. Gunter Narr Verlag offered to publish the book. There is some gratification in having a volume of papers on English literature read at an Italian University published in Germany.

We hope to be able to have other series of lectures in the future — indeed the third is being organized as the present book goes to press — and also to publish them. It would be the best way of celebrating the memory of Jack Bennett, of furthering the study of literature, and of enjoying ourselves.

Perugia, June 1982   Piero Boitani
                                                   Anna Torti

INTRODUCTION:
AN IDEA OF FOURTEENTH-CENTURY LITERATURE*

PIERO BOITANI

The purpose of this paper is that of illustrating the scene of fourteenth-century English literary culture in its European context, and thus of anticipating some of the themes which are treated by the other essays in this collection. We are, I think, in a privileged position to do this. We can base ourselves on the work of a fourteenth-century Englishman who was himself a great poet — a part of that culture — and who seems to have been thinking a great deal about the literary context in which he wrote. And we can look at his view of that culture with a historical perspective in mind — aware of the gulf that separates him from us and at the same time of all that we have in common with him.

The poet is Chaucer and the work I will concentrate on is the *House of Fame.* In the *House of Fame* Chaucer gives us his *idea* of fourteenth-century literature — not only, though preponderantly, English, but also European. He also makes a series of decisive choices on the kind of literature — past and present — he prefers and he points, however tentatively, to the kind of literature he will write in the future. He does this obliquely, allusively, and with a good deal of puzzled humour and irony, but he does it in earnest and with an astonishing thoroughness. Moreover, Chaucer builds in the *House of Fame* his own imaginary world of myth. To the 'fables' mentioned in this poem he will remain faithful throughout his career, and some of the mythological characters evoked in the first two Books seem to represent temporary — and ironical — incarnations of the poet in search of himself.[1]

The *House of Fame* is dominated by five central images or *loci,* those of the Dream, the Temple, the Flight through Space, the Castle-Palace and the Whirling Wicker. Each of these images is, as we shall see, associated with a

---

* This is the title of my inaugural lecture for the first series of J.A.W. Bennett Memorial Lectures. A part of the paper as printed here reproduces, with many alterations and additions, section 1 of my essay, 'Chaucer's Labyrinth: Fourteenth-Century Literature and Language' as published in the *Chaucer Review,* Winter, 1983.

1 At this regard, I have read with profit both J.P. McCall, *Chaucer among the Gods* (University Park and London, 1979) and J.M. Fyler, *Chaucer and Ovid* (New Haven and London, 1979), but, as I hope the present essay will prove, my drift is different. The best reading of the poem is still J.A.W. Bennett, *Chaucer's Book of Fame* (Oxford, 1968).

particular field of literary culture. All together, they indicate a deliberately secular choice (there is no Chapel, no Monastery, no Dark Wood, no Paradise in the *House of Fame*), one that moves from order towards disorder, from static iconography to swift movement, away from Love (the absence of a Garden in the *House of Fame* is an interesting departure from convention), away from tradition (in the sense that the House of Rumour, in spite of its Ovidian features, is much less 'traditional' than the Temple of Venus). All together, they constitute an exceptional achievement of poetic imagination.

The *House of Fame* itself is a Dream — complex, full of colours and sounds, all the apparent disorder, the incongruity, the lack of conscious logical connections typical of dreams —a poem chaotic and ironical. Yet it is also clear that this December dream is a vision of the poet's literary universe — past, present and future. No reader will fail to notice the presence in the *House of Fame* of the *Aeneid* and of the writers standing on the pillars, and Chaucer's continuous mentions, quotations and adaptations from many authors. Nor is it by chance that the poem opens with a discussion on the causes of dreams. Considered as veils of a profound truth in the Middle Ages as well as today, in the course of the fourteenth century dreams became more and more metaphors for poetry, and they had come to constitute a separate literary genre.[2] Cicero's *Somnium Scipionis,* on which the poet of the *Parliament of Fowls* will muse before going to bed, is a vision of the inner meaning of the universe. The 'Pleynt of Kynde' of Alanus, which Chaucer will also recall in the *Parliament,* is a dream. Visions are scattered throughout the Bible, from that of Ezekiel to that of John in the Apocalypse. The *Roman de la Rose* — the most widely read book of the four-teenth century after the Bible — is a dream-poem: born as an 'erotic' dream, it grows larger and more complex until it becomes an encyclopedia. Shorter French poems, such as some of those written by Machaut and Froissart in the fourteenth century, are dreams. And Boccaccio's *Amorosa Visione* and Petrarch's *Trionfi* are visions. Dream-poems embrace the whole of reality, factual and imaginary.

Chaucer knew these dream-poems: he mentioned, translated and adapted them in his own works. He himself wrote dream-poems — the *Book of the Duchess,* the *Parliament of Fowls,* the Prologue to the *Legend of Good Women,* the *House of Fame* itself. He may well have been acquainted with the extraordinary book of William Langland, who was at work endlessly on the many and multistratified dreams of *Piers Plowman* — which is discussed in this volume by Bruce Harbert — in those very last decades of the century and was resident in London itself.[3] He might have known — though they

---

2 See A.C. Spearing, *Medieval Dream-Poetry* (Cambridge, 1976).
3 J.A.W. Bennett, 'Chaucer's Contemporary', now in *The Humane Medievalist and other Essays* (Rome, 1982).

belonged to a tradition with which he seems to have had little acquaintance — that dream-poems such as *Death and Life, Winner and Waster,* the *Parliament of the Three Ages* (if already in circulation) discussed themes far wider ranging than that of love — youth, middle and old age, life and death, the economic world. On the other hand, it is unlikely that he knew of a northern poet who was writing a short but ambitious dream-poem, a heavenly vision and a parable revolving around a jeweller-dreamer and a pearl-maiden set in the midst of fantastic landscapes. It is, however, certain that in the Proem to the *House of Fame* Chaucer mentions visions, revelations, dreams, *phantasmata, oracula,* dreams caused by 'reflexions', sickness, meditation, melancholy, contemplation, love, foresight — all dreams, all literature, the literature of the past, of the present, of Chaucer's country, of all Europe. Medieval man falls asleep and dreams. In his dreams, he idealizes his world creating marvellous gardens, maidens, deities, temples, heavenly cities, and he discusses it, meditating on its philosophical, religious, economic, social, and literary problems. His dreams are voyages, ascents, debates, quests for truth, explorations of his mind and of all reality. Chaucer's dream in the *House of Fame* aims at precisely this comprehensiveness.

When, at the beginning of his dream, the protagonist finds himself in a 'gothic' and strangely decorated Temple and contemplates on its walls an image of Venus, naked and floating on the sea, accompanied by Cupid and Vulcan, we realize that we are entering the ambiguous universe of Eros. Yet once more this coincides with the world of literature. Venus and her Temple, with which Chaucer authoritatively enters the mainstream of the iconographic and poetic tradition of Europe, are the inheritance of classical poetry, of Virgil, Ovid, Claudian, the descendants of the late Latin and medieval mythographers who transmitted their *ecphrases* — Fulgentius, Hyginus, the Mythographi Vaticani, Pierre Bersuire and his *Ovidius Moralizatus.* The goddess and her 'chirche' are the sons of Guido delle Colonne, Andreas Capellanus, the *Roman de la Rose,* the products of the medieval 'survival of the pagan gods' in the figurative arts and in literature.[4] It is in the fourteenth century that Venus Anadyomene reappears in Petrarch's *Africa* and in Boccaccio's *Genealogie,* whilst a Venus and a Temple identified with concupiscible appetite occupy a great deal of space in Boccaccio's *Teseida,* which Chaucer was to peruse throughout his career.[5]

---

4   See J. Seznec, *The Survival of the Pagan Gods* (Princeton, 1972). Myth survives in love poetry, both in Latin and the vernacular. See, for instance, F. Goldin, *The Mirror of Narcissus in the Courtly Love Lyric* (Ithaca, N.Y., 1967), and J.B. Friedman, *Orpheus in the Middle Ages* (Cambridge, Mass., 1970).
5   See P. Boitani, 'Chaucer's Temples of Venus', *Studi Inglesi,* II (1975), 9-31, and references therein.

14

The world of classical mythology penetrated not only the private studies of Italian poets, but also the severe theologically-minded rooms of Oxford University. The so-called 'classicizing friars' wrote voluminous commentaries on Scripture and the Fathers, inserting descriptions of pagan deities in their treatises. Waleys, Ridevall, Holcot, Lathbury used mythology to illustrate points of ethics and theology but also enjoyed with undeniable pleasure its fascinating world.[6]

Attention to the classics was not, on the other hand, due simply to inter- est in mythology. Already in the twelfth century the English 'humanist' John of Salisbury had read classical authors with great fervour. Robert Grosseteste and Roger Bacon had already recommended the study of Greek.[7] At the beginning of the fourteenth century John of Wales begins the explo- ration again, Nicholas Trevet comments on Seneca, Richard de Bury — the patron bishop of Durham, whom even Petrarch considered 'non literarum inscius'[8] — searches monastic libraries for ancient texts.[9]

Mythology and 'classicism' were not the exclusive concern of scholars. They permeated the literary production of vernacular poets and through them reached the Court and the households of aristocrats and merchants. Chaucer himself, stimulated by the Italians, exploits mythology in all his works. His great friend and colleague, Gower, uses Venus as the supreme narrative device of the *Confessio Amantis,* and his stories in the collection are very often drawn from mythology. A general yearning for classical Antiquity — that mythic Golden Age which had not been Christian but which appeared so rich, so wise, so orderly — seems to spread once again throughout Europe. Perhaps it had never really disappeared.

It is not strange, then, that Chaucer should find the story of Aeneas painted on the walls of his dream-temple. This is indeed the shrine of litera- ture and the temple of Virgil. Here, Chaucer contemplates the *Aeneid* as supreme model of art — Dante's 'alta tragedìa' — and faces the 'altissimo poeta' who was also considered a *sapiens,* a magician and a prophet.[10] Virgil saved Dante from the Dark Wood (he had, according to Dante himself, showed the true light to Statius), he will be Chaucer's 'lanterne' (*Legend of Good Women,* 926).

6 See B. Smalley, *English Friars and Antiquity in the Early Fourteenth Century* (Oxford, 1960).

7 See H. Liebeschütz, *Medieval Humanism in the Life and Writings of John of Salisbury* (Kraus Reprint, 1980), and D.A. Callus, 'Robert Grosseteste as Scholar' in D.A. Callus, ed., *Robert Grosseteste* (Oxford, 1955), pp. 36-7 and notes.

8 *Familiares,* III. i, 4-6.

9 *Philobiblon,* VIII, 20-48 (ed. A. Altamura, Naples, 1954, pp. 99-100). J.A.W. Bennett also rightly mentions Bishop William Reed as an important book collector and donator *(Chaucer at Oxford and at Cambridge,* Oxford, 1974, p. 65 ff.).

10 For Virgil in the Middle Ages see D. Comparetti, *Virgilio nel Medio Evo* (repr., Florence, 1967).

Chaucer gives us an English translation of the first lines of the *Aeneid* and then a summary which replaces the 'ordo artificialis' of the original with the 'ordo naturalis' characteristic of medieval narrative,[11] for instance of the *Roman d'Eneas*, and which concentrates on Dido's episode (as did the 'Epistle of Ovyde' the poet mentions to counterbalance 'Virgile in Eneidos'). The moment is indeed solemn for English literature: to place at the beginning of a poem a 'table of bras' inscribed with the words, 'Arma virumque cano', means pointing to an ideal and an ambition which will dominate the literary scene until the eighteenth century. Chaucer, however, operates within the existing tradition. He adapts a complex classical epic to the linear narrative of the Middle Ages[12] and to his audience's interest in the theme of love. The Middle Ages loved the labyrinthic, 'interlaced' structure of the romances.[13] Chaucer's audience might have been able to understand the initial lines of the *Aeneid* in Latin. Langland inserts Latin quotations throughout *Piers Plowman*, and Gower writes an entire poem in Latin. But Chaucer makes a precise choice for the vernacular and a straightforward type of narrative. He will be faithful to both throughout his career. Indeed the great arcades which the five Books of *Troilus* build as narrative units, the series of frescoed chambers 'de claris mulieribus' which the *Legend* is meant to complete, the clearcut division 'in partes' of some of the *Tales* — all these are witnesses of Chaucer's adoption of a 'classical' model of narrative structure. His attempts in this direction are not very different from Boccaccio's in the *Filostrato*, the *Teseida*, and in some of his late works in Latin. And the constancy with which Chaucer pursues exclusively the ends of his vernacular, discarding (unlike Gower) French and Latin, is even more extreme than Dante's passion for the 'volgare', which does not stop him from writing two major works in Latin.

In the *House of Fame*, as in his *Boece*, his *Romaunt*, his adaptations and translations from French, Latin and Italian, Chaucer shows us a fundamental aspect of his attitude as a man of letters. He is the 'grand translateur' that Deschamps praised. Once more, he is not isolated in this activity, indeed he incarnates that tendency to translate and popularize which Georges Duby has seen as the culmination of the encounter between the chivalric culture of the courts and the clerical culture of the schools which took place in fourteenth-century Europe.[14]

Significant examples of this tendency are to be found in England, and in all fields. Trevisa translates Bartholomaeus Anglicus' encyclopedia, the *De Proprietatibus Rerum*, and Higden's history, the *Polychronicon*. Mannyng

---

11   Bennett, *Chaucer's Book of Fame*, p. 29.
12   See W.W. Ryding, *Structure in Medieval Narrative* (The Hague-Paris, 1971).
13   See E. Vinaver, *The Rise of Romance* (Oxford, 1971), p. 68 ff.
14   G. Duby, *Le Temps des Cathédrales* (Paris, 1976), pp. 241-5.

translates Langtoft's *Chronicle* and adapts William of Wadington's *Manuel des Pechiez*. Others translate Jacobus de Voragine's *Legenda Aurea*, the *Travels* of a mysterious Sir John Mandeville. Still others adapt the *Seven Sages of Rome*, or French romances like Chrétien's *Yvain*. Some translate the *Mystica Theologia* of Dionysius the Areopagite (*Deonise Hid Divinite*), and offer summaries or adaptations of works by Richard of St. Victor and St. Bernard (*A Tretyse of þe Stodye of Wisdome* and *A Tretis of Discrescyon of Spirites*). Wyclif and his circle, finally, dare to begin to translate the Bible itself. And Wyclif, a famous Oxford master, is a protegé of John of Gaunt no less than Chaucer.

The Temple, in other words, can be seen as the image of a flourishing literature — linked to the classical past, even ready, to a certain extent, for its 'revival', its 'renaissance', but also prepared to popularize, to translate, to mediate, to adapt itself to new needs. The desert which surrounds the Temple is the sandy waste around Carthage in the *Aeneid*, and also the desert of Mandeville. Nor is it surprising that the eagle the dreamer sees in the sky should be derived from Dante — the greatest figure in what must have been for Chaucer the literary avant-garde of his century.

With the Flight through Space which the eagle imposes on the protagonist a new horizon opens up for the poet. This is of course a journey and it will follow the pattern of travel literature: not, however, the exotic literature of pilgrimages and travels to the East, but that of the voyage to the centre of things, where man discovers the hidden order of the universe. It will be the literature of philosophical visions: the *Cosmographia* of Bernardus Silvestris, the *Anticlaudianus* of Alanus (which Chaucer mentions in the *House of Fame*), Dante's descent and ascent through the cosmos in the *Comedy* (of which the *Inferno* is explicitly recalled and *Purgatorio* and *Paradiso* imitated). It is again significant that Geoffrey should see the Galaxy draw near and the Earth fade to a point as the 'ayerissh bestes' — clouds, rain, snow — are formed and generated. It is particularly interesting that he should see the whole 'meynee' of 'many a citezeyn' who people this region of the air. These are the *daimones* and demons of William of Conches, Alanus, Layamon, Martianus Capella, Augustine, Apuleius and 'daun Plato'. They are beings in between men and gods, linked from late Antiquity onwards to the elements (the 'ayerissh bestes'), and on the other hand, fallen angels, evil spirits. In the *De Civitate Dei* (VIII, xvi), Augustine says that Apuleius (*De Deo Socratis*) 'ait daemones esse genere *animalia,* animo passiva, mente rationalia, corpore *aeria,* tempore aeterna'. He adds that 'ad eos pertinere *divinationes* augurum, aruspicum, vatum atque *somniorum;* ab his quoque esse *miracula magorum'* (*ibid.*). Finally, he maintains that, according to the Platonists, the *daemones* 'etiam ludorum obscenitatibus et *poetarum figmentis* delectantur' (VIII, xiv).[15]

The entire fictional world of the *House of Fame* seems to have an inner coherence built by sudden, oblique references and by apparently mysterious images that partake of many dimensions. Here, philosophy and myth conjure up the universe of dreams, illusions (the magicians will appear shortly in the poem) and poetic fictions. Indeed Geoffrey compares and contrasts his dream with the visions and the flights of Croesus, Isahiah, Scipio, Nebuchadnezzar, Pharao, Enoch, Elijah, Romulus, Ganymedes, Alexander, Daedalus and Phaethon. His journey is suspended between the worlds of natural philosophy, mysticism and myth.

Once more, Chaucer appears to be an extraordinarily sensitive observer and interpreter of the general trends of English culture in the fourteenth century. After William of Ockham, who limits the field of action of theology, the two dominating tendencies in English (and not just English) philosophy and religion seem to centre precisely on 'science' on the one hand and mysticism on the other, as if philosophers felt they could no longer safely venture into the traditional realm of metaphysics.[16] It is natural philosophy that makes decisive progress in fourteenth-century England. The Merton 'scientists' – the 'barbari Britanni' despised by Petrarch and the Italian humanists[17] – work on matter and space, mechanics and dynamics, and

---

15 On the 'ayerissh bestes' see Bennett, *Chaucer's Book of Fame*, pp. 85-6. For the presence of Alanus and Bernardus in Chaucer, see P. Dronke, 'Chaucer and the Medieval Latin Poet's (Part A), in D. Brewer, ed., *Geoffrey Chaucer* (London, 1974), pp. 154-72, and in particular 161-4. Chaucer himself is not clear about the identity of the 'eyryssh bestes', which are identified with the 'many a citezeyn' in line 932 and are then seen as clouds, mists, snow, rain, winds in lines 966-7. This link between elements and *daimones* goes back at least as far as Philippus of Opus (fl. c. 350 B.C.): see Eisler, Ritter, *Historisches Wörterbuch der Philosophie* (Basel-Darmstadt, 1972), s.v. *Dämonen.* References to Layamon (*Brut,* 7874-6 in the EETS edition), Apuleius, Chalcidius and Chaucer in C.S. Lewis, *The Discarded Image* (Cambridge, 1964), pp. 2-3, 118 and *infra.* References to William of Conches, Chalcidius and Plato in P. Dronke, *Fabula* (Leiden-Köln, 1974), pp. 37, 42, 77. Martianus talks about daemonas in *De Nuptiis,* II, 152 ff. The passage in Alanus ('aerios cives') is *Anticlaudianus,* IV, 273-84 ff.; and see J.M. Fyler, *Chaucer and Ovid,* p. 50. B.G. Koonce, *Chaucer and the Tradition of Fame* (Princeton, 1966), pp. 163-4 and notes 47-48, refers to passages in Paul's Epistles and to the *Hamartigenia* of Prudentius.

16 This of course does not mean that theology is altogether abandoned. See G. Leff, *Bradwardine and the Pelagians* (Cambridge, 1957); J.A. Robson, *Wyclif and the Oxford Schools* (Cambridge, 1961); G. Leff, *The Dissolution of the Medieval Outlook* (New York, 1976).

17 E. Garin, 'La cultura fiorentina nella seconda meta del '300 e i "barbari britanni" ', *Rassegna della Letteratura Italiana,* LXIV (1960), 181-95.

elaborate a mathematical physics.[18] Swineshead, Heytesbury, Burley, Bradwardine (the scientist, theologian and archbishop whom Chaucer recalls in the *Nun's Priest's Tale*), Strode (the 'philosopher' to whom Chaucer dedicates *Troilus)* are but the best known names.[19] During the Flight the eagle significantly expounds a physics of sound, speaking by logical deduction and promising a 'preve by experience'. And 'experience', which in Chaucer's works is constantly opposed to 'authority', has played an important part in English medieval philosophy (setting the tone for future empiricism) ever since Grosseteste laid the foundations of experimental science and Bacon elaborated its theory: 'nulla scientia sine experientia'.[20]

As Derek Brewer shows in his article in this volume, Chaucer himself was interested in science (he had a good knowledge of astronomy, alchemy and medicine at least) and in popularizing it, in making it available to those who cannot read Latin like 'lyte Lowys' his son.[21] But in the *House of Fame* Chaucer refuses to listen to the eagle when he offers to launch on a lecture in astronomy and astrology even though his guide explicitly links knowledge of 'sterres names' and 'hevenes sygnes' to 'poetrie' — indeed to the poetry of classical myth and of transformation of 'bridd, fissh, best, or him or here', in short to Ovid's *Metamorphoses* (993-1010) He protests that he is too old, that he believes 'hem that write of this matere', and finally that stars are too bright here to be looked at. Though this accumulation of excuses makes for an overall comic effect, it is clear that Chaucer, whilst acquainted with the literature on the subject,[22] sets a precise limit on the kind of scientific-didactic literature that the eagle would impose on him. He will not be a Dante. But he will not be an Ovid, either.

On the other hand, Chaucer is tempted by mysticism. At one point in his Flight, he does not know whether he is there 'in body or in gost' — a phrase

---

18   See A.C. Crombie, *Augustine to Galileo* (Peregrine ed., 1969), ch. 5.
19   And see Bennett, *Chaucer at Oxford and at Cambridge,* pp. 58-85.
20   See A.C. Crombie, *Robert Grosseteste and the Origins of Experimental Science* (Oxford, 1953), ch. 7.
21   *Astrolabe,* 1-40, 50-55, 61-64. These passages represent Chaucer's most explicit statement of his choice of the vernacular. It is significant that this should be expressed at the beginning of a 'scientific' treatise, and with the admission, 'I n'am but a lewd compiler of the labour of olde astrologiens, and have it translatid in myn Englissh oonly for thy [his son Lewis'] doctrine', where Chaucer once more confirms his interest in translation. The *Equatorie of the Planetis,* if that work is to be attributed to Chaucer, would be another instance of his dedication to science.
22   It is interesting to note that Geoffrey, as if anticipating the eagle's 'preve by experience' in astronomy as well as in the physics of sound, declares that he will not look on the stars because they are too bright and that he is content to rely on 'authorial' tradition. This is the other extreme of the 'experience-authority' polarity on which I have remarked above — and a nice contrast to Galileo's future ideas and the personal, physical tribute of blindness he paid to them.

which echoes St. Paul's second Letter to the Corinthians (12: 2-4) and shows that Chaucer seems to be thinking of himself as ready for a *raptus* similar to that of the Apostle. A few lines earlier, moreover, he had quoted Boethius' 'Thought' which 'may flee so hye, With fetheres of Philosophye, To passen everych element' (*De Consolatione*, IV, m. 1). Chaucer is alluding to the two ways in which a man can try to attain a vision of God — the purely mystical one, experienced by St. Paul, and the philosophical one, which Boethius describes at the beginning of Book IV of the *Consolatio*. Nor can we exclude the possibility that Dante's beatific vision at the end of the *Paradiso* — the supreme example of how poetry can tackle such a theme, and one well known by Chaucer — is on the poet's mind at this point.[23]

Here again Chaucer is a man of his time and of his country. English poetry, too, attempts a description of the 'gostly drem' with the splendid lunar landscape and the shining Heavenly Jerusalem of *Pearl* — the poem which is the topic of Anna Torti's essay in the present book. English mysticism goes far beyond this in the fourteenth century. It shows the ways which interior spiritual discipline must follow so that the soul may gradually abandon itself to the union with God, and it does this with powerful images and a beautiful prose. Fire, song and sweetness are the three characteristics of contemplative life for Richard Rolle, the famous mystic who had been a student at Oxford, became a hermit, and wrote commentaries on the Bible and religious lyrics. The image of the cloud dominates the writings of an anonymous author who follows the theology of Dionysius the Areopagite: for him, man is suspended between the cloud of unknowing and the cloud of forgetting, between the intellect's ignorance of God and the senses' oblivion of things created. For Walter Hilton, the scale of perfection, divided into the two stages of purification 'in faith' and 'in feeling', is characterized by the 'dark night' in which the soul detaches itself from earthly things and moves towards those of the spirit. And finally, in 1373 Julian of Norwich has sixteen 'revelations', by bodily sight, by words and by 'ghostly' sight.[24]

The dreams, the visions of which Chaucer speaks in the Proem to the *House of Fame* (7-8 and 33-35) can be of this kind, too. Geoffrey, however, does not take up this opportunity. He avoids mysticism and makes once more a decidedly secular choice. The eagle invites him to 'lat be' his 'fantasye'. Geoffrey does not altogether reject philosophy and philosophical poetry. He does indeed seem to choose for himself the kind of philosophical poetry represented by Alanus and Boethius (972 and 986). Yet just at this point (985) he also mentions Martianus Capella, the poet of the nuptials

23   See P. Boitani, 'What Dante Meant to Chaucer' in P. Boitani, ed., *Chaucer and the Italian Trecento* (Cambridge, 1983).
24   On the mystics see D. Knowles, *The English Mystical Tradition* (London, 1961), and W. Riehle, *The Middle English Mystics* (London, 1981).

between Mercury and Philology, who sets in the context of a Flight to the Heavens a celebration of grammar and *literature* with all the liberal arts. The author of the *Merchant's Tale* will go back to Martianus with a splendid *reductio,* to celebrate *himself:*

> Hoold thou thy pees, thou poete Marcian,
> That writest us that ilke weddyng murie
> Of hire Philologie and hym Mercurie,
> And of the songes that the Muses songe.
> To smal is bothe thy penne, and eek thy tonge,
> For to descryven of this mariage. (1732—37)

What Chaucer has the eagle promise him at the beginning of their Flight are, on the other hand, 'tidings of love' and information about the real world, both 'fro fer contree' and from his 'verray neyghebores'. Chaucer evokes here the primary muse of his inspiration, Love, which has made him compose 'bookys, songes, dytees' and which is an endless source of literary material, of fictions and poetry (672-98). Love inspires the young Chaucer and his friend Gower, their colleagues on the Continent and the authors of countless 'courtly' or 'popular' lyrics. It is the love of Troilus and Criseyde, of Petrarch for Laura, of Usk's *Testament* — love, the literary universe *par excellence* of the Middle Ages.

At the same time Chaucer shows himself ready to look upon the world of reality. He points with self-irony to the life of a bureaucrat and passionate reader he lives and seems to pay a new attention to his neighbours and all human kind, moving away from books. We shall see where this readiness will lead him in the *House of Fame*. Meanwhile we arrive with Geoffrey and the eagle at the House itself. Significantly, this is called both 'castle' (1161) and 'palace' (1398). And indeed the great fortresses of fourteenth-century European aristocrats were both castles closed to the outside world, strongholds built to defend barons and their retinues, and manifestations of their pride and prestige, of what Georges Duby has called 'possession du monde'.[25] Inside they are palaces, the places where courts meet and entertain themselves with feasts, games, erotic and chivalric fictions. It is this kind of Castle-Palace that appears to Geoffrey — as fantastic as the castle of Bercilak in *Sir Gawain* (the poem which Enrico Giaccherini discusses in this collection) or as those which the Limbourg brothers were to illuminate for the Duke de Berry in his *Très Riches Heures*.

Around and inside his Castle-Palace Geoffrey finds heralds, coats of arms, the 'chevalrie' of Africa, Europe and Asia, the 'armes' of Alexander and Hercules, the 'olde gestes' in which medieval man delights. This world of tales ancient and 'modern' is very much a part of the culture of Chaucer

---

25 Duby, *Temps*, pp. 296-327, and particularly pp. 308-11.

himself. The story of Troy is wrought 'in the glasynge' of the room where the dreamer finds himself in the *Book of the Duchess* (326-31). In that same room, the whole *Roman de la Rose,* 'bothe text and glose', is painted on the walls (332-4). Ceyx and Alcyone, Jason and Medea, Demophon and Phyllis, Dido and Aeneas, Narcissus and 'Ecquo', Samson and Delilah, Hester, Socrates, Alcybiades, Penelope, Lucrece, Orpheus and Daedalus — all find their place in the *Book of the Duchess*. So do the 'olde gestes' of the Charlemagne romances, of 'Genelloun', 'Rowland' and 'Olyver' (1121-3). Hercules and Alexander — the latter a hero widely known in the Middle Ages and the protagonist of many romances[26] — are recalled there (1058-60) as well as in the *House of Fame*. Both will be celebrated in the *Monk's Tale* together with the Samson of the *Book of the Duchess* and the Croesus, Nebuchadnezzar and Caesar of the *House of Fame*. Dido, Hypsipyle, Medea, Phyllis and Ariadne (*House of Fame*, 397-426) will be five of the 'Good Women' whose stories are narrated in the *Legend*. Phyllis, Medea and Dido were already present in the *Book of the Duchess* (725-34). Penelope and Lucrece will be mentioned in the *Anelida* (82), and the former appears as an alternative subject of poetry in *Troilus* (V, 1777-8). Orpheus will be evoked as paragon of 'melody' in the *Merchant's Tale* (1716). Joab and Thiodomas, shortly to appear in the *House of Fame,* will be recalled in the same tale — significantly in the context of the 'mynstralcye' at a wedding feast. The story of Pluto and Proserpina, here celebrated by Claudian, will occupy a hundred lines in the *Merchant's Tale* (2219-2319), where, interestingly enough, they will be defined king and queen of 'Faerye'. Venus, the naked Anadyomene[27] of the *House of Fame*, will dominate Chaucer's fiction. Planet and goddess, courtly and conjugal love, 'holy bond of things' and sheer lust, violence and death, perennial Muse, she is at the centre of the *Complaint of Mars* and the *Parliament of Fowls*. She will haunt Palamon in the *Knight's Tale* and will help Troilus (II, 680-5) and inspire his Narrator (III, 1-49) as much as the poet of the *House of Fame* (II, 518-9). Chauntecleer in the *Nun's Priest's Tale* and Aurelius in the *Franklin's Tale* are her servants (3342-4; 937); Damyan is hurt by her 'brond' in the *Merchant's Tale* (1777); the Wife of Bath is 'al Venerien in feelynge' (604-18). Her son Cupid, the God of Love, who accompanies her here in the Temple of glass, will dictate the composition of the *Legend of Good Women*. The world of Venus which Chaucer thus enters in the *House of Fame* has no limit of space or time. From Greece to Troy, from Rome to Carthage, from Arthurian to contemporary England, Venus reigns supreme. She is indeed —

26 See G. Cary, *The Medieval Alexander* (Cambridge, 2nd ed., 1967).
27 M. Twycross, *The Medieval Anadyomene* (Oxford, 1972), and P. Boitani, 'Chaucer's Temples of Venus'.

pagan Eve — at the beginning of the imaginary world. Immersed in a lulling atmosphere, floating in the sea or lying in a dark room, this ambiguous Venus is both *voluptas* and *appetitus*, pleasure and desire — two of the basic, non-rational impulses of the human being. It is not without meaning that Venus should be the first image to appear in Chaucer's dream and that he should pray her to 'alwey save us' just before he leaves her Temple.

The *House of Fame* is the cradle of Chaucer's myth. Here, following on his own footsteps in the *Book of the Duchess,* he defines his imaginary world. The very first mythological reference in the poem, in the Invocation in Book I, is to that god of sleep whom Mercury visits in the *Book of the Duchess,* or rather in the Ovidian tale of Ceyx and Alcyone inserted within the *Book of the Duchess.* Chaucer seems to be starting his way right where he had left it in the earlier poem, and the fact that the lines which describe the dwelling of the god of sleep in the *House of Fame* (70-6) are inspired by *Metamorphoses* XI as much as their counterparts in the *Book of the Duchess* (153-65) is significant.

Chaucer's mythological universe begins to take shape in a remote world — near the land of the Cimmerians — and in a 'cave of stoon' upon the banks of Lethe. The golden age is gone. Jupiter, 'fader of delicacye', has already come into the world. Nimrod has already built the tower of Babel (*Former Age,* 56-9), and the language of men has already been confounded. The Bible and classical myth are once more coupled in the *imaginaire.* We are now in the 'derke valeye' of the *Book of the Duchess* (155). It is here, in darkness and total silence (*Met.,* XI, 601-2), away from animals and men, that Chaucer's journey through mythology starts. It will continue, later, with an invocation to the god of light in Book III, and it will end with the ever increasing noise of the houses of Fame and Rumour. Here, the imaginary is born upon the river of oblivion, a 'flood' that comes from Hell (71-2). The 'unmerie' god of sleep presides over Geoffrey's phantasy with his thousand sons. In the *Book of the Duchess,* following the Ovidian model, Morpheus had taken on the shape of Ceyx. Here, more subtly, the unnamed sons of Sleep identify with poetic inspiration itself, as the context of the Invocation suggests. The poet creates deceptive shapes — a theme which runs throughout the *House of Fame,* and which Ovid had underlined with key words in the *Metamorphoses* when he had Sleep pass by two of his sons, Icelos and Phantasos, and choose Morpheus to appear to Alcyone:

> At pater e populo natorum mille suorum
> excitat *artificem simulatoremque figurae*
> Morphea: non illo quisquam sollertius alter
> exprimit *incessus vultumque sonumque loquendi;*
> adicit et vestes et consuetissima cuique
> *verba;* sed hic solos homines *imitatur,* at alter
> fit fera, fit volucris, fit longo corpore serpens:

hunc Icelon superi, mortale Phobetora vulgus
nominat; est etiam diversae tertius artis
Phantasos: ille in humum saxumque undamque trabemque,
quaeque vacant anima, fallaciter omnia transit;
regibus hi ducibusque suos ostendere vultus
nocte solent, populos alii plebemque pererrant.   (XI, 633-45)

The themes of language and imitation which pervade the *House of Fame*[28] dominate in this passage. Sleep, dream, craft – they all counterfeit Kind (*House of Fame*, 1213). This cave of stone, remote and dark, deserted and silent, where a gloomy god lies next to a stream that comes from Hell and where his sons take on the shapes of all animate and inanimate beings of the universe – the mythological pendant of Plato's cavern – is the cradle of the imaginary and of art.[29]

Art and myth are indeed but two faces of the same thing. Like Morpheus, Geoffrey will take on many shapes 'that shall seem true form': all of them – Alexander, Phaethon, Daedalus – will bear mythological names. Furthermore, he invents in the *House of Fame* a short 'mythological' episode modelled on Ovid and parallel to Mercury's visit to Sleep in the *Book of the Duchess*. This is the visit which Fame's messenger pays to Aeolus to bid him come with his two clarions to her Palace (1567-1604). Indeed it is with this episode that the references to mythology in the *House of Fame* end – with Aeolus (Alcyone's father) holding the winds 'in distresse' in another 'cave of ston' (1584), and then flying, accompanied by Triton, to Fame's hall. Thus the image of the cave opens and closes the imaginary-mythological space of the poem.

There is no discontinuity between these 'classical' myths and their medieval counterparts. 'Chevalrie' dominates the whole world – Africa, Europe and Asia. The 'olde gestes' tell of Dido as well as of Roland and the 'bele Isawde' evoked later (1796) by Fame herself. In the *Parliament,* the stories painted on the walls of the temple of Venus will similarly cover Semyramis and Hercules, Dido and Troilus, Cleopatra and Helena, Tristram and Isolde (284-92).

The dreams of adventure and mystery which people medieval tales – studied in this volume by Jörg Fichte – are full of forests, fortuitous encounters, duels, tournaments, castles, queens, enchanted swords, the Grail, the faeries. Is it by chance that Geoffrey sees here the harpers – Orion, Chiron,

---

28   See my analyses in *English Medieval Narrative in the Thirteenth and Fourteenth Centuries* (Cambridge, 1982), 6, 1, and in 'Chaucer's Labyrinth', section II.

29   For 'moralizing' interpretations of the Ovidian passage and its significance in Chaucer, see B.F. Huppe and D.W. Robertson, *Fruyt and Chaf* (Princeton, 1963), pp. 39-40 and n. 10; and B.G. Koonce, *Chaucer and the Tradition of Fame* (Princeton, 1966), pp. 55-7.

Orpheus and 'Bret Glascurion'? There is more than one connection between the harp, Orpheus, and the Celtic substrata of English medieval culture. One of the manuscripts of *Sir Orfeo*, the beautiful, enchanted fourteenth-century poem, maintains that the Bretons used to take their harps and sing stories of adventure and above all of love.[30] *Sir Orfeo* itself is a lay and, like *Sir Launfal*, it is dominated by the world of faeries, from which Orfeo, here a minstrel and a harper, frees Heurodis.

And it is the world of the minstrels and the 'gestiours' that Geoffrey contemplates around the Castle. The 'mynstralles' who 'tellen tales Both of wepinge and of game' are the creators (perhaps), the reciters (certainly) of ballads, interludes, fabliaux. They are the 'jongleurs' who fill the halls of medieval lords and enliven their feasts, like Archambaut's in the Provençal *Flamenca*.[31] The feast for the wedding between January and May in the *Merchant's Tale* is full of just this kind of entertainment. These are the ballads of Robin Hood, of Adam Bell, of Glasgerion (Chaucer's 'Glas-curion'[32]), comic tales of foxes and wolves, of clerks and procuresses, par-odies of Parodies, of the 'Land of Cockaygne' — the interludes of that secular drama which will be examined later in this volume by Peter Dronke.

They are accompanied by music, dances, carols — 'cornemuse' and 'shalemyes', pipes, horns, trumpets. Geoffrey hears them now (1214-68), Richard II must have listened to them at Kennington, in 1377, when the Commons of London offered him a mumming show.[33] There are 'love-daunces, sprynges, Reyes' (1235-6), carols such as the famous 'Blow, northerne wynd', roundels such as the one the birds sing at the end of Chaucer's *Parliament*, 'Now welcome, somer, with they sonne softe': these are the songs and the lyrics of Douglas Gray's essay in the present book. Medieval *bergerie* appears (1223-6),[34] together with its classical ancestry, pastoral poetry and music, here represented by 'Atiteris', 'Pseustis' and 'Marcia' (1227-9).[35] There are trumpeteers, jugglers, magicians, illusionists,

---

30 MS Brit. Mus. Harley 3810, lines 1-24. See A.J. Bliss, *Sir Orfeo* (Oxford, 1954), and J.B. Friedman, *Orpheus in the Middle Ages*.

31 See P. Dronke, *The Medieval Lyric* (New York, 2nd ed., 1977), pp. 25-6.

32 See T. Percy, *Reliques of Ancient English Poetry* (London and Edinburgh, 1879), p. xxx and pp. 206-7.

33 See R.L. Greene, ed., *A Selection of English Carols* (Oxford, 1962), p. 19, and the reference there to E.K. Chambers, *The Mediaeval Stage* (Oxford, 1967 repr.), I, p. 394 and n. 4.

34 See H. Cooper, *Pastoral: Medieval into Renaissance* (Cambridge and Totowa, N.J., 1977), p. 54.

35 Whether or not 'Atiteris' corresponds to Tityrus and 'Pseustis' to the shepherd in the *Ecloga Theoduli*, it is clear that Chaucer has pastoral poetry and music in mind. For Pseustis, see P. Dronke, 'Chaucer and the Medieval Latin Poets' (Part A), p. 163. Dronke notes that in the *Ecloga* Pseustis sings of pagan myths.

witches (1259-81).[36] In short, we have here all the pre-literary, para-literary, peri-literary universe of the feast, of Carnival — Bakhtin's Carnival, Le Roy Ladurie's Winter Festival.[37]

The more specifically literary nature of Chaucer's dream, however, comes increasingly to the fore. Chaucer seems to accept with joy and without prejudice this world shared by aristocratic castle and popular market-place (interestingly, he omits any reference to the mystery plays discussed by Agostino Lombardo in this volume), and which is so distant from the Temple and its *Aeneid*. But he will soon return to literature proper. Together with the clarion players of Aragon and Catalonia, he introduces the trumpeteers of the 'great tradition': Virgil's Misenus, Statius' Thiodomas, the biblical Joab. Inside the Castle — now significantly called Palace — Chaucer assembles novel and traditional elements, to create a completely new picture. A Virgilian and apocalyptic Fame dominates the scene. Chivalry, 'olde gestes', precious decorations, gold, the *Lapidarium* surround her. The nine Muses, and in particular Calliope, the Muse of sublime poetry, sing her praises.

Chaucer is the first English poet to invoke the Muses, here in the *House of Fame*.[38] It is significant that he owes this to the example of Dante and Boccaccio, the two vernacular poets who thus act as intermediaries between him and classical tradition. And Dante and Boccaccio find their places in the poetic pantheon of the *House of Fame*, in the literary universe of fourteenth-century England. The *Inferno*, mentioned here by Chaucer (450), is on the same level as Virgil's Avernus and Claudian's Hades. Indeed the image itself of the Castle of Fame might have been inspired by Dante's Castle of Lim-

---

36 It is interesting to note that the reference to Ballenus (= Belinous) is at the same time an allusion to Hermes Trismegistus, whom the Canon's Yeoman will call 'of philosophres fader' *(Canon's Yeoman's Tale*, 1434). The *Corpus Hermeticum* and the philosophical writings of Hermes became increasingly popular in fourteenth-century England, where it appears that Bradwardine and some scholars in De Bury's circle knew them. See J. Coleman, *Piers Plowman and the Moderni* (Rome, 1981), pp. 162-70 and references therein. In the same passage of the *Canon's Yeoman's Tale* (1428) Chaucer also mentions 'Arnold of the Newe Toun', the astrologer, alchemist and physician who devoted part of his *De Improbatione Maleficiorum* to 'magik naturel'. Roger Bacon, who was himself considered a magician, was another strenuous advocate of 'magik naturel'. In the fourteenth century, Bradwardine was influenced by the pseudo-Ovidian *De Vetula*, and his own *De Causa Dei* was important for the development of western hermetism. See F. Cardini, *Magia, stregoneria, superstizioni nell'Occidente medievale* (Florence, 1979).

37 M. Bakhtin, *Rabelais and his World* (Cambridge, Mass., 1968); E. Le Roy Ladurie, *Carnival* (London, 1980), ch. 12. But see also F. Bruni, 'Modelli in contrasto e modelli settoriali nella cultura medievale', *Strumenti Critici*, XLI (1980), 1-59 and particularly 40-9.

38 See J.A.W. Bennett, 'Chaucer, Dante and Boccaccio', Accademia Nazionale dei Lincei (Rome, 1977), Quaderno Nr. 234, p. 20; now in P. Boitani, ed., *Chaucer and the Italian Trecento.*

bo.[39] Dante himself will be recalled by Chaucer's friend, Gower.[40] Boccaccio, here called 'Lollius', is celebrated with Homer and the other writers of Troy (1468). 'Laureat' Petrarch is shortly to come to the attention of the poet and of his king.[41] England is the first country to become acquainted — and through her greatest poet — with the greatest writers of Italy.

By invoking Parnassus and Helicon, the Muses and Apollo, Chaucer implicitly indicates that he considers himself the heir of the Ancients and presents his candidacy for the place of 'sesto tra cotanto senno' which Dante had been accorded by the great poets of Antiquity in his Castle of Limbo. Once more indirectly, but more explicitly than in the *House of Fame,* Chaucer will do this at the end of his greatest romance, *Troilus* (V 1791-2). Here, Geoffrey contemplates in Fame's hall the great writers of the past and their 'matters' — Josephus Flavius and seven other Jewish authors, Statius and Thebes, the writers of Troy, Virgil and Aeneas, Ovid and Love, Lucan and Rome, Claudian and Hell. Myth and history, history and poetry, truth and 'fable' are thus placed on the same level. Chaucer shows himself aware of this when, picking up a traditional medieval rumour, he humourously remarks:

> But yet I gan ful wel espie,
> Betwex hem was a litil envye.
> Oon seyde that Omer made *lyes,*
> *Feyninge in hys poetries,*
> And was to Grekes favorable;
> Therefor held he hyt but *fable.* (1475-80)

For what interests Chaucer here is not a clearly demarcated distinction between historical truth and poetic fiction but the *imaginaire* — as Georges Duby would call it — of the whole West. It is the image of himself that Western man has consecrated and transmitted in his entire literary tradition that Chaucer sees on the metal pillars of Fame's hall:[42] 'in hem' there is indeed 'hy and gret sentence' (1425). The case of Troy, whose fame is so heavy 'That for to bere hyt was no game', is emblematic. Homer is the founding father, and he is followed by Dares and Dictys, by Guido delle Colonne and Boccaccio ('Lollius'), and finally by Geoffrey of Monmouth. 'Englyssh Gaufride' has brought the Trojan cycle to Britain, where Brutus, grandson

---

39 See P. Boitani, 'What Dante Meant to Chaucer', section I.
40 *Confessio Amantis,* VII, 2329-37.
41 Through a letter of Philippe de Mézières to Richard II (1395), now published by G.W. Coopland (Liverpool, 1975), p. xxix and n. 53.
42 Interestingly enough, there is no specific mention here of Germanic or Anglo-Saxon legends (the ,Tale of Wade' is mentioned in *Troilus,* III, 614), nor of the Charlemagne chansons and romances. They could of course be comprised within the 'olde gestes' of line 1515.

of Aeneas, 'settez wyth wynne', as the *Gawain*-poet says, 'siþen þe sege and þe assaut watz sesed at Troye'. Troy (whose haunting presence is felt also in Statius' *Achilleid,* alluded to by Chaucer in lines 1462-3) survives, through Aeneas and Virgil's poem, in that Rome whose 'grete werkes' Lucan and other 'clerkes' have sung — that Rome which is New Troy like London in the fourteenth-century English *St. Erkenwald* (1. 25).[43] The shadow of Troy dominates Western imagination, as Foscolo was to realize four centuries after Chaucer: 'finché il Sole risplenderà su le sciagure umane' (*Dei Sepolcri*, 295). Chaucer himself will pay his great tribute to the Trojan cycle with his *Troilus*. In the same manner, and once more following Boccaccio, he will put in his Knight's mouth a Tale which is also an episode of the Theban cycle.

Chaucer's stroke of genius in the *House of Fame* consists in having painted such a wide and interwoven picture of literature and culture in one panel. 'Jewerye', the other great branch of Western tradition, is celebrated side by side with Troy and Rome. War, 'olde mervayles', Love and Hell are all parts of the *imaginaire.* Geoffrey himself seems to be aware of the importance of the 'great tradition' when he declares that, after admiring Ovid's copper pillar, he saw the hall itself grow higher, longer and wider than it was before (1493-6).

Chaucer's choices, however (except for 'Lollius') are not uncommon among English intellectuals of the fourteenth century, for example among people as diverse as Gower and Bishop Reed. In the *Mirour* (22129-52), for instance, the former presents 'Renomée' and 'Desfame' blowing their 'messages' 'par les paiis' with their horns. Some illustrious names — for instance those of Theocritus, Pindar, Lucretius, Sallust, who are mentioned by Richard de Bury in his *Philobiblon* (X, 35-40) — are even absent in Chaucer's list. De Bury, however, had been to Avignon, had met Petrarch there and had perhaps breathed the pre-humanistic atmosphere around him. In *his* 'House of Fame', the *Triumphus Fame* inspired by Boccaccio's *Amorosa Visione,* Petrarch is much more thorough, more precise and more historically conscious than Chaucer. We find in his garden all the heroes of Roman and Greek history and of ancient myth, all the great characters of the Old Testament, and then Arthur, Charlemagne, Godfrey of Bouillon, Saladin, even

---

43 C.D. Benson, *The History of Troy in Middle English Literature* (Cambridge and Totowa, N.J., 1980), examines only some of the Troy narratives of the English Middle Ages. P. Dronke, 'Chaucer and the Medieval Latin Poets' (Part A, II, 'Trojan Poetry and Rhetoric'), points to Chaucer's possible indebtedness to the Latin *Ilias* of Simon Chèvre d'Or for one detail in his summary of the *Aeneid* in Book I; he also agrees with R.K. Root's statement that 'the "Dares" to whom Chaucer refers ... is in fact the epic *Frigii Daretis Ylias* of Joseph of Exeter' (p. 168).

Henry of Lancaster, but above all philosophers, historians, orators, poets of that world of Greece and Rome which Petrarch and his friends wanted to recover.

Chaucer is more limited, more insular, less extreme, yet probably more representative of the average culture of his time. The *House of Fame* is the literary universe of a fourteenth-century Englishman with a rich cultural formation. These are his songs, his music, his tales; these, above all, his books. When, after a day of 'labour', of 'rekenynges', Geoffrey returns home, he sits, 'also domb as any stoon', 'at another *book*'. It is this obsessive and slightly ridiculous bibliophily (not very different from that of Richard de Bury) that the eagle's mission purports to correct, offering instead 'tidings' of the real world and of love.

To find these, Geoffrey goes down a valley under the Castle and reaches the House of Rumour. Chaucer dissolves the Temple and the Palace into the twigs, the holes, the sounds of this gigantic Whirling Wicker. He himself declares that it is made more 'wonderlych' and 'queyntelych' than the House of Daedalus, the original Labyrinth. Here at last literature as such is not present. The *House of Fame* has its own way of de-composing a work of literature. This appears as a comprehensive, unitary 'opus' in the *Aeneid* of the first Book. It becomes fragmented in the great 'matters', the cycles and their individual authors of the second Book. In the third, it is atomized into the many 'tidings' which fill the House of Rumour and which are spoken or carried around by messengers, pardoners, shipmen and pilgrims.

It will eventually be Geoffrey's task to put these very messengers, pardoners, shipmen and pilgrims on the way from the Tabard Inn to Becket's tomb, to make them tell their 'tidings', their tales, in short to write a book of stories told orally — the *Canterbury Tales*. Thus the image, the intuition of a re-composed 'opus' which will include oral and written, reality and fiction, 'ernest' and 'game' begins to take shape behind the Whirling Wicker of the *House of Fame*. This design which we can only see *a posteriori* will not, significantly, be fully realized. Like the *House of Fame,* the *Canterbury Tales* will remain incomplete. Yet they will authoritatively take their special place in the panorama of fourteenth-century English literature. It is in this context that they will be examined in the present collection by Jill Mann and A.C. Spearing.

Aeolus blows away all ancient and medieval fables. After his appearance, myths vanish from the *House of Fame,* and only one image slowly takes shape and then dominates the poem — that of the Labyrinth. Geoffrey has compared and contrasted himself with Isahiah, Scipio, Nebuchadnezzar, Pharao, Enoch, Elijah, Romulus, Ganymedes, Alexander, Phaethon and Daedalus. The latter seems to be his incarnation in the last section of the poem.[44]

---

44   See P. Boitani, 'Chaucer's Labyrinth', section II.

Thus Morpheus and Daedalus cast their shadows on the *House of Fame*, one at the beginning and one at the end — both *artifices*, both *simulatores figurarum*. It is not without significance that the Castle of Fame should be surrounded by

> . . . clerkes eke, which konne wel
> Al this magik naturel,
> That craftely doon her ententes
> To make, in certeyn ascendentes,
> *Ymages*, lo, thrugh which magik
> To make a man ben hool or syk. (1265-70)

These — from the mythological Medea, Circe and Calypso to the biblical Simon Magus and Limote (= Elymas?), to Hermes Trismegistus' disciple Belinous, to the contemporary Colle — are some of the agents of Fame: 'by such *art* don men han fame' (1276). We should not be surprised if Chaucer, after invoking Sleep and God in Book I, Venus and the Muses in Book II, asks in Book III for the help of Apollo, god of *knowledge, wisdom and light* (1091), oracle of prophecy. For in the maddening, confusing vision of Fame and Rumour Geoffrey will need clarity, measure, a definitive answer. But, as Heraclitus said,[45] 'the Lord whose oracle is in Delphi does not either say or hide — he signifies'. And this is the kind of answer Chaucer receives in the *House of Fame*.

Geoffrey identifies in turn with Ovid, Virgil, Dante, Paul and Old Testament prophets, Boethius, Alanus and Martianus Capella; with the countless artists — minstrels, harpers, shepherds, magicians — who surround the Palace; and with the great authors who fill the hall of Fame. Each of these identities is only a fleeting incarnation and is soon discarded. Finally, just before the protagonist enters the House of Rumour, authors and mythological characters disappear. Geoffrey faces the oracle — his own consideration of himself as a poet:

> Sufficeth me, as I were ded,
> That no wight have my name in honde.
> I wot myself best how y stonde;
> For what I drye, or what I thynke,
> I wil myselven al hyt drynke,
> Certeyn, for the more part,
> As fer forth as I kan myn art. (1876-82)

Once more, this is a double-edged image. There is, on the one hand, the humble clerk who does not look for fame, who only wishes that 'no wight have *his* name in honde' 'as *he* were ded', who even limits the extent to

---

45 *I Frammenti e le Testimonianze,* eds. C. Diano and G. Serra (Milan, 1980), fr. 120, p. 52.

which he knows his art ('as fer forth as I kan myn art', 'certeyn, for the more part'). Geoffrey does not want glory in Dante's or Petrarch's way. He begins to construct here an image of himself which he will pursue for his entire career. He is a bookworm, unsuccessful and unknowing in love, dumb as a stone, incapable of 'maistrye' and 'art poetical'. This will be the Narrator who says that everything he tells is derived from his Author ('therfore blameth nat me'), the pilgrim who looks at the ground and tells the absurd story of *Sir Thopas*.

On the other hand, Geoffrey wants no fame because he knows himself best how he stands. With quiet self-assurance, he asserts that he knows his worth and his limits, knows at least how far his 'art' can go. It is suffering, feelings, experience and thought translated into the 'maistrye' he says he does not want to show. Like Christ during the Passion, Geoffrey is ready to 'drink' what he suffers and what he thinks as far as he can — almost the whole cup ('for the more part').[46] This is the Chaucer who will build the great architecture of *Troilus*, who will implicitly proclaim himself 'sesto tra cotanto senno' after the 'Virgile, Ovyde, Omer, Lucan and Stace' who appear here in the hall of Fame.

The two aspects are complementary, and the image Chaucer builds of himself is a Janus-like figure. He will call *Troilus* a tragedy, i.e., the highest form of poetic compositon, but he will call it 'little'. He will consider *Troilus* a 'little book', but he will also recommend posterity not to 'mys-write' or 'mysmetre' it. It is this double-edged vision of himself that Chaucer consecrates in the *House of Fame* as his own *myth*, and it is with this ambiguous figure that, as A.C. Spearing shows in his contribution to the present volume, his successors will have to cope.

If the *House of Fame* is, as Johannes Kleinstück maintained,[47] the story of Chaucer's initiation into his own self, then this initiation ends in a cul-de-sac. For the moment Geoffrey utters his own oracle, his own ambiguous oath of allegiance to poetry, he is ready to enter the House of Rumour, where he does not find traditional myhts, but tidings, μῦθοι being born under his own eyes. Does Geoffrey see himself as collector and creator of his own 'myths' from now on? We shall never know, for the *House of Fame* breaks off suddenly at the end of a line. But we are entitled to suspect that Geoffrey did not know it, either, because he has his newly found 'myths' fly back to Aeolus, to Fame, to the great hall of the poets, the Castle of min-

---

46 The expression (1880) might be proverbial, as both Skeat and Robinson main-
    tain, but the echo from the Gospels is not unlikely. Typically, this serious mood
    is immediately overcome by Geoffrey's search for 'thynges *glade*'.

47 J. Kleinstück, *Mythos und Symbol in englischer Dichtung* (Stuggart, 1964) pp.
    25-55, and particularly p. 55.

strels and magicians, the 'opus perfectum' of the *Aeneid*.[48] Chaucer is stuck with the circularity of his vision, and his problem can have no solution.

When the man of great authority appears in the poem's last line, we are back at square one. The *auctoritates* with whom Geoffrey has identified and into whom he has refused to incarnate himself — Virgil, Ovid, Dante — rise again. Chaucer, as the line's derivation from *Inferno* IV testifies, is about to enter another Castle of Limbo. The *House of Fame*, like a short story by Borges, would repeat itself forever. 'Auctorite' can be taken as the sign of Chaucer's impotence and of his triumph. In all his works he will fail the moment he succeeds. *Parliament, Troilus, Legend, Canterbury Tales* — his greatest claims to the fame he will receive without looking for it — will have disturbing, unsatisfactory, ambiguous, problematic, incomplete conclusions. This is perhaps the reason why twentieth-century readers — used as they are to 'open' forms of art — feel that his failures are, beginning with this in-finite *House fo Fame,* his most exciting successes.

---

48   See above, p. 28, and 'Chaucer's Labyrinth', section II.

TRUTH, LOVE AND GRACE IN THE B-TEXT OF "PIERS PLOWMAN"

BRUCE HARBERT

In Passus I of *Piers Plowman* the dreamer asks Holy Church *tel me þis ilke,/How I may saue my soule.*[1] The whole poem can be read as an answer to that question. To understand the answer Langland gives, formed as he was by the study of theology, we need to have some grasp of the way in which medieval theologians viewed the soul. They were not, of course, unanimous in their views: in Langland's own day the nature of the soul and the means of its salvation were the subject of much controversy. But the controversies were conducted against a background of shared understanding inherited from the theologians of earlier centuries. Since Langland was a poet rather than a technical theologian, we cannot locate him precisely in relation to contemporary theological controversy, saying what view he held on this or that topic. But a knowledge of the theological mainstream, the common traditions, does throw light on his poem, helping us to see shape and order where the mind unaware of theological resonances perceives only chaos.

The standard theological textbook in Langland's time was still the *Sentences* of Peter Lombard, written over two hundred years earlier. Every teacher of theology began his career by lecturing on the *Sentences* and every student studied them. By his comprehensive coverage of theology as then understood and by his copious citation of patristic authorities on the topics raised Lombard determined the shape of scholastic theology. He may not have given all the answers, but he did determine most of the questions. In the thirteenth century theology was revolutionized by the discovery of the works of Aristotle, whose insights were incorporated by Thomas Aquinas into a new synthesis of philosophy and theology. Aquinas is often thought of as *the* medieval theologian, but alongside the new Thomism another tradition flourished that looked back to Augustine as its master. The most important disagreement between the two schools was on the nature of the soul, Augustinians seeing the Will as a more important and fundamental element in the soul than the Intellect, while Thomists set them more on a par. The outstanding representative of the Augustinian tradition in the

---

1 lines 83-4; all references are to the edition of the B-text by George Kane and E. Talbot Donaldson (London, 1975).

thirteenth century was the Franciscan Bonaventure: he and Thomas are the classics of scholastic theology as Plato and Aristotle are of ancient philosophy. The Augustinian tradition nurtured an affective piety such as we find in Jacopone da Todi or in the Middle English religious lyrics produced under Franciscan influence, while Thomistic piety, cultivated among the Dominicans, is more intellectual, represented for example by the subtle hymns of Thomas himself on the Eucharist.

In England the Augustinian tradition was stronger than the Thomistic, flourishing in the Augustinian and Franciscan orders. In 1344 interest in Augustine was given new encouragement by Thomas Bradwardine's *De Causa Dei,* an attack on a group of contemporary theologians whom Bradwardine called 'neo-Pelagians' because, like Pelagius at the time of Augustine, they minimised the role of God's grace in bringing about man's salvation, and trusted too much in human effort. The great volume of writing that Augustine had produced in combating Pelagius' heresy earned him the title of *Doctor Gratiae* and made him the authority *par excellence* from his day to ours on the means of salvation. The *De Causa Dei* was a call to the fourteenth century to return to the teaching of Augustine. There is evidence also of a revival of Augustinian studies in Oxford among the Austin Friars, who had a large number of Augustine's works copied afresh for their library.[2] It is in the Augustinian tradition that Langland belongs, as will become apparent in what follows.

The fourteenth century was a time of complex theological developments, and many scholars have tried to place Langland precisely on the intellectual map of his time. In this essay, no attempt will be made to do this, and his thought will deliberately be illustrated, not from fourteenth-century authors, but from Augustine, Lombard and Bonaventure. This is done, not to suggest that any of these authors was a direct source for Langland — though he can hardly have been unacquainted with a least the first two — but in order to sketch the broad lines of medieval theological tradition, the background against which fourteenth-century developments took place, and the common heritage of even the most advanced thinkers.

Holy Church, Truth and Love

The question posed by Langland's dreamer regarding the salvation of his soul is answered by Holy Church in a speech that falls into two parts, stressing the necessity first of Truth and then of Love (I 85-209). This patterning

---

2   D. Trapp, 'Augustinian Theology of the Fourteenth Century', *Augustiniana* 6 (1956) 146-274.

corresponds to a way of understanding the soul common to both the Thomistic and the Augustinian traditions, which divided the faculties of the soul into those of the Intellect, concerned with knowing, and those of the Will, concerned with loving. *Tota anima dividitur in cognitivam et affectivam*, says Bonaventure (*Breviloquium* II 9,7). The business of the Intellect is to know the Truth, that of the Will to love the Good. Holy Church's Truth and Love, then, correspond to Intellect and Will respectively. The dreamer has asked about his soul and received an answer that reflects the way in which the soul is constructed. But there is more to Langland's Truth than is dreamed of in scholastic philosophy.

Truth is used in Middle English to translate Latin *veritas*. This can have a purely intellectual meaning 'conformity with fact' or, to use the classic definition given by Bonaventure, *adaequatio rei et intellectus* (*In I Sent* XL a.2 q.1). But already in classical Latin *veritas* had moral as well as intellectual connotations, being used to mean 'truthfulness of character' by Cicero and others. These connotations were reinforced in ecclesiastical Latin since *veritas* was the standard translation of Hebrew *'emeth* 'steadfastness', used especially for the steadfastness of God, a word from the same root as the familiar *Amen*. ME *truth* received moral meaning also from its Germanic origins, cognate as it is with *troth, trust* and *true*. Truth is the quality of being trustworthy, steadfast, reliable, fulfilling one's promises. It is the virtue for which Gawain was renowned before he met the Green Knight, Gower calls it the chief among the virtues (*CA* VII 1723ff.), and the plot of Chaucer's *Franklin's Tale* hinges on Dorigen's preservation of her Truth, of which Arveragus says:

Trouthe is the hyeste thyng that man may kepe (*CT* V 1479).

Langland is in good company in setting so high a value on Truth.

When Holy Church begins to speak about Truth, the intellectual connotations are prominent: she commends the man who is 'true of his tongue' (88), speaks as if Truth were a judge whose business is to find out what is true (98), and tells how Christ taught the angels to *know* Truth (109). But Holy Church is speaking of Truth as a virtue, and so the moral connotations are there as well: those who 'end in Truth' can be sure that their souls will go to heaven (130-2). Finally, Truth is a name of God the Father, as Holy Church has already made clear in explaining the Tower of Truth that had been seen in the opening vision, she now speaks of heaven as the place where 'Truth is in Trinity' (133). Here she is following Augustine, who taught that men only know truth because the divine light shines in their minds: what seems to be human truth comes in fact from God. A concise formulation of this view was reproduced in the *Sentences* (I 46,3) and hence widely familiar: *omne verum a veritate verum est: est autem veritas Deus: Deum igitur habet auctorem omne verum.*

Although the dreamer now claims that he still does not understand what Truth is, Holy Church, instead of attempting to explain further, goes on to speak of Love: Intellect and Will are not two watertight compartments in the soul, but rather one activates the other, Truth engendering Love. This process in man is a reflection of the begetting of the Son from the Father in the divine Trinity, and so Love, like Truth, is the name both of a human virtue and of a person of the Trinity. In making these parallels between the life of the soul and the life of God, Langland was following theological tradition, for a standard starting-point for discussion of the soul was the words of God in Genesis 'let us make man in our own image and likeness' (Gn 1,26). As God is a spiritual being, the divine image in man was sought chiefly in his spiritual part, his soul (e.g. *Sentences* I, III 2). We meet this doctrine in the speech of Thought in Passus IX (33-52), and it becomes even more important later in the poem, but is already implicit in the speech of Holy Church, where the operation of the soul's faculties is seen as a mirroring of the life of God.

The Search for Truth

The diptychal patterning of Holy Church's answer to the dreamer's initial question is now repeated on a much larger scale. The dreamer begins a search for the Truth about which Holy Church has told him that lasts until the end of the third dream, when Imaginative utters a eulogy of Truth (XII 287-294) that echoes the one given by Holy Church. From that point the dreamer becomes less concerned with the Intellect and Truth, more with the Will and Love, and this brings him to his encounter with Anima who again echoes Holy Church in the long speech on love that fills most of Passus XV.

The search for Truth begins with a question about its opposite, the false (II 4), in response to which Holy Church plunges the dreamer into the vision of Lady Meed. The chaos that ensues is eventually subdued by the appearance of Reason, whose name associates him closely with the Intellect and hence with Truth, and who seems to offer some promise that the rule of Truth will be restored. The search continues in the second dream as the pilgrims, after confessing their sins, set out to find Saint Truth. The directions Piers gives for finding him are based largely on the Ten Commandments, with added exhortations to truth-telling and right belief appropriate for such a quest, showing that the Truth sought by the pilgrims is not purely intellectual but moral as well, but he ends by saying that Truth is to be found not outside a man but within him, sitting in his heart in a chain of charity (V 606-7). Not surprisingly, then, the external pilgrimage proves inconclusive, and Piers expresses exasperation with this fact when he tears the Pardon that Truth has sent. Piers resolves to be less concerned with external works, and the dreamer follows his example, for the third dream is set, not in the concrete contemporary world, but in a landscape populated with personifications most of whom are associated with the human Intellect: Thought, Wit, Study, Clergy, Scripture, Reason, Imaginative.

This journey into the soul is in the tradition of Augustine's *Confessions* and Bonaventure's *Itinerarium Mentis in Deum.* Augustinian too is the fact that Langland gives the Will more importance than the Intellect. This is made clear by Wit in the directions he gives the dreamer at the beginning of the inner journey (IX 56-60): Anima (the soul) lives in the whole of man's body, but is most at home in the heart. The head, by contrast, is inhabited by Inwit (Mind in the C-text), an intellectual faculty. The meaning is that the Will is a more fundamental part of the soul than the Intellect, the Augustinian or voluntarist view, which is indicated also by the very fact that the dreamer's name is Will. The primacy of Will over Intellect, of Love over Truth, is established poetically as the action proceeds.

There is much discussion in the third dream (VIII 67 – XII 297), of the value of intellectual activity, and specifically learning. Study is strongly opposed to it, and asserts the greater importance of Love. Clergy, whose very name means 'learning', takes a more positive attitude, inveighing not against learning itself but against its corruption. His wife, Scripture, is more opposed to learning itself. The theological issues of predestination and the value of baptism are raised, but nobody seems able to resolve the problems discussed, and so the limitations of human understanding are shown up. The value of reason is questioned further in the dream within the third dream (XI 5-406) since although reason was held to be the property in man that distinguishes him from the beasts, it is the beasts who are seen living according to reason, while man fails to do so. When the dreamer awakes from this dream-within-a-dream he thinks he knows what Dowel is, and it has nothing to do with learning.

However, Imaginative now appears and redresses the balance. The *vis imaginativa* was closely associated with the memory,[3] and Imaginative has the role of raising again issues that have been discussed already and establishing more order in the discussion. As soon as he appears, it is clear that he values reason and learning more than the dreamer is prepared to do, and he goes on to show that learning does have its place, ending with a eulogy of Truth.

---

3   B.J. Harwood, 'Imaginative in Piers Plowman', *Medium AEvum* 44 (1975)249-63.

Love and Charity

The fourth dream continues the movement away from the Intellect towards the Will. The Doctor represents corrupt learning, and the dreamer's departure from Clergy and Scripture in the company of Conscience and Patience (XIII 215) indicates that learning will no longer be a preoccupation. The final dialogue between Conscience and Clergy (202-214), however, suggests that they will meet again, that learning has its place as Imaginative has taught, and Conscience does in fact call for Clergy's help in the final dream (XX 375).

As the poem's concerns move in this bridge-passage from Truth to Love, Conscience is an appropriate companion for the dreamer, since conscience belongs to the Intellect but is connected with the Will, *voluntatis quaedam regula directiva* (see Bonaventure *In II Sent* XXXIX a.1 q.1), a link between knowing and willing, the faculty with which a man decides what to do.

We now meet Haukyn or *Activa Vita*, whose sins show the temptations and drawbacks of the active life as distinct from the contemplative, but the important point about him is not that he is in the world rather than out of it, but that his life of activity, of doing, contrasts strongly with the life of knowing and thinking exemplified by the Doctor. The Doctor's life is dominated by the Intellect, Haukyn's by the Will. Moreover, Haukyn is a poor man, and poverty comes to be more and more associated with Love, which is about to become the dominant theme with the appearance of Anima. The introduction of Haukyn, then, assists the thematic progress of the poem, although the drastic revisions that Langland made to this section in the C-text suggest that he was not satisfied with this scene as it stands in B.

Anima means 'soul', and Anima proves to have several other names all of which are faculties of the soul and some of which we have met before. Names belonging to both Will and Intellect are listed, including Reason, associated with Truth as we should expect (XV 27-8), Conscience the link-faculty, *Animas* associated with willing (24) and *Amor*. Anima, then, represents the whole soul, and looks back on some of the themes that have already been discussed in the inner journey, but in true Augustinian tradition he is especially associated with Love, with the heart rather than the head as Thought had predicted. He speaks of the corruption associated with learning, but most of his speech is concerned with Love, for which Charity is now coming to be the preferred name. Charity is not discovered by learning but through the Will (XV 209-10): the manner of life that favours its growth is one of patience and poverty. Still, however, at the end of Passus XV the dreamer does not understand what Charity means, and so Anima tells him about the Tree of Charity, which grows in the heart of man and is farmed by Liberum Arbitrium.

One of the sources of the vision of the Tree of Charity is a passage in the

De Gratia Christi (XVIII 19 – XIX 20) where Augustine comments on Pelagius' comparison, based on Matthew 7, 18, of a good man and a bad man to two trees bearing good and bad fruit respectively. A look at that passage helps to explain the Tree in *Piers Plowman*. Pelagius had said that it was in the power of the cultivator's free will to determine whether the fruit of his tree should be good or bad. Augustine replies that Pelagius, by making good and bad trees spring from the same root, is contradicting both Christ, who said a good tree cannot bring forth bad fruit nor a bad tree good fruit (Mt 7, 18), and Paul, who called cupidity the root of all evil (I Tim 6, 10), thus implying that charity is the root of all good. A man can have either a good or a bad root: if his root is evil, this is because of original sin. A man produces a good tree when he receives the grace of God, which heals the disease that infects evil roots. Charity does not come from us, but is given to us by God.

Although Langland makes Charity the fruit of the tree rather than its root, his meaning is the same, that man's ability to do good depends, not on himself, but on God. Liberum Arbitrium is the most fundamental and noble part of man, what most makes him human and most clearly bears the divine image, *nobilissimum quod est in homine* (*In II Sent* XXV p.1 q.1) and *sub Deo potentissimum* (*In II Sent* III p.2 a.1 q.2) as Bonaventure puts it. But this image was defaced at the Fall, and so Liberum Arbitrium is powerless to bring forth the fruit of Charity unless helped by God: hence the Tree of Charity is supported by three props representing the three persons of the Trinity, which Liberum Arbitrium uses to help ward off the temptations that threaten the fruit.

The precise nature of Liberum Arbitrium and its relationship to the other faculties of the soul was one of the most debated matters in medieval psychology. It has an intellectual and an affective aspect, and hence by some was held to include Intellect and Will: *cum de libero arbitrio loquimur, non de parte animae loquimur, sed certe de tota* (Bonaventure, *Breviloquium* II 9, 8, quoting Ps-Augustine *Hypomnesticon* III, 5, 7). Aquinas insisted that Liberum Arbitrium and the Will were identical. Others saw it as separate from Intellect and Will but linking them: Bonaventure compares Liberum Arbitrium to Conscience, saying that both terms can be used to mean the same thing, and that they both relate in the same way to Intellect and Will: *quemadmodum libertas arbitrii consistit in ratione et voluntate . . . sic conscientia (respicit) rationem et voluntatem* (*In II Sent* XXXIX a.2 q.2). Bonaventure is here following the classic definition in the *Sentences* of Liberum Arbitrium as *facultas voluntatis et rationis* (II, XXIV 3), and this seems to fit Langland's concept too: his Liberum Arbitrium is a link between Intellect and Will, but more fundamental than either.

Triadic Images

Hitherto we have considered the soul as composed of two parts, intellectual and affective, in conformity with medieval theory. But it is also thoroughly scholastic to discern in the soul a triadic structure. This approach was developed most fully by Augustine in the *De Trinitate*, where he sees Gn 1, 26 fulfilled in the existence of the three interdependent faculties of memory, intellect and will in the human soul: this triad of faculties constitutes the image of the Trinity in man's nature of which God was speaking when he said 'let us make man in our own image'. Scholastic theologians drew heavily on the *De Trinitate* in their accounts of the structure of the soul without seeing any incompatibility between its tripartite analysis and the bipartite one discussed earlier: rather the two approaches are seen as complementary. Langland does not use the Augustinian triad of memory, intellect and will, but seems to have in mind the triad of Intellect, Will and Liberum Arbitrium, which underlies much of the imagery of Passus XVI and XVII. This is a fuller picture than had been implicit in Holy Church's speech, and suggests that a view of the soul that fails to see in it an image of the Trinity is inadequate in a discussion of the means of the soul's salvation. Triadic images abound in this section of the poem. It will be convenient to list these before discussing them:

Faculties:	Intellect	Will	Liberum Arbitrium
Props:	Father	Son	Holy Spirit
Temptations:	World	Flesh	Devil
States of Life:	Matrimony	Widowhood	Continence
Theological Virtues:	Faith	Hope	Charity
Biblical Characters:	Abraham	Moses	Good Samaritan
Divine Commands:	sacrifice of Isaac	circumcision	offering of bread and wine
Images of the Trinity: (i)	fist	fingers	palm
(ii)	wick	wax	flame
(iii)	wicked wife	rain	smoke

Faculties: Intellect and Will are not mentioned explicitly but are included for the sake of completeness. As Intellect and Will had been associated with Father and Son in Holy Church's speech, so the Holy Spirit is associated with Liberum Arbitrium: he helps him with his grace (XVI 51-2), the sin against the Holy Spirit is equated with sin through free will (47a) and the Holy Spirit is called the *fre wille* of Father and Son (223; cf. *frenesse of spiritus sancti* 88).

Props: we have spoken of man's soul as an image of the Trinity, but when the dreamer reaches the centre of the soul he finds, not a mere image, but the Trinity itself. This conforms to the doctrine that God dwells within the soul that is in a state of grace. This doctrine was more explored among the theologians of Eastern christendom than in the West, but it does find a place in Augustine (*De Trinitate* XV 18, 32) and among the scholastics. In his *Itinerarium Mentis in Deum* Bonaventure shows how God can be found, not only by looking at the natural faculties of the soul, but also 'by the contemplation of his very self in the minds of those in whom he dwells by the gifts of most abundant charity' (IV 4). In the *De Causa Dei* Bradwardine, attacking those who paid too little attention to the influence of God on human conduct, asserted that 'God necessarily collaborates in every act of the created will'.[4] This is an extreme position, and problematic in that it seems to make God the cause even of sin.[5] Langland does not go as far as Bradwardine, but by introducing the divine Trinity at this point he stresses man's inability to do well on his own without the help of God. The dreamer's question in Passus I is thus shown to be mistaken: he cannot save his own soul. From this point on the emphasis is not on what man can do, but on what God has done and continues to do.

Temptations: There does not seem to be any reason why the Father in particular should defend charity against the world, though the Son, who took flesh, can perhaps be seen as an especially appropriate aid against its temptations. But the chief role in combating temptation belongs to the Holy Spirit, who not only checks the Devil, but sends grace when human power is insufficient to resist all three together. In giving the Holy Spirit the most prominent role within the soul Langland is following tradition which saw God's work in man as especially belonging to the Holy Spirit, following such texts as Christ's promise to send the Spirit to his followers in John 14, 16-17 (cf. 14,26; 16,13). When Faith explains his coat of arms — a symbol of the Trinity — he too lays special stress on the role of the Holy Spirit as an enlightener and comforter of creatures (XVI 189-90). Theologians associated the Holy Spirit closely with Charity (Augustine *De Trinitate* XV 17,27): Lombard taught that they were identical (*Sentences* I 17), but his view was later condemned. Bonaventure comments on it and refines it, arguing that the Holy Spirit, being the bond of love that unites Father and Son, is identical with Charity in the Trinity, but that in men he is its giver and exemplar (In I Sent XVII dub.5). He inflames the soul with Charity (*In II Sent* I a.2 q.1) and is present in every soul that has the gift of Charity. The Holy Spirit therefore properly has a prominent role at the Tree of Charity.

States of Life: The three states of matrimony, widowhood and continence, briefly mentioned as fruits on the Tree (XVI 63-72), are later explained as another image of the three divine persons, separate and yet interdependent (XVI 202-224).

---

4   Quoted by G. A. Leff, *Bradwardine and the Pelagians* (Cambridge, 1957), p. 94.
5   Ibid., pp. 57ff.

Theological Virtues: Although many medieval allegories were written to be interpreted in more than one sense, rarely are the different senses so clearly indicated as in the scene that follows the dreamer's awakening from his *louedreem* (XVI 167ff: cf. XVI 20), where the two characters he meets have two names each, Faith and Hope, alias Abraham and Moses.

Faith and Hope belong to the triad of virtues enumerated by Saint Paul in I Co 13,13, the third of which is Charity. The Good Samaritan whom they meet must therefore represent Charity, although he is not given that name explicitly. Faith, Hope and Charity are known in theology as the 'theological' virtues because they direct man to divine things and, as it were, make him divine (Bonaventure *In III Sent* XXXIII dub.5). Faith and Hope without Charity are called 'unformed' and accounted insufficient to save a man (*Sentences* III, XXIII 4,2; 8,2). This is acted out when Faith and Hope do nothing to help the wounded man they meet, but the Samaritan takes charge of his healing.

Such is the inadequacy of Faith and Hope on their own that their teachings even seem to be incompatible, so that the dreamer does not know which to follow (XVII 127ff.). This brings to a climax the indications there have been from early in the poem that man's Intellect tends to be at odds with his Will. Although Holy Church had spoken of Love as flowing from Truth, a process whose supreme example is seen in the sending of God the Son by the Father, attempts to seek or define Truth have proved unsatisfactory. Love, too, has come to seem an inadequate concept, so that the very law of Love itself, given to Moses on Mount Sinai (XVII 11-16), is insufficient to save the wounded man for all Hope's boasting (XVII 18-21; 62-5). The implication is that Truth and Love, being natural virtues, are not enough for salvation, which needs God's gift of the supernatural triad of Faith, Hope and Charity. So a triad supersedes a pair in Langland's account of virtues as it had done in his account of the soul's faculties.

Charity is usually located by theologians in the Will together with Hope, while Faith resides in the Intellect. Bonaventure sees in the theological virtues another image of the Trinity, called the *imago recreationis* because it is found in the soul recreated by supernatural grace, as distinct from the *imago creationis* found in the purely natural powers of the soul as created by God. He comments that whereas in the *imago creationis* two faculties, Memory and Intellect, belong to the intellectual part of the soul and only one, Will, to the affective, the *imago recreationis* has two virtues in the affective and one in the intellectual (*In II Sent* XVI a.2 q.3). Langland seems to be working with a more symmetrical model: for him, just as Liberum Arbitrium unites Will and Intellect but is more fundamental, and the Holy Spirit proceeds from Father and Son but plays a more prominent role in the soul, so the dramatic function of Charity, represented by the Samaritan, is to reconcile the opposing claims of Faith and Hope and to transcend them. For Langland, as for Augustine in the *De Gratia Christi*, Charity resides in Liberum Arbitrium remade by grace.

Biblical Characters: Until Passus XVI the poem, although nominally set in fourteenth-century England, has dealt with matters that affect men in every time and place. With the appearance of biblical characters among the fruits on the Tree — Adam, Abraham, Isaiah and so on (XVI 81f.) — attention begins to focus on a particular historical situation, that of the just who lived before Christ. Although their presence on the Tree shows that they had Charity, it was finally unable to resist the Devil. The struggle to rescue them leads to the throwing of the prop *Filius* by Piers, an image of the Incarnation and the turning-point of the poem, when the focus shifts decisively from atemporal themes to history and from man's actions to God's. We are plunged into history as we witness the Annunciation, followed by the whole drama of salvation, encompassing the life, death and resurrection of Christ, the sending of the Holy Spirit, the growth of the Church and the coming of Antichrist.

One of the greatest problems facing any Christian theologian is to demonstrate that the condition of all men in all times and places is affected by a single brief series of events which happened at a particular time and place, the death and resurrection of Christ. Langland's use of an allegory with both an atemporal moral sense and a historical sense is his way of solving this problem. He is seeking to show that the salvation of the human soul through Charity, of which the Tree is an image, is impossible

> Wiþouten þe blood of a barn born of a mayde   XVII 96.

For the moment we are concerned only with the just who live before Christ, the hoard of holy men whom the devil stole from the Tree (XVI 84). Although Moses was not named among these, he is there by implication, and in Passus XVII he and Abraham represent all of them awaiting their salvation by Christ.

Divine Commands: Abraham's list of the three things he was ordered to do by God (XVI 231-46) is yet another example of Langland's preoccupation with triads in this section of the poem.

Images of the Trinity: The Samaritan plays the role of Christ but is not explicitly identified with him. In Passus XVIII the Christ-figure is *Oon semblable to þe Samaritan and somdeel to Piers þe Plowman* (10), while in Passus XIX it is Piers who appears *riȝt lik in alle lymes to oure lord Iesu* (8). Langland is being deliberately vague about the identity of Christ, avoiding identifying him simply as a man, and so hinting at the mysterious coexistence in him of divine and human natures, the beginning and source of that interpenetration of human and divine life of which the Tree with its props was an image.

The same theme runs through the three triadic images that the Samaritan uses to teach the dreamer (XVII 140-349), all of which follow the pattern that we have already observed, the third member reconciling and transcending the first two. In each case the third member is associated with the Holy Spirit. Thus, it is worse to be maimed in the palm than in the fingers or fist, a sign that the sin against the Holy Spirit is the greatest sin. Here the image of the hand is used in a simple, explanatory way. The second image is more complex: as a flame burns with wick and wax, so the Holy Spirit melts to mercy the might of Father and Son when there is love in a man's soul, but when there is its opposite, unkindness, his grace is quenched because unkindness harms the life and love of man, which is guarded by the Holy Spirit, giver of life. Here Langland is not simply drawing a parallel between man and God, but expressing the union of their lives in Charity. Finally smoke, the worst of the three trials that plague a man in his house, is like the unkindness that quenches the mercy of God, engendered in the soul, as the image of the torch had illustrated, by the work of the Holy Spirit. The notion that to hurt a man is to offend God, springing from the view of man as made and remade in God's image, runs through the whole of the Samaritan's speech.

Structure of the triads

We have discussed the triadic images as though each member were separate from the other two, the first two members often being in opposition to each other, but when we consider all these images together, we see that the situation is more complex. A glance back at the table will help to make this clear, for the divisions between the columns are not so watertight as our neat tabulation might make them seem. Love appears by implication both in the second column, being the content of the law taught by Moses, and in the third, being related to Charity though not identical with it. We remember that Holy Church had shown Truth overflowing into Love, and that these virtues had only later been seen in opposition to one another. The implication seems to be that without God there is disharmony in man's soul, but when God is present, Truth flows into Love and Love into Charity.

A second question raised by the table is whether God the Son belongs in the second column or in the third. He is the second person of the Trinity and appropriately appears as the second prop at the Tree; Holy Church had associated him with Love, which would also place him in the second column with the Will, but he is also represented by the Samaritan and associated with Charity, and both of these appear in the third column. So the neat association of Father with Truth, Son with Love and Holy Spirit with Charity to which Holy Church's speech and our table might seem to point proves to be an oversimplification. No such sharp division is maintained between the work of the Son and that of the Holy Spirit, but the salvation and sanctification of man is shown to be the work of both. The Passus that follow will show the work of the Spirit flowing from that of the Son and thus completing the movement whose beginning was described by Holy Church when she spoke of the Father engendering the Son as Truth engenders Love.

Truth and Love reconciled

Of the four maidens whom we meet in the sixth dream (XVIII 110ff.), Truth and Righteousness belong to the Intellect and Mercy and Peace to the Will. Love also appears, still associated with the Will in being Peace's lemman (182; 423). Righteousness and Truth insist on the facts, which they say cannot be changed (148; 199f.), so that what is in Hell can never come out. Mercy, although she argues against Truth, does not set the facts aside, and insists that her proof is based on evidence (152). Similarly, Peace argues that God allowed man to suffer sorrow in order that he might *know* happiness better (205). So they argue for a Love that is not at the expense of Truth but in harmony with it. Their debate suggests a conflict between Truth and Love in God himself in which neither conquers the other but the claims of both are reconciled.

The discussion between the devils covers similar ground, Lucifer taking the side of Righteousness and Truth while Satan and Goblin follow Mercy, again stressing the reasonableness of her argument. Similarly, Christ when he appears insists that he ransoms souls *by right and by reson* (349) and that *I may do mercy þoruȝ my rightwisnesse* (389). In this context he speaks of his love and mercy in lines that are justly among the most celebrated in the poem (361ff.), where the pattern that we have become familiar with appears again: having reconciled the claims of Truth and Love he now speaks of a third element that transcends them, grace. By grace he will save not only the righteous who lived before him, who have been the concern of the debate so far, but also sinners, even in the future. The perspective of the poem broadens out as Christ proclaims to Satan

> Now bigynneþ þi gile ageyn þee to turne
> And my grace to growe ay gretter and widder   (361-2).

His work of redemption, far from ending with the Harrowing of Hell, will be complete only on the Last Day. The dance of the four maidens to Love's melody is an image of the reconciliation of opposites. The new, transcendent element introduced by Christ is developed further in the next dream.

Dowel, Dobet and Dobest

The speech of Conscience in Passus XIX contains three triads: the titles of Christ (26-62), the gifts of the Magi (75-95) and Dowel, Dobet and Dobest (108-187). Christ's titles of knight, king and conqueror indicate the growing universality of his mission until he is able to redeem all men. We find here the pattern of crescendo that we see in other triads, but no correspondence between members of the triad and the parts of the soul. There is such a correspondence in the Magi's gifts, for Reason, represented by incense, and Pity or Mercy, represented by myrrh, belong to Intellect and Will respectively, while the third member of the triad, gold, represents both Righteousness, which is primarily intellectual, as we saw in the debate of the four maidens, and Leautee, which is elsewhere associated with Love (IV 36, 161; XI 145, 167) and hence with the Will.

Most problematic of all are Dowel Dobet and Dobest. Although this triad appears more in the poem than any other, making its first appearance as early as Passus VIII (78ff.), discussion of it has been postponed until now in the belief that Conscience's explanation in Passus XIX is the definitive one. The explanations offered by other characters are notoriously inconsistent and inconclusive, but there are some indications that this triad follows the pattern that we have been considering. Dowel is associated with Truth (VIII 81) and belief (X 238-256), Dobet with Love (VIII 86; IX 97f., 201) and Dobest comes from both (IX 208; XIII 128f.) and is above both (VIII 96; IX 14). Conscience shows how Dowel, Dobet and Dobest are exemplified in the life of Christ: Dowel when he taught law and evoked belief, Dobet when he did acts of love and mercy, and Dobest when he granted forgiveness and mercy to all men through the Church, fulfilling the claim that he made during the Harrowing of Hell that his grace was growing greater and wider. It is important to note that Conscience nowhere says simply that Jesus did well, better or best: it is *God* who began to do well at Cana (116), the doing well being associated specifically with Jesus' divinity (122f.); Dobest is a name of Jesus (128f.) and he *þouȝte* Dobest (182). This directs us to the essential point about Dowel, Dobet and Dobest, that they are not within the power of man, but man only does well, better or best in so far as God works in him. The divine character of this triad had already been hinted at by Clergy in speaking of Piers Plowman who

> demeþ þat dowel and dobet arn two Infinites,
> Which Infinites wiþ a feiþ fynden out dobest,
> Which shal saue mannes soule.   (XIII 128-30)

The way in which this triad appears in the titles to the Passus as given in Skeat's edition also helps to indicate how Langland conceived it: Dowel begins with Passus IX and the part of the journey into the soul that concentrates on the Intellect; when the greater importance of Love is being established Dobet begins (Passus XV) and continues to the end of the story of Christ. Dobest is the last two dreams (Passus XIX and XX), the age of grace, the Holy Spirit and the Church.

Money and the Soul

Having explained Dowel, Dobet and Dobest, Conscience ends his speech by recalling Piers' Pardon, which had contained the first reference to Dowel in the poem and had instigated the quest of the *Vita*. In Passus VII its terms had appeared harsh, but now Conscience says that all sins can be forgiven save debt, which alone will cause a man to be numbered among those *qui mala egerunt* and condemn him to eternal fire. The price of the Pardon is accordingly *redde quod debes*, pay what you owe. This has a double resonance, and looks back to Holy Church's discussion of Jesus' words in Matthew 22, 21, *reddite Caesari* (I 46-57). What bears Caesar's image, a coin, must be rendered to Caesar, while what bears God's image must be rendered to God. This, as we have seen, is man's soul. Man cannot 'save' his soul: the whole poem has shown up the error implicit in that financial metaphor. Rather he must surrender his soul to God in order that God may save it as Piers had done when, in response to the Pardon, he had consecrated himself to a life of prayer and penance. Only by such an attitude of passivity, of patient poverty, can a man prepare himself to receive God's grace, without which he cannot do well, better or best. A similar commendation of poverty is made by Need at the beginning of Passus XX when, contradicting Conscience and the King, he says that Temperance, not Justice, is the highest cardinal virtue, for it teaches us to be like Christ in taking no more than we need. This in turn looks back to Holy Church's teaching that man should be content with the necessities of life, which God will provide, a teaching that is repeated again in the confusion of the final dream by Kind, who advises the dreamer not to worry about clothing or food but to

> Lerne to louse ... and leef alle opere (208)

Langland is urging both material and spiritual poverty, and *redde quod debes* is an injunction to pay both financial debts and the spiritual debt of the soul to God in order to share in the reward proclaimed by the Pardon. We see now why Holy Church, in spite of the dreamer's request *Teche me to no tresor* (I 83), had persisted in using financial metaphor, calling Truth the best of treasures (I 85, 137): questions about salvation and questions about money cannot be separated. The doctrinal and economic themes of the poem coalesce, for Langland's preoccupation with money is at root theological.

The Time of the Church

In response to Kind's advice the dreamer confesses his sins, thus paying his personal debt to God, since every Christian was expected to make a sacramental confession once a year. This moment has been prepared for by the narrative in Passus XIX of Pentecost, the founding of the Church and the institution of the sacraments. In this section Christ is no longer seen, his place having been taken by the Holy Spirit, his messenger, through whom Christ's grace grows greater and wider and is made available to men in the Church. The dreamer himself has been drawing gradually closer to the Church, witnessing the death and resurrection of Christ at the time when they are commemorated in the liturgy. It was on Midlent Sunday, a week before the liturgical commemoration of the Passion begins, that he had met Abraham; during Holy Week he had witnessed the Passion, Harrowing of Hell and Resurrection, falling asleep on Palm Sunday and awakening on Easter morning. At this point he had gone to church to fulfil his Easter duty of receiving Communion, but had been prevented by falling asleep during Mass. His statement that after his confession he *cam to unitee* (213) may mean that he received Communion then. Certainly it means that he is reconciled to the Church, following the way of salvation that his dreams have taught him by seeking grace in the Church: his participation in the redemption wrought by Christ is through the liturgy and sacraments. Thus his personal quest for the means of salvation is over and we hear no more of him.

Passus XX returns us to the contemporary world, the field full of folk of the Prologue where, notwithstanding the dreamer's individual conversion, the general picture remains unchanged: mankind still stands in need of grace but fails to seek it. The arrival of Antichrist would have indicated to a medieval reader, especially perhaps one familiar with the mystery-cycles, that the end of the world and the second coming of Christ were at hand. Thus this latter part of the poem has sketched the whole history of humanity from Adam to the eve of *resurrectio mortuorum,* of humanity's sharing in the resurrection of Christ when, according to his prophecy (XVIII 368ff.), his thirst of love is to be slaked and he will have out of Hell all men's souls. It is to that moment, when all will be judged according to the terms of Piers' Pardon, that the last lines of the poem look forward, and Conscience's cry for Grace with which the poem ends echoes the cry at the end of the Bible, 'Come, Lord Jesus' (Apoc. 22, 20).

AUENTURE, CNAWYNG AND LOTE IN "PEARL"*

ANNA TORTI

Since the discovery of the manuscript at the end of the nineteenth century, *Pearl* has captured the interest of the critics who have often offered contradictory readings. The traditional interpretation, based on the biographical elements which can be found in the text, considers *Pearl* an elegy in which the poet laments the death of his two-year-old daughter, possibly called Margery from Margarita = Pearl, and, in the vision form favoured by medieval writers, is consoled by her, now a 'quene' in Heaven. In 1904, Schofield was the first of a long series of critics to give an allegorical interpretation of the work.[1] He maintained that the poet's intention was to illustrate the qualities of the virtue of purity, by linking them with the image of the pearl, which had figured as the emblem of perfection ever since the parable of Matthew on the pearl of great price.[2] Emphasis on the elegiac and symbolical elements — considered either separately or together — has dominated subsequent criticism, along with a particular consideration of the poem's circular structure.[3]

Without underestimating these interpretations, my intention is to use a close reading of the language of *Pearl*, in order to analyse the allegorical process from the beginning of the dream to the poet's awakening. This will be seen as developing a progression in the author's knowledge of himself both as a man — a natural, earthly being with a spiritual existence — and as an artist who wants to evaluate the significance of his poetry.

As allegorical works point to the protagonist's or the characters' changes within the story (normally in the form of a journey or a quest), and must,

* I thank Jill Mann and Piero Boitani for reading an earlier draft of this paper and making many suggestions to improve it.

1 See W.H. Schofield, 'The Nature and Fabric of *The Pearl*', *PMLA* XIX (1904) 154-215, and 'Symbolism, Allegory, and Autobiography in *The Pearl*', *PMLA* XXIV (1909) 585-675. Schofield's allegorical analysis is questioned by G.G. Coulton, 'In Defence of *The Pearl*', *MLR* ii (1906) 39-43. For this debate on elegy and allegory in *Pearl* see further the introduction in E.V. Gordon, *Pearl* (Oxford, 1953), pp. XI-XXXVI, and more recently W.A. Davenport, *The Art of the Gawain-Poet* (London, 1978), pp.34-54.

2 Matthew, XIII, 45-46.

3 On the circular structure of the poem, see Nelson's important study: *'Pearl:* the circle as figural space' in C. Nelson, *The Incarnate Word. Literature as Verbal Space* (Urbana, Chicago and London, 1973) 25-49, in which the pearl is seen as an emblem of the 'circularity' of life.

therefore, present the possibility of transformation, my first hypothesis, i.e. that *Pearl* illustrates the poet's progression towards knowledge, can be verified. It is the aim of this analysis to show that such knowledge, despite the dreamer's efforts, will prove nearly impossible to achieve.

The extreme perfection of the poem's form, its subtle numerological and metrical structure[4] and its complex language — by which the ambiguous meaning of each word is exploited to the full, — reveal the artistic ability of the author.[5] Even though the dreamer's effort to gain knowledge will eventually fail, the poem will satisfy its didactic function by offering itself as a memoir, a concrete sign of the experience of the man-poet, an *exemplum,* although a negative one, to mankind. One can, therefore, say that the poet is equally interested in the poetical language both as 'means' (signifier) and as 'message' (signified).[6]

The real beginning of the 'auenture' is to be found in the fifth stanza of the first section:

> Bifore þat spot my honde I spenned
> For care ful colde þat to me caȝt;
> A deuely dele in my hert denned,
> Þaȝ resoun sette myseluen saȝt.
> I playned my perle þat þer watȝ spenned
> Wyth fyrce skylleȝ þat faste faȝt;
> Þaȝ kynde of Kryst me comfort kenned,
> My wreched wylle in wo ay wraȝte.
> I felle vpon þat floury flaȝt,
> Suche odour to my herneȝ schot;
> I slode vpon a slepyng-slaȝte
> On þat precios perle wythouten spot.
>
> II
> Fro spot my spyryt þer sprang in space;
> My body on balke þer bod in sweuen.
> My goste is gon in Godeȝ grace
> In auenture þer meruayleȝ meuen.   (49-64)[7]

It is the dreamer who relates his past experience; it is through his description of the events, before, during and after the dream, that the poet with his fictitious 'I' offers an *exemplum* of the simplicity and smallness of man in the face of mysteries such as death, divine reward and the hereafter. The

---

4 On numerology in *Pearl,* see M.S. Rostvig, 'Numerical Composition in *Pearl:* a Theory', *English Studies* XLVIII (1967) 326-332.

5 See C. Muscatine, *Poetry and Crisis in the Age of Chaucer* (Notre Dame & London, 1972), pp. 46-50.

6 On the didactic function of language in St. Augustine, see D.W. Robertson, Jr., *A Preface to Chaucer* (Princeton, 1962), pp. 65-69.

7 I have used the edition of *Pearl* by E.V. Gordon (Oxford, 1953).

autobiographical element, though important, is not, at least in the first section, a basic factor, and this can be observed in the frequent use of anaphoric deictics[8] such as *that* and *there* which refer to the preceding text/context up to:

> Perle, plesaunte to prynces paye
> To clanly clos in golde so clere   (I-2)

Here the pearl is not identified as a person yet, but only described as a splendidly luminous and precious gem, ideal for an earthly prince, and destined to cause an intense 'luf-daungere'. The ambiguity of the Pearl is still more evident if one observes the deliberate contiguity of two clauses (1.1 and 11.3-4) which signal on the one hand a certain familiarity with and on the other a distance from the thing (pearl) or the person (Pearl). This is the case with the elliptical vocative clause 'Perle, plesaunte to prynces paye', which consists of a noun and appositional elements (familiarity), and the normal coordinate clause, 'Oute of oryent, I hardyly saye, / Ne proued I neuer her precios pere', where the anaphoric feminine possessive adjective in the third person — and not in the second as one would expect — indicates the distance. The use of both 'hyr' and 'hit', on this as on other occasions, sums up this ambiguity.

In the first section, the *repetitio* of 'wythouten spot' and 'þat spot' with the word play on *spot* is the only precise referent. The obsessive use of the deictic *that*, to mark distant reference both at the beginning and at the end of the poem, places the experience of the extra-earthly vision of the dreamer in a temporal and spatial gnomic past, which is of value to all men.

The contrast between *dreamer* and *maiden* is pre-figured in the opposition present in the narrator's mind between his 'resoun' which tries to console and his 'wylle'[9] which is in 'wo' for the loss of the 'so-called' pearl and which wants to know the reason for this loss. His 'wylle' is not satisfied with Christ's words, that the grain must die in order to give fruit.[10]

At this point, a deep sleep conveys the spirit into a world in which everything is 'adubbement'.[11] The brilliance of the landscape and the singing of

---

8 On the use of deictics and on cohesion in English, see M.A.K. Halliday and R. Hasan, *Cohesion in English* (London, 1976) and W. Gutwinski, *Cohesion in Literary Texts* (The Hague, Paris, 1976).

9 'Wylle' would thus indicate *voluntas;* but the M.E. term also includes the meaning of *desire, wish,* (see *O.E.D.* s.v. 'will', I, and *Chaucer Glossary,* eds. N. Davis, D. Gray, P. Ingham, A. Wallace-Hadrill (Oxford, 1979) — a meaning which the *Gawain*-poet is clearly aware of (see references in M. Andrew and R. Waldron, eds., *The Poems of the Pearl Manuscript* (London, 1978), p. 362 s.v. 'wylle').

10 See John, XII, 24.

11 For discussion of the particular category to which the dream experienced by the poet belongs, see L. Blenkner, 'The theological Structure of *Pearl', Traditio* XXIV (1968) 43-75; E. Wilson, 'The 'Gostly Drem' in *Pearl', Neuphilologische Mitteilungen* LXIX (1968) 90-101; A.C. Spearing, *Medieval Dream-Poetry* (Cambridge, 1976), pp. 111-129, and P. Boitani, *English Medieval Narrative* (Cambridge, 1982) pp. 103-108.

the birds intoxicate the dreamer who, not knowing who or what has brought him among those wonders, is only capable of referring to 'fortwne' (1.98 and 1.129) and can only wish to see and have more and more.

The climax, the appearance of the maiden, is reached through a gradual process marked by a type of language which belongs to the human, earthly sphere, with expressions in the refrain such as 'to haue ay more and more'; 'me longed ay more and more'; 'Þat meued my mynde ay more and more' up to 'I knew hyr wel, I hade sen hyr ere' (164). The contrast between *knew* and *hade sen* (underlined in 167-168) indicates for the first time a subtle relationship between knowing and seeing which will be a recurring theme throughout the poem. Knowledge of the Pearl depends on the protagonist's memory of an actual physical *sight* ('I hade *sen* hyr *ere*', i.e. in past life), but also, more interestingly, on his present vision of her in the 'sweuen':

> On lenghe I loked to hyr þere;
> Þe lenger, I knew hyr more and more. (167-168)

Knowledge is authenticated by both experience (*sight*) and spiritual vision. Yet the Pearl will later slight both by putting forth the model of absolute knowledge:

> We þurȝoutly hauen cnawyng (859)

Seeing the maiden in such a strange place, the man is confused and bewildered and needs time to measure the vision in human terms. The dreamer's awe is such that his 'lyste'[12] is unable to play any role. The maiden appears to him completely adorned with pearls (and the poet uses various synonyms: 'perleȝ', 'margarys', 'mariorys').[13] The pearl on her breast is so extraordinarily beautiful as to baffle his reason:

> A manneȝ dom moȝt dryȝly demme,
> Er mynde moȝt malte in hit mesure.
> I hope no tong moȝt endure
> No sauerly saghe say of þat syȝt, (223-226)

Here, the poet reaffirms what he has said before: neither 'lyste', nor 'dom',[14] nor 'tong' (language) can describe that event which is beyond the range of human experience. The 'mesure' of the pearl, and by 'mesure' he means

---

12 'Lyste' has, according to *M.E.D.*, s.v. 'list', 1. (a), the meaning of *desire, wish, will, longing*, etc. It might thus be seen as a particular case of 'wylle' (see note n. 9 above). The two terms could perhaps be seen as parallel to the two poles in Thomas Aquinas's definition of *voluntas:* 'voluntas media est inter *rationem* et *concupiscibilem*, et potest ab utroque moveri' (*S.T.* 2,2.q. 155, a.3 ad 2.).

13 and even, as in the Anglo-Saxon alliterative tradition, a formulaic line with *variatio*, 'Of mariorys and non oþer ston' (206) and 'Wyth whyte perle and non oþer gemme' (219).

14 See *M.E.D.* s.v. 'dōm', 5 b. (c), the meaning of *imagination*.

measure, but also value, significance, is not understood, nor can it be, since the dreamer's mind is faced with something beyond his mental capacity (note the insistence on 'mo3t').

Without doubt, the dream-vision tradition enabled the medieval poet to narrate strange, or in any case unusual events, and the characterization of the maiden follows the canons of medieval courtly love poetry. Nevertheless, the emphasis given to the contrast between human reason and human mind on the one hand and divine 'mesure' on the other suggests the importance placed on spiritual matters in this dream and lays the ground for the maiden's speech which is fundamental to the significance of the work.

Before addressing himself to her, the narrator specifies that the maiden was closer to him than an aunt or a niece, and these words, which are not the poet's but the narrator's (in fact, the poet never intervenes except through his *personae* — Pearl and dreamer), serve as a means of beginning the dialogue, without playing down the autobiographical element. The first remarks indicate the 'worldliness' of the dreamer who ascribes the loss of his 'juel', the pearl, to 'wyrde'.

The maiden focusses her speech upon the folly of the dreamer and of man in general, who thinks that he can judge the other world in human terms. The theme of folly is here introduced with the function it has in the morality plays. It represents man's inclination to err, above all to talk nonsense, and ultimately to misunderstand and, therefore, his vulnerability to evil.[15] The maiden wants, first of all, to put the dreamer in his place and make him understand that his folly, an act of language, can be the cause of more serious evils, this being signalled on the semantic level by the use of lexemes such as 'mysetente' (257), 'mad porpose' (267), 'raysoun bref' (268), and of syntagms like 'Wy borde 3e men? So madde 3e be!' (290); 'Py worde byfore þy wytte con fle.' (294); '3e setten hys worde3 ful westernays' (307). Once more, the maiden applies the metaphor of the jeweller, this time correctly: to be a happy jeweller is not enough, the dreamer must be 'jueler', 'gentyl', 'gente', 'kynde', in order to gain Paradise. That gem which the jeweller has mourned is but a rose with a life and death cycle, from the moment it blossoms to the moment it fades, while what is before him is the pearl of great price to which he cannot ascribe earthly qualities. He seems not to have understood: he thinks he has attained happiness ('þis blys', 286), by simply seeing the pearl.

---

15   See A. Torti, 'La funzione dei 'Vizi' nella struttura del *Morality Play* del Primo Periodo Tudor', *Annali della Facoltà di Lettere e Filosofia dell'Università di Perugia* XIV (1976-1977) 177-217.

The maiden reprimands the dreamer for the three thoughtless statements he has just made: one cannot expect to see what God has prepared, nor aspire to go to Heaven without first having asked permission — and this permission can be denied. Nor can one enter the gates of Paradise without having died and returned to the earth from which one came. Man's judgement ('deme') is nullified when confronted with the 'deme' (supreme judgement) of the Lord.[16] The maiden contrasts a life of true love in God with the poet's pearl which, however 'precios' a 'tresor' (330 and 331), is yet earthly. For a moment, the narrator acknowledges his folly: 'If rapely I raue, spornande in spelle' (363), but then maintains that his pain has been assuaged by seeing the pearl, once again revealing a 'mysetente' judgement. True bliss, in fact, is found only in the Lamb, in Christ, who has made the girl a queen.

The dreamer shows himself linguistically unable to express the significance of the pearl, both as queen and equal to the other queens of Heaven (he uses mercantile hyponymic expressions such as 'precios', 'margarys', 'tresor'). The maiden attempts to explain this significance by means of some of the most problematic parables of the Gospel. The protagonist's misunderstandings and the Pearl's explanations reveal with dramatic irony the unintelligibility and ineffability of divine messages.

The first link-word used in its various meanings is 'cortaysye',[17] attributed in a negative way to the dreamer (the person who needs to see in order to believe is 'vncortayse', 303), and in a positive way to the Virgin and the elect in Heaven, where all are kings and queens 'by cortaysye', without anybody being diminished, 'depryue' (449). The dreamer seems to have understood that in Heaven one lives in 'Cortaysé . . . / And charyté grete, . . .' (469-470), but he cannot comprehend how a two-year-old girl could have attained the rank of queen (in fact, he uses hyponyms like 'countes', 'damysel', 'lady', as the most suitable to her status).

The contrast between human measure and heavenly measure is further signalled by the word 'date' (section IX), in its various meanings of limit, season, end, sunset (in general a point in time), and by the adverbs 'more' (sect. X) and 'innoghe' (sect. XI) functioning as intensifiers. Paradoxically

---

16   'Deme' has both the meaning of *to think about, imagine* (see *M.E.D.* s.v. 'dēmen', 14. (d): the example quoted is *Pearl,* 336-337) and, of God or destiny, *to ordain* (see *M.E.D.* s.v. 'dēmen', 8. (a): *Pearl* 360).

17   On link-words, see W.S. Johnson, 'The Imagery and Diction of *The Pearl:* Toward an Interpretation', *ELH XX* (1953) 161-180; O.D. Macrae-Gibson, *'Pearl*: The Link-Words and the Thematic Structure', *Neophilologus* 52 (1968) 54-64; J. Milroy, *'Pearl*: The Verbal Texture and the Linguistic Theme', *Neophilologus* 55 (1971) 195-208, which is focussed on the linguistic aspect of the poem. See also E. Wilson, 'Word Play and the Interpretation of *Pearl', Medium AEvum* 40 (1971) 116-134. On the meaning of 'cortaysye' see D.S. Brewer, 'Courtesy and the *Gawain*-Poet' in J. Lawlor, ed., *Patterns of Love and Courtesy* (London, 1966) 54-85, and J. Milroy, *The Verbal Texture,* pp. 199-205.

the amplifier 'more' is used for the parable of the Labourers in the Vineyard, in which the astonishment of those who have worked harder, upon receiving the same salary as those who have worked less, is a metaphor for the earthly measure — while the downtoner 'innoghe' is attributed to the grace of God.[18] The paradox of the relationship earthly life/reward after death lies in the subtle opposition between the labourers who have worked harder and therefore want more (and the dreamer himself cannot conceive the possibility that a higher salary can be given to those who work less), and the grace of God, 'gret innoghe'.

The equality of the kings and queens in the kingdom of 'cortaysye' and the 'mesure' of divine grace are incomprehensible to the poor jeweller who is forced to admit:

> Me þynk þy tale vnresounable.
> Goddeʒ ryʒt is redy and euermore rert,
> Oþer Holy Wryt is bot a fable. (590-592)

The incompatibility of the dreamer's ignorance with the pearl's wisdom is reaffirmed in the long treatise on the innocence and the salvation of the newly baptized children and in the ironical refrain, 'Þe innosent is ay saf by ryʒt' (sect. XII). The supreme justice of God which the dreamer has just doubted cannot be compared to man's justice. It is no longer a question of using terms such as 'cortaysye' or adverbs of human measure: God is justice *tout court*.[19]

The other paradox of becoming children in order to enter Heaven like pure pearls is introduced through the words of Christ. The fact that the refrain is eliminated at the beginning of section XIII, with the consequent break in the structural symmetry, emphasizes the gulf between the earthly identity of man and the spotless heavenly pearl. The refrain is 'perle maskelles', that pearl for which the jeweller sold everything he possessed and which the dreamer must earn by abandoning the world 'wode' (743), senseless and mad, and by forsaking earthly terms of comparison that do not correspond to the heavenly ones.[20]

The maiden goes on to present the 'gostly drem' (790) of John in which the New Jerusalem, Christ, the Lamb, the brides of the Lamb and the death

---

18 For the linguistic terminology, see R. Quirk and S. Greenbaum, *A University Grammar of English* (London, 1973), pp. 214-220.

19 On the characterization of the maiden and on the doctrinal aspects of her speech, see I. Bishop, *Pearl in Its Setting* (Oxford, 1968), pp. 101-125.

20 In fact, the dreamer continues to address the maiden with expressions such as 'Ouer alle oþer so hyʒ þou clambe / To lede wyth hym so ladyly lyf' (773-774) and 'A makeleʒ may and maskelleʒ' (780), without understanding. The irony is evident in that he uses superlatives to indicate the heavenly condition, whereas the maiden had only used 'innoghe' with reference to God's grace.

of Christ in the earthly Jerusalem are described. In section XIV, the stanza which relates Christ's sacrifice (805-816) is set between the first and last two which, through John's vision and Isaiah's prophecies, reveal the miracle of the transformation of the earthly Jerusalem into the Heavenly Jerusalem.[21] This miracle is due to the death of Christ, 'My Lombe, my Lorde, my dere juelle, / My ioy, my blys, my lemman fre' (795-796). These words, formerly used by the dreamer for the maiden as a human being, now acquire their true significance. In the Heavenly Jerusalem, the brides of the Lamb, among them the maiden, enjoy perfect equality and harmony (marked by the understatement of the intensifier 'neuer þe les'), and complete knowledge, expressed in the line 'We þurȝoutly hauen cnawyng' 859) and by deictics relating to nearness: 'Thys Jerusalem Lombe' (841), 'þys perle' (854), 'Þe Lombe' (861).

The sixth stanza is considered supernumerary:

> 'Neuer þe les let be my þonc',
> Quod I, 'My perle, þaȝ I appose;
> I schulde not tempte þy wyt so wlonc,
> To Krysteȝ chambre þat art ichose.
> I am bot mokke and mul among,
> And þou so ryche a reken rose,
> And bydeȝ here by þys blysful bonc
> Þer lyueȝ lyste may neuer lose.
> Now, hynde, þat sympelnesse coneȝ enclose,
> I wolde þe aske a þynge expresse,
> And þaȝ I be bustwys as a blose,
> Let my bone vayl neuerþelese.   (901-912)

Through the repetition of lexemes found in the first part of the dialogue,[22] it does in fact function as a means of reaffirming the 'worldliness' and the incredible ignorance of the dreamer who is the object of the poet's self-irony. Here 'wyt' denotes the wisdom of the maiden, whereas in line 294 it was used with contempt in reference to the dreamer: 'Þy worde byfore þy wytte con fle'. The error for which the protagonist has been so severely reprimanded is made evident by the word 'mul' (which had already appeared in line 382), and by the false relationship between dust and rose (false because the rose has become the pearl of great price).

Section XVI amplifies with *variatio* the same type of error, that is to say the confusion between the two Jerusalems, which requires the clarification of the maiden on the spotless Jerusalem as the eternal dwelling place of the

---

21 Section XIV presents a highly thematic symmetry: Christ's sacrifice stands at the centre, preceded by quotations from the Apocalypse and Isaiah (stanzas 1 and 2) and followed by quotations from Isaiah and the Apocalypse (stanzas 4 and 5).
22 See J. Milroy, *The Verbal Texture*, pp. 204-205.

perfect pearls. The characteristics of the city which no one can enter unless he is pure, without stain, are indicated by the expressions 'mote wythouten moote' (sect. XVI), 'As deuyseʒ hit þe apostel Jhon' (sect. XVII), 'bryʒter þen boþe þe sunne and mone' (sect. XVIII). The dreamer can only catch a glimpse of the city from the other side of the stream. In the description of the city, 'þat cyty of gret renoun' (986), the use of both the deictic *this* suggesting nearness — 'þis ilk toun' (995); 'þise stoneʒ' (997); 'Þise twelue degres' (1022); 'þis manayre' (1029) — and *that* suggesting distance — 'þat place' (1034); 'þat water' (1077); 'þat bayle' (1083); 'þat bone' (1090) — and in continuous reference to the Apocalypse signal a sense of the dreamer's participation in the life of the Heavenly Jerusalem which, however, is denied to him by his awakening at the moment of crossing the stream.

The narrator wants to say that, like the Apostle, he, too, has seen the wonders of the city, and identifies himself with John's descriptions; but this increases the suspicion that it is a further illusion created by the poet's artistic imagination. For a moment, the dreamer becomes the poet (or does the poet push the dreamer aside?) and with a richness of alliteration describes what, with the simple glimpse that the maiden allows him, he could not have described without the help of the apostle: a fantastic city, made of gold and precious stones, of an exceptional brilliance (God himself is the light and the Lamb the lamp). The wonder of that splendour is such that:

> For I dar say wyth conciens sure,
> Hade bodyly burne abiden þat bone,
> Þaʒ alle clerkeʒ hym hade in cure,
> His lyf were loste an-vnder mone. (1089-1092)

Human wisdom is incapable of bearing the sight of heavenly events and the gulf between heaven and earth becomes ever wider. The dreamer tries to lessen this gulf by participating in the 'gret delyt' of the maiden and of the other brides of the Lamb. An examination of the intensity and the characteristics of this delight would, if need be, give further proof of the superficial and thoughtless nature of the dreamer, in spite of the rigorous lesson the maiden has given him. He says:

> Delit þe Lombe for to deuise
> Wyth much meruayle in mynde went.
> Best watʒ he, blyþest, and moste to pryse,
> Þat euer I herde of speche spent; (1129-1132)

> Þat syʒt me gart to þenk to wade
> For luf-longyng in gret delyt. (1151-1152)

> Delyt me drof in yʒe and ere,
> My maneʒ mynde to maddyng malte;
> Quen I seʒ my frely, I wolde be þere,
> Byʒonde þe water þaʒ ho were walte. (1153-1156)

The delight in contemplating the Lamb is compared to the joy in seeing the pearl, which has once again become the little queen with earthly features — so much so that the 'luf-longyng' of line 1152, at the end of the vision, recalls to mind the 'luf-daungere' of line 11, at the beginning of the poem. Here we witness a change of emotions from passive to active — from the power of love which the lost pearl has on him the dreamer passes to the pressing desire to reacquire the pearl. The 'wreched wylle' of line 56 is reaffirmed in line 1155: 'I wolde be þere', the dreamer having forgotten the lessons learned in the past. The senses ('yȝe' and 'ere'), confused by delight, bring the dreamer to the point of semi-hysteria, but also allow the narrator to tell what he has seen, even if only from the other side of the stream.

As he is 'So mad arayde' (1166), the dreamer is not accepted by the divine Prince: only through the Eucharist which renews Christ's sacrifice, can he be purified and become a precious pearl of Christ's pleasure. Nevertheless, what had seemed to be an admission of his sins, above all the sin of pride relating to his wish to understand God's plans, and the acceptance of the maiden's teachings, is belied by a doubt which might upset the very significance of the vision. The narrator says:

'O Perle', quod I, 'of rych renoun,
So watȝ hit me dere þat þou con deme
In þys veray avysyoun!
If hit be ueray and soth sermoun
Þat þou so stykeȝ in garlande gay,
So wel is me in þys doel-doungoun
Þat þou art to þat Prynseȝ paye.' (1182-1188)

In the light of what I have said above on the dialogue between the maiden and the dreamer, one can ask if there has been a true vision and if this vision has brought about the desired enlightenment. The poet, with the opposition between his two *personae,* the narrator-dreamer and the pearl-maiden, has always denied the possibility that the human mind can understand. Only the maiden, who lives the life everlasting in the kingdom of Heaven, has a perfect comprehension which, however, cannot be communicated to those who are separated from Heaven because of their earthliness. Moreover the dreamer's wits are often confused by an experience which is so out of the ordinary.

The maiden has shown that truth and the five senses of man cannot be reconciled. The happiness of the dreamer in the valley of tears is an illusion. Cannot the vision itself be an illusion? The *dubitatio* ('In þys veray avysyoun! / If hit be ueray and soth sermoun / Þat þou so stykeȝ in garlande gay', 1184-1186) would be a simple rhetorical expedient indicating resignation as a consequence of the consolatory vision were it not for the deep pain and despair of the narrator for the loss of the pearl. This despair is shown to us as overwhelming at the beginning of the *tale* – *after* the experience of the dream, which the poet's *persona* is relating, has taken place.

If it is true that the dreamer has found 'A God, a Lorde, a frende ful fyin' (1204), it is also true that he is '. . . outfleme / So sodenly of þat fayre regioun' (1177-1178) and '. . . kaste of kytheȝ þat lasteȝ aye' (1198), and must admit 'Lorde, mad hit arn þat agayn þe stryuen, / Oþer proferen þe oȝt agayn þy paye' (1199-1200). The foolishness of the human attempts to penetrate God's mysteries, the terrible exile in the prison of pain, the desire for more ('Bot ay wolde man of happe more hente / Þen moȝte by ryȝt vpon hem clyuen', 1195-1196) remain. All these themes were already present in the 'erber' before he received the vision. Far from consoling him, the vision sharpens the sense of impotence of the man, who, confronted with the mysteries of life and death, tries to find a rational and natural explanation which is no more than folly and illusion – as St. Paul notes when he states that natural man does not know the plans of the Holy Ghost nor can he judge them, whereas spiritual man judges all and is judged by no one.[23]

The division between his natural 'I' *in actu* and his spiritual 'I' *in potentia* is superbly rendered by the poet with the creation of the two figures, the dreamer and the maiden, in contradiction with one another. As long as the dreamer is on earth, body and soul, his earthly being dominates, in spite of the vision. Despite the maiden's attempts to make superior concepts understood, the dreamer's whole understanding is reduced to human terms – desire, sight, possession. But is it the poet's wish, that the maiden reveal the truth she possesses to the dreamer? There is, in *Pearl*, a reaffirmation of St. Paul's teachings: that which is mortal is not to be confused with that which is heavenly; human understanding is limited, insufficient, and human reason cannot completely grasp the mysteries of God. In this way the journey, the 'auenture', has only served to reconfirm the impossibility of reconciling on earth the experience of any one thing desired by the dreamer and the perfect 'cnawyng' of everything voiced by the maiden.

In the poem, a strong opposition between the two *dramatis personae* is in fact evident. This is produced by the completely intellectual debate of one man, the poet, who, probably shaken by a painful personal experience, sets himself a series of vital questions, creating the two characters of the dreamer and the maiden. The paradigmatic connotations of the two characters can be summed up in the following manner: on the one hand, the dreamer is characterized by sorrow, ignorance, folly; the delight at seeing the maiden and the Lamb is interrupted at the end of the dream. On the other hand, the maiden possesses wisdom and happiness above and beyond any possible human measure.

---

23   I Cor., II. 14-15.

If this dichotomy between the finite nature of the dreamer and the infinite nature of the Pearl is irreconcilable, why does the maiden reproach the dreamer, who, moreover, errs again and shows himself ridiculous in his stubborness? Why does she propound yet further explanations, when the dreamer is unable to understand but in purely human terms? The answer comes from the poet:

Ouer þis hyul þis lote I laȝte   (1205)

Lote sums up the ambiguous and complex significance of *Pearl*. *Lǒt* (OE hlot) means, as all critics have read it, *fortune*, though it also contains the meaning of *experience, adventure*.[24] But, as Gordon has pointed out,[25] lōt(e) (ON lāt) means *utterance, song*, or, as the *MED* puts it, *word, speech, talk*.[26] The *Gawain*-poet uses both words,[27] and critics have often disagreed as to which one he meant on a particular occasion. In view of the extraordinary ability which this poet shows at word-play and ambiguity, it seems obvious to conclude that the meanings of *fortune, adventure*, and *talk* or *song* are all present in this line. If the dreamer with his 'resoun' and 'wylle' is unable to grasp the significance of the maiden's speech — within the vision he has (or has not) had the 'fortune' of having — the poet is still left with 'þis lote', with his poem. The deictic 'þis' reinforces the impression of the poet's familiarity with the object of his imagination — the narrative as a record of his journey, a search for the knowledge of himself and of his destiny.

Pearl thus points to the poet's reflection, however oblique and indirect, on his poetry. Nor is this the only occasion in which this author shows his self-consciousness as a poet. The last fifty lines of *Sir Gawain*, as Piero Boitani has shown,[28] constitute an extraordinary example of 'artistic self-consciousness'.

Auenture and *meruayle* have an important part to play in this conception. From the beginning of the dream, the poet is aware that his mind is not capable of understanding and that the means at his disposal are insufficient to describe his experience. As soon as the spirit leaves the body, the dreamer

---

24   See *M.E.D.* s.v. 'lǒt' 1. (c) *fortune, destiny, experience, adventure*. The example quoted by *M.E.D.* for 1. (c) is precisely *Pearl* 1205: 'Ouer þis hyul þis lote I laȝte'
25   E.V. Gordon, p. 86.
26   *M.E.D.*, s.v. 'lōte', 3. (b).
27   'Lōte' (= *talk)* especially in *Sir Gawain* (244, 988, 1086, 1954), but also in *Cleanness* (668). In *Pearl* 238: 'And haylsed me wyth a lote lyȝte', 'lote' is interpreted by *M.E.D.* as *facial expression, aspect, glance, look*, but it is seen by Gordon and Andrew and Waldron as meaning *word, speech* (Gordon), *voice* (Andrew and Waldron). Gordon interprets 'lote' at *Pearl* 986: 'As lyk to hymself of lote and hwe' again as *word, speech*.
28   Boitani, *English Medieval Narrative*, pp.69-70.

says that he is going 'In auenture þer meruayleȝ meuen' (64). Later he repeats this: 'More meruayle con my dom adaunt' (157). Here the reference to wonders is not merely a *topos* dear to chivalric literature, but also a way of presenting — by means of the *topos* — the *tale* of an *event*, of a *journey*,[29] to the reader capable of receiving his message. Prompted by fate or God ('dom'), he undertakes this journey amongst the 'meruayleȝ' of artistic creativity,[30] even if *his* 'dom' — his reason, judgement and imagination —[31] quails at the idea of such a difficult task.

This concept is reaffirmed many times, for instance when at the sight of the 'wonder perle' (221) on the maiden's breast the poet exclaims:

> I hope no tong moȝt endure
> No sauerly saghe say of þat syȝt,   (225-226)

Here we find a clear admission of the inadequacy of human language and therefore, of the poet's own words to describe such an experience. Later, it is still his human judgement that forces the poet to 'speke errour' (422) and to fear that 'Bot my speche þat yow ne greue' (471).

When the maiden compares the pearl on her breast to Heaven and invites the dreamer to acquire that pearl, he does nothing more than admire it from an aesthetic point of view, as an artist. He insists on the ability of the person who has formed the 'fayre fygure' (747) since

> Þy beauté com neuer of nature;
> Pymalyon paynted neuer þy vys,
> Ne Arystotel nawþer by hys lettrure
> Of carped þe kynde þese properteȝ.
> Þy colour passeȝ þe flour-de-lys;
> Þyn angel-hauyng so clene corteȝ.   (749-754)

Certainly this contrast between the work of nature and of Pygmalion and Aristotle is a *topos*, probably taken from the *Roman de la Rose;* nevertheless

---

29 On the meaning of 'auenture' as *tale of adventures,* see *M.E.D.* s.v. 'aventūre', 6. The most relevant example quoted there is *Gawain* 27, 29.

30 On the association of 'meruayle' with poetry, see Aristotle's *Metaphysics* and St. Thomas's commentary: 'Fabula namque ex miris constituitur', S. Thomae Aquinatis *In Duodecim Libros Metaphysicorum Aristotelis Expositio* (Taurini — Romae, 1971, sec. ed.), p. 17. On the poetry-marvel relationship in Dante, see now P. Boyde, *Dante Philomythes and Philosopher* (Cambridge, 1981), ch. I.

31 On the various meanings of the word 'dom' see *M.E.D.* s.v. 'dōm'. For *imagination* the *M.E.D.* (s.v. 'dōm', 5b. (c)) quotes *Pearl* 157: 'More meruayle con my dom adaunt'.

the poet's use of these conventions is important.[32] Once again he underlines the difficulty of expressing a concept of beauty which is above nature and which neither the artist nor the philosopher *par excellence,* Pygmalion and Aristotle, can grasp. Neither mimetic capacity nor philosophical speculation can fully comprehend divine beauty, which is 'supersubstantiale pulchrum'.[33]

Only John, directly inspired by God, has succeeded in his book of *Revelations* in reconciling perfect wisdom with human finiteness. The poet of *Pearl* has failed. If the Apostle's book can be sealed by Christ's words which at the beginning and at the end assert the truthfulness and the 'necessity' of the vision, the poet can only reaffirm the wonder and the exceptional favour granted to him and paradoxically doubt the validity of his vision.

Yet this poem, 'lote', is left. Its setting is in a didactic timelessness in which the contrast between natural being and spiritual being presents itself each time man questions his own destiny. The poem can only express what is finite, mortal and what is *not* infinite, immortal. For this reason the poet uses the pearl as a symbol which represents a girl, the jeweller's precious stone, celestial beauty, an emblem of moral purity, salvation and the kingdom of Heaven.

In the poem the opposition between earthly happiness (the natural aspect of man) and spiritual happiness, which is attained only with the aid of divine grace (the spiritual aspect of man) is always present. Being a polysemous symbol the pearl goes beyond this opposition, but at the same time it is an element of contradiction and confusion, representing both the rose that dies and the pearl that enjoys everlasting life. In this way, the poem, with its perfect structure,[34] constitutes a whole, a synthesis, but also expresses, through the two *personae,* an antithesis between the earthly and the spiritual elements, which is ubiquitous and which the ambiguity of the pearl as a whole and a part continuously both resolves and denies.

---

32 For the influence of the *Roman de la Rose,* see Gordon, *Pearl,* p. 72. The primary source of the story of Pygmalion is found in Ovid's *Metamorphoses,* Book X, 243-297 (Ovide, *Les Métamorphoses,* ed. by G. Lafaye (Paris, 1960), in which the association of the purity of the gem with the whiteness of ivory and lilies is also present. 'Interea niueum mira feliciter arte / Sculpsit ebur formamque dedit;...' (247-248) and 'Hyr vysage whyt as playn yuore' (178); 'Liliaque pictasque pilas et ab arbore lapsas / Heliadum lacrimas; ...' (262-263) and 'Quen þat frech as flor-de-lys' (195) and 'Þy colour passeȝ þe flour-de-lys' (753). On Pygmalion and the *Roman de la Rose,* see R. Tuve, *Allegorical Imagery* (Princeton, 1966), pp. 262-263 and Robertson, *Preface,* pp. 99-103.

33 For this concept of God's beauty, see S. Thomae Aquinatis *In Librum Beati Dionysii De Divinis Nominibus Exposition* (Taurini – Romae, 1950). C. IV, 1. v, 333-356, pp. 113-115; see U. Eco, *Il problema estetico in Tommaso d'Aquino* (Milano, 1970)

34 But there are 'imperfections' such as the missing line, the supernumerary stanza, and the refrain which is lacking in section XIII. See Gordon, *Pearl,* p. 88; Milroy, *The Verbal Texture,* pp. 204-205 and Nelson, *The Circle,* p. 33.

To conclude with the words of the poet, the poem, like the pearl on the maiden's breast, is '. . . wemleȝ, clene, and clere, / And endeleȝ rounde, and blyþe of mode' (737-738) — beautiful, infinitely circular, serene for the joy and consolation that the 'writing' of it gives to the author and to the reader.

GAWAIN'S DREAM OF EMANCIPATION

ENRICO GIACCHERINI

I

Historically speaking, romance constitutes, within the area of medieval western literature, a narrative genre with an adventurous subject, whose protagonists are knights, kings and queens. The specific motives that drive the romance hero to action can be various, but, in the last analysis, find their own justification in themselves: the hero is driven toward adventure for adventure's sake.

The most peculiar trait of romance is, however, that of being a free product of the imagination, free, that is, from a representational conception of reality in terms of verisimilitude. The world of romance is the realm of the marvellous, within which natural laws are often suspended or infringed by an act of magic, or by divine intervention. This transgression, on the other hand, is not perceived as an alteration of the balance of forces keeping that world under tension, but only as one of the aspects in which that order manifests itself. As such, it will arouse none of those feelings of awe and anguished terror that we normally associate with supernatural phenomena.

Our access to this enchanted garden is consequently dependent on a spontaneous rejection of all the ideological paraphernalia which our familiarity with the canons of realism has made an integral part of our critical approach to literary texts, especially of a narrative kind. In order to penetrate into the utopian space of man's desire represented by the world of romance, and to understand from within the peculiar laws by which it is governed, it is therefore indispensable to exercise a willing suspension of our disbelief and an unconditional surrender to its magical atmosphere. In other words, romance as a literary genre has its own specific conventions, which our approach to the protagonists must also take into account.

Although they have in common an essentially human nature, the figures that populate this universe — no matter what cultural and linguistic area they belong to — do not meet the requirements of a psychological characterization in terms of individuality; they are rather the result of a process of stylization aimed at an emblematic portrayal of idealized types. Nevertheless, it is essential to notice that the typical romance hero is no mirror of virtue, no Galahad impervious to all temptation; he is, on the contrary, a sinner who is always repenting, and whose idealization takes on mostly ethical and social connotations, largely determined by the historical matrix of medieval romance itself: as Auerbach put it, 'A self-portrayal of feudal knighthood with its mores and ideals is the fundamental purpose of the courtly romance'.[1] This does not however imply that the circulation of the romances was restricted to that social class. The romance, as well as its derivations in later ages, has always met with extraordinary favour among all layers of society, becoming a pre-eminently popular genre. Indeed, the Middle Ages saw the development of a process through which the aristocratic ethos of the dominant class, mirrored in the romances, became gradually detached from the feudal *humus* from which its historical and political function originated, to assume, in the courtly society, an intrinsically absolute value. It is thanks to this quality of absoluteness that the genre has maintained its hold over a public belonging to such different ages and social classes, reflecting as no other literary form the aspirations and desires of mankind. The concept of 'class', then, as used in socio-literary criticism, is only applicable to the 'superstructures' of romance, but is of little help in understanding the nature and efficacy of its basic structures, which are characterized to a large extent by an element of idealization, that is of projection of 'deep' desires, common to all human beings, in the various shapes determined by historical circumstances.

As regards the formal principles that regulate romance, a generally valid structural pattern is given by the quest — the ideal narrative framework for generations of romancers, thanks especially to its non-coercive nature. The action of the romances, in fact, is syntactically characterized by the predominance of parataxis, according to a principle of simple spatial and chronological contiguity, rather than causality. Every adventure is for the hero a test he has to submit to, but the link with the events that first set him off on his journey is nearly always tenuous to the point of evanescence; the reader is then forced to strain his memory in order to tie up the loose ends of a thread which, in the meantime, has become entangled with a hundred others. But Professor Vinaver's now classic analogy with the *entrelacement* structure of romanesque ornamentation, through which he has admirably characterized the *ductus* of the romance, discloses the organic and dynamic quality of the logical and syntactical relations forming the 'deep' layers of this genre.[2] The rhythms and modules into which a romance deploys itself

---

1   *Mimesis*, trans. W.R. Trask (Princeton, 1957) p. 131.
2   The parallel, originally formulated by Ferdinand Lot, was several times reelaborated by the late Professor Vinaver beginning with his 'A la recherche d'une poétique médiévale', *Cahiers de Civilisation Médiévale* 2 (1959) 1-16. The dynamic function of this structural device has been particularly stressed by R. Tuve, *Allegorical Imagery* (Princeton, 1966), pp. 359 ff. and P. Zumthor, *Essai de poétique médiévale* (Paris, 1972), ch. 8 *passim*.

are therefore essentially, albeit variously, iterative, while movement, which is at any rate always perceptible, is often distinguished, in space as well as in time, by circularity.

The distinctive features of romance can thus be summed up as fantasy, non-naturalism, abundance of the marvellous and the supernatural, stylization, popularity, and an apparent lack of structural logic.[3] All these elements underline the analogies that relate romance to other phenomena such as fairy-tale, myth, and dream, the characters of which belong to a prevailingly psychological and mythical dimension. Its latent affinity with the realm of dreams is also stressed by the presence and ready acceptance of fantastically improbable events within the framework of everyday reality, on whose surface they form only ripples that are soon smoothed away. In this respect, there is no more instructive example than the ambiguous greenness of Gawain's adversary in the best Middle English romance of the fourteenth century.

Once the validity of these premises is accepted, we can observe that ever since remotest antiquity an interpretation in symbolic terms of the images produced by dream activity has been regarded as not only possible, but as necessary.[4] The hypothesis that the motifs and images recurrent in texts like the romances possess a meaning that reaches beyond the explicit, literal level of the narration, can be verified by the adoption for these literary texts of exegetical criteria having as their foundation the concept of symbolism, as in the case of the dream and its manifestations.

If the language of dreams is characterized by 'primitiveness', consisting as it does not of conceptual abstractions but of representations of images which have an immediate effect — a trait it shares, as we have pointed out, with myth, ritual, popular narrative, romance, in short with all 'naïve' literary forms[5] — their content can be defined as a pictorial history of the dreamer, that can only be interpreted in an individual key. The absolute protagonist in this activity is in fact the dreamer himself, who expresses his innermost wishes, conflicts and feelings by means of materials drawn from his personal experience.[6] The analogy between romance and dream could

---

3   See Derek Brewer's interesting article 'The Nature of Romance', *Poetica* 9(1978) 9-48.

4   See for instance R.L. Van de Castle's helpfully synthetic essay 'The Psychology of Dreaming', in *Dreams and Dreaming*, ed. S.G.M. Lee, and A.R. Mayes (Harmondsworth, 1973) pp.17-32, with bibliography.

5   With 'naive', a term he derived from Schiller, Northrop Frye defines a literary form that aims at communicating through space and time with special immediacy and efficacy, therefore also 'popular'. See his *Anatomy of Criticism* (Princeton, 1957) p. 35.

6   See C.G. Jung's very clear exposition of this concept in his last published work 'Approaching the Unconscious', in *Man and His Symbols*, ed. C.G. Jung (London, 1961).

then be further extended to identifying the romance hero with the protagonist/dreamer, and to analyzing the former, and the specific characters and actions which make up the story, in terms of projections. As in dream analysis, it is only through a process of this kind that the interpreter can go back from the projection to the matrix that generated it, and to do this he must combine the exigency of maintaining a safe critical distance from the object of his enquiry with the deepest possible penetration of the psychic universe from which it originates. A certain degree of identification will become inevitable, and the critic's position will then be partly similar to that of a reader emotionally involved in a story to the point of 'becoming' its hero. In a way, the critic may be said to take part in a creative process that unites the narrator, the protagonist of the story and all its potential public.[7] It is worth noticing at this point that the effect of profound gratification produced in the reader − or listener − by his instinctively letting himself become absorbed by a story, would indicate that traditional narratives of this kind body forth motifs that are latent in the unconscious layers of the psyche. However, I do not here take 'unconscious' in its canonical meanings of Jung's 'mythical realm of racially inherited experience' or of Freud's 'seat of irrational libidinal forces', to quote Erich Fromm,[8] but, following his suggestion, in the less rigid one of the seat of experiences to which the mental schemes that characterize external reality cannot be applied.

Needless to say, this is but one critical approach among many that are equally valid. Far from exhausting at all levels the literary work that constitutes its object, its aim is to bring to light the deep motivations, the basic themes that underlie its imagery, and the narrative patterns implicit in the work, rather than to account for its 'artistic' merit − if by this expression we mean the author's capacity to give an aesthetically accomplished shape to those latent contents by means of traditional verbal and rhetorical structures, constantly regenerated in the poetic process.[9]

---

7   See A.D. Wilson, *Traditional Romance and Tale* (Ipswich, 1976), p. 30: 'the protagonist . . . is how we most wish to see ourselves in the story, and while he is as much an image as are other characters representing the hero in the story, it is correct to see him as the essential representative of ourselves, creating the story. We, if we join the story-teller, are the actual hero, recreating the story through the acknowledged hero.'

8   *The Forgotten Language* (London, 1952), pp. 35-36.

9   It is also indispensable to avoid the danger − always threatening all symbolic interpretations − of privileging the 'fruyt' to the detriment of the 'chaff', in other words, of denying all relevance to the manifest content, the *littera* of the text. As Derek Brewer points out − to whom sec. II of this essay is very much indebted − in literary interpretation 'the latent may well govern the manifest content, but it is the manifest which realises the latent and gives it some uniquely interesting force' ('The Interpretation of Dream, Folktale and Romance with Special Reference to *Sir Gawain and the Green Knight*', *Neuphilologische Mitteilungen* 77[1976] 569-81. The passage quoted is at p. 572).

II

The portrait of King Arthur, as it emerges from *Sir Gawain and the Green Knight,* shows him as very different from the superior, detached, old monarch of a largely spurious Victorian tradition; he is, on the contrary, 'þe comlokest kyng þat þe court haldes' (53),[10] 'Kyng hyȝest mon of wylle' (57), young, in love with life, with a restlessly exuberant personality.[11] These highly idealized features inevitably present him as a projection of the desires of the hero, whose figure — as we have suggested — can be identified with the anonymous Gawain-poet (in that he is the author's mental creation) as well as with every actual or potential reader, eventually with man himself. Arthur's bride too is, in equally idealized terms, 'Þe comlokest to discrye / . . . / A semloker þat euer he syȝe / Soth moȝt no mon say' (81-4); similar characteristics are shared by all the inhabitants of the court of Camelot, the noblest knights and the loveliest ladies, gathered there for the Christmas season in glee and serenity. If we look beyond its historically and socially determined aspects, it is evident that Arthur's court represents, thanks to the warm, serene and festive atmosphere that pervades it, an ideal habitat. It is, in other words, every man's ideal kingdom, one's own home. Camelot, then, with its young and active ruler and his equally young, fair and beloved bride, can easily be seen as an idealized version of the basic family nucleus.[12] However, assuming that the situation as a whole is but a projection of the hero's desires, it follows that the latter feels excluded from that state, to which he would like to have access. Now, the nearest model of such a situation that is offered to the protagonist, as well as to any man in certain periods of his existence, is of course the family, where the paternal and maternal figures dominate. King Arthur, the embodiment of the hero's ideal aspirations — whose concrete model is normally given by the paternal figure — will then inevitably result from a condensation of several valencies, among which we recognize 'the father'. Indeed Gawain introduces himself as the king's nephew, seated next to the queen, and it is well known that 'the uncle' is quite often a substitute of the paternal figure, thus making possible the manifestation of hostile feelings which would otherwise be censored and repressed.[13]

---

10   All quotations and line references from *Sir Gawain and the Green Knight* are taken from the text edited by J.R.R. Tolkien and E.V. Gordon, rev. N. Davis, 2nd ed. (Oxford, 1968).

11   See 96-99.

12   On a sociological plane, the power of the sovereign in a monarchy finds at once a correspondence and a justification in the exercise of the *patria potestas* within the microcosm of the family nucleus, of which the state, mathematically speaking, is but an involution.

13   The 'Freudian' school of criticism has made of this one of its favourite points. See, for all, E. Jones' classic study *Hamlet and Oedipus* (London, 1949).

While the Green Knight's epiphany seems to fall unexpectedly on a surprise-stricken assembly, it nonetheless responds to an implicit desire on the king's part: 'Oþer sum segg hym bisoȝt of sum siker kniȝt / To joyne wyth hym in iustyng, in jopardé to lay, / Lede, lif for lyf, leue vchon oþer' (96-8). On a latent level, the event is therefore elicited by the protagonist, but his mental conflict induces him to project the expression of that desire onto the uncle-king; this hypothesis is confirmed, on a manifest level, by Arthur's by no means frightened reaction to such an extraordinary event. The irrational and fantastic substance of what has been going on, a dream-like parenthesis within the narrative flow of time, is underlined by Arthur's words to Guinevere, which describe the episode as 'such craft vpon Crist-masse, / Laykyng of enterludez' (471-2), while earlier on in the text the reader had already been offered explicit hints as to its peculiarly oneiric quality when, after the Green Knight's first words, the courtiers 'stonstil seten / In a swoghe sylence . . . / As al were slypped vpon slepe' (242-4).

Also the Green Knight, the most bewildering figure in the poem, presents essentially ambiguous connotations, seeming to point now to a terror-striking titanism, now to the perfection of a demigod:[14] yet, in the latter form, the boundary between what is human and what is superhuman tends to become blurred, and the two natures eventually coincide. A similar uncertainty is raised by the Green Knight's behaviour and speech, halfway between that of a courteous guest and that of an arrogant challenge-bearer; a challenge, at any rate, which for him is little more than 'a Crystemas gomen' (283), a game, therefore a fiction, a mental fiction.

The hero shows his eagerness to go through this test, but at the same time is so scared at its possible consequences that the manifestation of his wish is attributed to the very enemy he has just evoked. This image, on the other hand, is marked by characteristics of imposing nobility, beauty, invincibility, that enable us to recognize in the Green Knight an unmistakable father-figure. Furthermore, Gawain himself had previously identified his own role as that of the 'son' in the Knight's description of all the courtiers he was addressing − which is consequently also the hero's description of himself and of his own 'double' Arthur: 'Hit arn aboute on þis bench bot berdlez chylder' (280). But this strong feeling of antagonism against this figure objectifies another conflict between different urges at work in the hero's psyche: the will to confront and defeat the paternal figure on the one hand, and, on the other, the inevitable sense of guilt and fear induced by the acknowledgement of such opposition. The 'fantoum'[15] thus conjured up must necessarily possess such features as may justify this feeling in the eyes of an ever vigilant conscience. This task is obviously fulfilled by the Knight's

---

14   See ll. 136-40; 142-6; 181-6; 199-202.
15   'Forþi for fantoum and fayryȝe þe folk þere hit demed' (240).

most shocking trait, his green colour. Whatever its traditional sources may be, the most relevant aspect of this complex image is certainly its 'deep' effect of dismay and terror. This is originated by the fact that the green colour is the visible sign of a totally alien, non-human nature, conveying, as such, a bottomless horror[16] — exemplified, for instance, by the 'Martians' or 'monsters from outer space' of science fiction in its pioneering stage, creatures that were so often green, and always hostile and death-bearing. Another, and more striking example is the fisherman, as ugly as a sea-monster, who threatens Pinocchio, and whose head, 'Instead of hair . . . was covered with a thick bush of green grass, his skin was green, his long beard that came down to the ground was also green'.[17] The idea thus objectified takes on a paradoxically reassuring shape, for it presents the antagonist as a dangerously perturbing element, and by so doing eliminates those hindrances that might have prevented the hero from assuming his own responsibility by confronting 'the enemy'.

The specific form of Gawain's rebellious act — the beheading — adds an explicitly sexual dimension to the father-son opposition that has been gaining consistence, thanks to its well-recognized status as a castration symbol. Yet this is not enough to outline an Oedipal situation, at least not in the Freudian sense.[18] So far, in fact, a fully maternal figure has been largely absent from the scene: Queen Guinevere is in the first place 'the king's wife', an expression, as such, of the protagonist's desire to have a wife and an independent family of his own. In *Sir Gawain and the Green Knight* the maternal archetype is certainly present, but under different shapes. On the one hand it is sublimated in the Virgin Mary, to whom her faithful servant Gawain turns in his moments of greatest despair; a prayer to her is sufficient to give him rest from the mental travail that is ravaging him, objectified in the rigours of the winter season and the dangerous waste land he finds himself in the midst of during his search for the Green Chapel. On the other hand, the Mother is also a repressive image, who opposes the son's escape from the family circle and his entering into adulthood — a principle embodied in our poem by Bertilak's wife. Indeed Bertilak represents an obvious father-

---

16 We can borrow here J. Speirs's words. In essence he is the *other* — the other than human —, but not the precise meaning Speirs attributed to them, nor his conclusions. See his *Medieval English Poetry* (London, 1957), p. 226

17 C. Collodi, *Pinocchio: The Tale of a Puppet*, trans. M.A. Murray (London,1911) p. 176.

18 See S. Freud, *The Interpretation of Dreams*, vol. 4 pt. I of *The Standard Edition of the Complete Psychological Works of Sigmund Freud*, ed. J. Strachey and A. Freud (London, 1953), pp. 255 ff.

figure in its most loving and protective aspect:[19] he is a mature man, noble in demeanour and speech, strong and proud, whose meeting with Gawain bears some resemblance to the 'prodigal son' episode. The reverse of the medal, the hostile and threatening side, as we have suggested, is embodied by the Green Knight, who will eventually reveal himself as none other but Bertilak. Analogously, the mother-figure too is split into two faces, whose contrast is only deceptive. To Bertilak's wife, whose undeniable sexual appeal can be seen as a symbol of the fascination she exerts on the hero (a regressive image, then, identifiable with the son's almost irresistible temptation to give up his efforts towards independence), can be added the awfully sombre aspect of the Mother, here present in the guise of the mysterious old woman who stands at her side, holding her by the hand in a gesture that stresses their basic identity.[20]

On the level of the manifest contents, Gawain's testing by the lady of the castle is the *clou* of the whole poem. But by this testing, of a patently sexual nature, the hero once again projects his own conflict with the paternal image, which he obliquely challenges by attacking 'the lord's wife', or, in other words, 'the father's property'. It goes without saying that, as the existence of this conflict is denied by the protagonist's conscious mind, the manifestation of his desire – the first amorous advances – is attributed to the woman herself, who thus becomes at once the subject and the object of the temptation.

The hunting scenes are fairly transparent allegories of the erotic ones that are simultaneously taking place.[21] In the first of the three days Bertilak goes hunting for hinds, whose flesh is pierced with arrows – the sexual allusion in the scene is quite evident – while at home the protagonist 'evokes' the lady who offers him her love in very explicit terms. Yet Gawain accepts but one kiss which, as was agreed, he will return in the evening to the lord: the mechanism at work is that of a confession that will absolve him from his sense of guilt. It is clear, however, that Gawain identifies him-

---

19   This has induced some critics to identify Sir Bertilak with king Arthur, like J.A. Burrow, *A Reading of Sir Gawain and the Green Knight* (London, 1965), pp. 65-66. This interpretation, supported by Tolkien's translation of 'hyghe eldee' (844) with 'in the prime of youth' (see the Glossary to his edn, s.v. *elde(e) n.*) is contradicted, in the first place, by Bertilak's white beard ('bryʒt' [845]) and by his demeanour, which is that of a more than mature man. In my view, there is a marked contrast with the youth of Arthur and his courtiers.

20   See 11. 943-60.

21   See especially the observations of J. Speirs, pp. 236ff. Without going into details, we can notice that the killing of the prey suggests the beheading scenes at the beginning and conclusion of the poem, while the exchange at the end of each day suggests the exchange of strokes Sir Gawain and the Green Knight have agreed on. See also C. Moorman, 'Myth and Medieval Literature: *Sir Gawain and the Green Knight*', Medieval Studies 18(1956) 158-72.

self to a certain degree also with the hunter, that is the paternal archetype, endowed with the power to 'kill' females: the state of confusion still present in the hero's mind at this stage[22] is however gradually giving place to an ever increasing self-assurance. In the course of the second day, Gawain receives two kisses from the lady: the atmosphere between them becomes more and more tense, while the hero's fears are sharply mirrored in Bertilak's beheading of the boar slain at the end of the chase. The protagonist of the third, and last, hunting party is a fox — cunning and shrewdness resisting the hunter-father, after the wild boar's physical strength; and just as Gawain is dreaming of his now imminent encounter with the Green Knight, the image he conjures up is that of the loosely-dressed woman who kisses him, and then 'With smoþe smylyng and smolt þay smeten into merþe, / Þat al watz blis and bonchef þat breke hem bitwene, / and wynne.' (1763-5). On a manifest level, that is, in the hero's conscious mind, the consummation is denied and rejected; at the crisis, Gawain appeals to the Virgin to help him out of that very embarrassing circumstance: 'Gret perile bitwene hem stod, / Nif Maré of hir knyȝt mynne' (1768-9). It is significant, in this context, that the image Gawain turns to is precisely the celestial sublimation of the mother-archetype, the Mother from whom the hero is desperately trying to escape. Yet Gawain's sexual desire for the woman is undeniable, and this, from our point of view, amounts to saying that, on a latent level, the final consummation has actually taken place. On this level, then, the challenge to the paternal figure is now brought to its extreme consequences through the hero's assertion of his own strength and independence. At the same time, sexuality is resolutely rejected to the degree that the embrace with the woman-mother symbolizes the temptation to seek refuge inside the maternal womb, and, consequently, the regression to a pre-natal stage of absolute dependence.[23] The fact that Gawain deliberately omits to return to Bertilak the girdle he has accepted from his wife can be explained if we interpret the object as the symbol of what he has conquered.[24] The girdle is thus doubly a talisman: it reassures the possessor, for by openly accepting it instead of what the woman was ready to give him he implicitly claims that he has committed no sin, whereas, on a latent level, the girdle gives him the kind of self-confidence deriving by the consciousness of his own power.

---

22 Cf. the analysis of the hunting scenes in A.D. Wilson, pp.100-2, to whom I am partially indebted.

23 According to D.S. Brewer instead ('The Interpretation. . .', pp. 579-80) the rejection of sexuality is totally unconditional, since it is associated to natural forces and, in the last analysis, to death; for him, then, only by refusing sexuality can man achieve independence.

24 The chromatic symmetry between the object in question and the Green Knight seems somehow to anticipate the revelation of the latter's identity with the lord of the castle, the legitimate owner of what Gawain has obtained.

74

The final clash with the Green Knight eventually takes place at what is known as the Green Chapel, but the scene that offers itself to the hero's eyes is rather that of 'a lawe as hit were, /A balȝ berȝ bi a bonke' (2171-2), and 'nobot an olde caue, / Or a creuisse of an olde cragge' (2182-3). If the first picture suggested by the text is that of a mound, the next focuses on a cave, or a fissure on the surface of the earth, whence, shortly after, the Knight emerges as if 'of a hole' (2221). His abode — as green, mysterious and frighteningly alien as its inhabitant — has all the appearances of a *mundus,* a cleft in the body of Mother Earth, whose archetypal connotations, obscurely complex though they are, always convey a feeling of deadly horror.[25] The very use of the term 'chapel', on the other hand, does not make sense unless it is understood as a 'sacred space', a place, that is, which by its own nature and destination communicates the kind of awe that is peculiar to divine epiphanies.

The hero's meeting with the paternal archetype represented by the Green Knight, in fact, cannot but occur in the womb of the Great Mother, while all the journey that has led him there reveals itself at last as a catabasis, where the recognition of the hero's father — the explicit subject of so many romances, from the French anonymous *Livre de Caradoc*[26] to the Italian *Guerin Meschino* — is nothing but the finding of the self, of one's own source and essence. On a psychological level, Gawain's quest is therefore the dramatization of the protagonist's descent to the lower regions of the psyche and, as such, follows a pattern we have learnt to recognize in a number of mythological and fabulous narrations, from that of Aeneas to that of Pinocchio and a thousand other heroes who, in the bowels of the earth or of a sea-monster, find their lost father, and finally reemerge as 'new', adult human beings.

Gawain's final testing in the beheading episode makes him realize that he is as strong as his opponent, who is discovered to be unable to hurt him seriously. The hero does not, however, come out totally unscathed from this experience, for no one is immune from the feeling of having somehow disappointed, or even betrayed one's own father and mother; the slight scar on Gawain's neck is the visible sign of the process he has gone through. The same sense of guilt may provide an adequate symbolic explanation for Gawain's attempt to excuse the Green Knight / Sir Bertilak from all the personal responsibility — thus providing a justification for his own behaviour,

25 Cf. E. Fromm, pp. 185 ff.
26 This French romance, one of the nearest analogues to our poem, offers decisive evidence for the symbolic interpretation presented here. It turns out, at its conclusion, that the knight who had been the bearer of the challenge taken up by the hero Caradoc — another beheading — was none other than Caradoc's own father, who spares him on this account. See Tolkien and Gordon's edn., Introd., p. xvi.

too: the cause of everything is Morgan le Fay (the old woman of the castle) who, we now know, is Gawain's aunt, and has learnt her craft from her lover Merlin. Their relation is therefore that of aunt and uncle, once again identifiable as parents-substitutes, which helps us to understand Morgan's motivations; her enmity toward Guinevere conceals the mother's antagonism toward the bride of the son (to whom the figure of the queen was reducible), in other words the most dangerous rival, for whom the son forsakes the mother.

The 'deep' analysis of *Sir Gawain and the Green Knight* has brought to light some internal lines of tension that confer to it the character of a psychodrama, whose subject is the passage of the individual from the state of adolescence to independent adulthood. In the course of this process the individual finds himself forced to break open the chrysalis of his family and of those forces, at once protective and repressive, that tend to suffocate him. In this struggle, the antagonist is represented by the paternal figure, flanked by that of the mother. In this critical phase, a threatening attitude is attributed to both figures, which, however, the conscious mind disguises in order to justify the individual's hostile reaction and the following sense of guilt. In our specific case, the camouflage is given by the 'alien' look of the Green Knight and the attribution to the maternal figure of the status of 'witch', endowed with magical powers directed toward evil.

One of the reasons for the rivalry between the protagonist and the father is certainly of a sexual nature, but it would be wrong to take this as the only motivation of the conflict, or even a decisive one: it is just one aspect of the prize at stake, and a means to reach it.

III

If the latent contents of romance lend themselves to a symbolic analysis based on methods more commonly applied to dream activity, the actual narrative form assumed by these contents shows a stricter affinity with another of those phenomena formerly identified as belonging to the same category of expression as myths, fairy-tales and dreams: the ritual.[27] Vladimir Propp noticed long ago that the roots of the fairy-tale lie deep in ritualistic soil, and that the closest connection is to be found with the most significant rite in the life of the individual as well as of the group in the

---

27 Northrop Frye has recognized in what he calls the formal phase of narrative, ' a recurrent act of symbolic communication', that is a ritual, and in its significant content – from the viewpoint of archetypal criticism – an element of 'conflict of desire and reality which has for its basis the work of the dream' (pp. 104-5). See also pp. 186 ff.

76

context of a 'primitive' society, that is the puberty initiation.[28] It is not my
intention here to apply to *Sir Gawain and the Green Knight* J.L. Weston's
well-known theories of a genetic kind about the role of the initiation rites in
the romance,[29] the initiation pattern — I believe — has a universal validity
that transcends its single manifestations tied to divers historical and cultural
situations. By means of a procedure analogous to that used in relation to
dreams, I shall limit myself to pointing out a number of analogies and corre-
spondences between the two orders of phenomena, in view of more generally
valid conclusions.

The affinity between the symbolic interpretation of our romance in
terms of dream activity, such as has been put forward, and the initiation
pattern emerges in the very nature of the latter, consisting — as Mircea
Eliade defines it — in 'un ensemble de rites et d'enseignements oraux, qui
poursuit la modification radicale du statut réligieux et social du sujet à ini-
tier', the equivalent, in philosophical terms, of an ontological change of the
existential regime of the individual. More precisely, puberty initiation consists in a series of rites, compulsory for all the young males of the tribe,
which give them the right to be admitted among the adults. Once the
adolescent has passed through a number of tests, 'c'est grâce à ces rites, et
aux révélations qu'ils comportent, qu'il sera reconnu comme un membre
responsable de la societé'.[30] The individual process of coming to maturity
on a psychic level is therefore homologous with the set of ceremonies that —
on a social plane — aim at introducing the subject to be initiated into the
status of adult. The principal stages of this ritual include, first of all, the
severance from one's family, or rather from the women's society, under

---

28 V.Y. Propp, *Istoričeskie korni volšebnoj skazki* (Leningrad,1946); the book has
    never been translated into English. Further references are to the Italian translation,
    Le radici storiche dei racconti di fate (Torino, 1972). Propp's main purpose, con-
    sistently with his rigid marxist orthodoxy, was to underline the transformations
    undergone by fairy-tales with the changing of the socio-economic structures of
    the peoples of whose cultural heritage they were part. See, however, M. Eliade's
    objections to Propp's thesis in his 'Les savants et les contes de fées', *Nouvelle
    Revue Française*, 1956.
29 *From Ritual to Romance* (Cambridge, 1920). The role of the archetypal pattern
    of initiation in *Sir Gawain and the Green Knight* has also been stressed by H.
    Zimmer, *The King and the Corpse* (New York and London, 1948), but his other-
    wise valuable work is diminished by a quantity of far-fetched and gratuitous hypo-
    theses. A similar case is presented by J. Speirs's study, which was the first to assert
    the necessity of a symbolic interpretation of our poem. On Zimmer's and Speirs's
    theses, vitiated also by a terminological confusion between 'ritual' and 'myth',
    see the observations of C. Moorman, not wholly exempt, however, from the same
    fault.
30 *Initiations, rites, sociétés secrètes: Naissances mystiques* (Paris,1959). p.12. This
    is a revised French translation of Eliade's *Birth and Rebirth* (New York,1958),
    originally published in English, not at present available to me.

whose jurisdiction the child normally falls. The parting, in most cases, happens in a highly traumatic and frightening way. The adolescents believe that they are about to be carried off by divine beings, who make their appearance wearing horrific mask-heads, with the purpose of 'killing' them, that is abducting them from the world that has been familiar to them, in order that they may be later reborn under a new guise: but a rebirth necessarily implies a passage through death, albeit a symbolic one. Sir Gawain's Green Knight shows close analogies with these beings; he too belongs to the subterranean world, the realm of death, to which his greenness indubitably connects him, while his effect on Gawain and everyone else is exactly that of an invincible horror.

Until the moment when the adolescents have completed their instruction, they are to all effects 'dead'. Their tutor, or mystagogue, is thus, in a very concrete way, their guide through the dark region of death, their psychopomp; his task, however, is of a maieutic kind, to lead them out again into the world of men, and in this capacity the psychopomp becomes an obstetrician, and obvious father-figure. The two are therefore but different faces of the same paternal figure and function, a role whose importance in the psychological process has already been stressed.

The symbolic meaning of death in initiation rites may be explained by the necessity — in order that the successive rebirth of the 'new' individual be efficacious — to actuate also in this specific manifestation the principle lying at the heart of all ritual, the repetition of an exemplary event. In the case of the birth of an individual, this event can only consist in the cosmogonical act itself, operated by a god, whose function is now fulfilled by the initiator. However, the existential plenitude of the original creative act can only be restored by abolishing the present time and the world itself, thus returning to primeval chaos. One of the means of achieving this in the ritual is the narration by the person who possesses the knowledge, namely the initiator, of the history of the tribe, which is equivalent to the history of the creation of the world. We can find an analogy between the necessity of narrating what occurred — according to Eliade's formula — 'in illo tempore', thus cancelling chronological time,[31] and the characteristic, shared by fables and romances alike, of taking the reader or listener back to a mythical past. This can also be verified at the beginning of our poem, where we are told of the series of events that, 'Siþen þe sege and þe assaut watz sesed at Troye' (1), led to Felix Brutus and the founding of Britannia, as well as by means of the story's setting in the mythical kingdom of Camelot.

---

31 This happens, of course, not only in puberty initiation rites, but practically on all important occasions in the life of a tribe. Cf. M. Eliade, *The Quest* (Chicago and London,1969), especially chs. 2 and 3.

The neophyte's ritual death is often represented by burial, one of whose symbols is the hut itself where, in many cases, the initiation ceremony takes place. This is, however, a multivalent symbol; the dark hut in the thick of the forest is suggestive of the cosmic darkness preceding the creation: rather than of death, we should therefore speak of regression to a state of embryo. The analogy with the individual's pre-natal state is evident; thus the burial, or the initiation hut, can also be seen to be homologous with the maternal womb, and, consequently, with man's origin from his telluric matrix, which takes us back once again to our interpretation of the Green Chapel as an opening of the earth's womb, whence emerged the Green Knight, an emanation of its most obscure forces. But this being, we know, is none but Bertilak himself, lord of the castle where Gawain finds shelter. The hero's initiation, therefore, is set in a place — the Chapel — ultimately indistinguishable from the castle, which is clearly homologous with what has been called the initiation hut. This is a fundamental element in the scenery of these rituals; it represents a sacred space, out of bounds with respect to the everyday world, in some cases consisting simply of an isolated, not necessarily enclosed patch of ground, even though a hut in the midst of a forest or of a wood — by themselves suggesting the impenetrable darkness of Chaos — seems more appropriate as far as pre-historic Europe is concernd. As Propp has amply demonstrated, a testimonial of this has reached down to us in the Russian folktales he analysed, showing how certain highly typical motifs, such as the 'hut on fowl's legs' (the abode of the witch Baba-Yaga) that rises in a forest clearing, or the big house the hero finds in his rambling through the woods, are to be connected to ancient initiation rituals.[32] The hut is at once the boundary between and the way of access from the world of the living to that of the dead, where the protagonist must penetrate, and in that hut he undergoes a series of tests. In describing some Oceanian tribal customs concerning initiation ceremonies, Propp also relates the departure of the adolescents, who are accompanied into the forest by the father (or eldest brother, acting in his stead), pointing out the analogy with the typical fairy-tale motif of the parent who abandons, or somehow gets rid of the son, who from that point sets off on his adventures.[33] All this closely recalls, as I have observed, Sir Bertilak's castle, situated at the centre of a waste land, with a moat that separates it from a surrounding park,[34] whose inhabitants have strong links with the world of the dead, and where the hero must face his toughest tests, that of sexual temptation as well as the combat with his father, having passed which he finally achieves his emancipation.

---

32   V.Y. Propp, chs. 3 and 4, *passim*.
33   Ibid., p. 132. To us, a more familiar example is the story of Snow-white, who is abandoned in the forest by a hunter — a transformation of the father-figure.
34   See 11. 763-802.

Puberty initiation marks the entrance into a 'perfect' adult state, in which man's participation in the sacred is the same as all those life manifestations, whose nature has become instead totally desacralized to modern man. Among these, a basic role is fulfilled by the revelation of sexuality, a function of the very first importance in all initiation rites. There is here a quite explicit analogy with Gawain's sexual initiation in the castle, but the symbolism of these ritual ceremonies allows us to dig further in our search for possible points of contact, or intersections between different spheres.

Among the puberty initiation rites connected with sexuality, the most relevant is no doubt that of circumcision, an almost universal practice, whose very nature identifies it, on a symbolic level, with castration. It has already been noticed, however, that the psychological fear of castration is often portrayed by beheading scenes, and the beheading is indeed the test Gawain is most afraid of, to the point that it becomes the leit-motif of all the drama that is upsetting his mind. The executioner who threatens the hero with this mutilation is the paternal figure, who by so doing 'kills' the son, while in initiation rites the man in charge of the operation is the instructor, the guide, a figure endowed in its turn with markedly paternal characteristics. Moreover, as Eliade again relates, one of the mytho-symbolical forms taken by the rite of circumcision among the Australian tribe of the Arunda is precisely the beheading; the novice is taken before the god, who orders him to look at the stars: 'Lorsque le garçon lève la tête, le Grand Esprit la lui coupe. Il la lui remet le lendemain, alors qu'elle commence à se décomposer, et le ressuscite'.[35]

The psychological, symbolic and ritual aspects of the initiation pattern thus converge — each in its peculiar embodiment — in the sexual sphere and in the image of the beheading; it is a complex and crucial phase of Gawain's experience, as well as of every individual, a phase whose memory is indelibly fixed in the collective mind.

Circumcision (often followed by sub-incision), an extremely painful test which the youth must stoically accept, may be substituted among different cultures by other physical trials, such as the extraction of an incisor, scarification, and so forth; after the ceremony is over, all these operations leave upon the flesh of the newly initiated some visible sign that will mark him permanently as a member of the group. This testimonial is comparable with the scar Gawain has to bear as a memento, of the test he underwent and which, on a manifest level, was meant to remind him of his not-quite-crystal-clear behaviour with the lady of the castle. By the time the hero returns to Arthur's court, the insistence is not so much on the scar as on the bauderyk, or belt he is wearing around his neck — the green girdle he had received

---

35   *Naissances mystiques*, pp. 60-61.

from the lady — only to discover that 'Vche burne of þe broþerhede' (2516) of course wears a similar one, since everyone there has already passed that test.

The final phase of the initiation ritual (whose complexity may change enormously with different ethnic groups, and which may even take years before it is completed in all its aspects) invariably includes, as in our poem, the hero's homecoming, the return into the world, a happy conclusion implicitly guaranteed by the nature of *rite de passage* of the process itself. It is a wholly 'new' individual, however, that goes back among his own people. The 'old' creature is dead, while the initiated man now leads an independent life with no relation to his previous condition; he can form a family of his own and beget children. Fundamentally analogous is the condition of the 'initiated' Sir Gawain who, having successfully overcome the combat with the repressive forces embodied by the much-feared image of the father, finally finds himself back in the place he had never actually left, but with a renewed consciousness of his own humanity, ready to fulfil, in the forms given to every man, his role in the world.

IV

In what Northrop Frye calls its archetypal phase, the work of literary art is a myth, and unites the ritual and the dream;[36] ritual, according to his view, is the social expression of dream, while it is myth that identifies both in itself.[37]

The validity of Frye's intuition appears to be substantially confirmed by the results so far obtained in my analysis of *Sir Gawain and the Green Knight*. Indeed the apparently heterogeneous paths I have been following in my approach to this romance naturally lead into the vast area of myth.

I have already insisted, following Jung's example,[38] on the essentially personal quality of the dream experience, in which mankind's communal memory is brought to the surface of consciousness, and moulded by the psychic history of the individual into unique images, whose symbolic meaning only the widest possible knowledge of that individual history can penetrate. Similarly, although the romance of Sir Gawain gives expression to complexes and conflicts common to all mankind by means of archetypal images that the critic must strip of all the veils and appendages peculiar to the age and culture that produced it, it nevertheless refers us to myth — not the conceptual category, but a particular myth, that of Oedipus. This does not deny the validity of my previous statement; in fact, what I have rejected,

---

36   *Anatomy of Criticism*, p. 118.
37   Ibid., pp. 106-7.
38   See above, pp. 4-5 of typescript and n. 6

rather than the existence of an Oedipal situation, is its exegesis in Freudian terms. The overwhelming importance attributed by Freud to Oedipus' incest with his mother Jocasta — the corner-stone of his theory on the development of the infantile psyche — finds no correspondence in the pattern that has emerged in the course of our reading of *Sir Gawain and the Green Knight*. Here, the mother-son relationship is simply a subordinate aspect of the protagonist's conflict with the paternal archetype, which is not determined by a primarily sexual rivalry, but by what we can define as a struggle for power. The homology between the romance of Sir Gawain and the myth as narrated by Sophocles stands out more clearly in Erich Fromm's analysis of the latter. He observes that it appears hardly conceivable that 'a myth, the central theme of which constitutes an incestuous relationship between mother and son, would entirely omit the element of attraction between the two';[39] in fact, the tragedy has practically nothing to say in this connexion. The only reason given for their union is that it implies the succession to Laius' throne. Fromm's hypothesis that the myth may be understood *as a symbol . . . of the rebellion of the son against the authority of the father in the patriarchal family; that the marriage of Oedipus and Jocasta is only . . . one of the symbols of the victory of the son, who takes his father's place and with it all his privileges'*,[40] is based on a reading of the three tragedies that make up the Sophoclean version of the story of Oedipus — *Oedipus Tyrannus*, *Oedipus at Colonus* and *Antigone*, whereas Freud only considered the first. In all three, the action revolves on the son's rebellion against paternal authority: the brothers Eteocles and Polynices versus Oedipus, and Haemon versus Creon in the latter two, as well as Oedipus himself versus his own father Laius in the more popular one.

Fromm's successive argumentations — based on Bachofen's well-known theories concerning the conflict between an original matriachal principle and a later patriarchal one[41] — are not to be subscribed to without reservations. However, what appears most significant and consistent with my premises is the way the recurrent father-son conflict, such as emerges from the latent structures of *Sir Gawain and the Green Knight*, is substantially reflected in Oedipus' myth, in a form, that is, whose very universality confirms the validity of its contents.

The initiation ritual we have alluded to here, and especially the one relating to man's admission into the society of the adults on his reaching the age of puberty, is characterized by being a collective ceremony. This does not only mean that the youth takes part in it together with other

---

39 *The Forgotten Language*, p. 174.
40 Ibid. (his italics).
41 J.J. Bachofen, *Das Mutterrecht*, vols. 2 and 3 of his *Opera Omnia*, ed. K. Meuli (Basel, 1948).

members of the same age-group by undergoing with them — and the initiators — the same experience at the same time; the fact has wider implications. The subject's reenactment, through a symbolic death-and-rebirth process, of a paradigmatic event — the creation of the first human being, in its turn a repetition of the cosmogony itself — by abolishing chronological time and entering a timeless dimension, brings about a *renovatio* which affects not only the individual, but the whole of the society he lives in, and eventually the whole world. Thus, the ritual of initiation does not refer us to a single mythic epiphany, but to myth in itself, to the narration of the sacred history of the world;[42] in other words, to that narrative of the first and fundamental ontological modification which reveals to man the sanctity of the world and of his own existence.[43]

The romance of *Sir Gawain and the Green Knight,* therefore, also qualifies as a mythic narrative, in so far as its structures trace the ritual pattern; by following the track it provides, the reader is led through the process of the hero's personal emancipation, and hence to the common experience of psychological emancipation, hence again to man's 'birth' into the world and to the sacred origin of the world itself.

The path unwinds itself, then, in a basically centripetal direction,[44] since it draws us from the periphery — Gawain's adventure, as expressed by historically determined linguistic, literary and social conventions — near to the real thematic and structural centre of the work.

---

42 Cf. M. Eliade, *Naissances mystiques,* p. 56.

43 The reception of Eliade's formula of myth as the narration of a 'creation' (see for instance *The Quest*, p.9), or in terms of a 'vessel' made to contain a 'substance' (the creation itself) — whose concrete and historical forms we can and must investigate — does not seem to me to be in contradiction with the necessity of a 'scientific' study (which, after Lévi-Strauss, no one can afford to ignore) of the ways the mythological machine works, before facing the problem of the existence of a mythical 'substance'. In my view, on the other hand, the latter problem can only be solved in terms of an ideological choice.

44 A route, which is at least as worthy to be followed by the critic as the opposite, centrifugal one advocated by C. Moorman: 'In short, having discovered the myth core of a piece of literature, the critic must go on to examine in their own right the other literary aspects of the work' (p. 235).

SONGS AND LYRICS

DOUGLAS GRAY

It is a common generalization of literary and cultural historians that – in Northern Europe at least – the fourteenth century was an age of violent change or crisis. One recent book on poetry in the age of Chaucer has the word 'crisis' in its title; among historical books, one has the subtitle 'The Calamitous Fourteenth Century',[1] and there is the even more famous *Waning of the Middle Ages*. There is, of course, evidence for this view in the history of the period. The Black Death of 1348/9 ravaged Western Europe: England suffered, in addition, from a series of wars – against the Scots and the French – and from internal disruption (two kings – Edward II and Richard II – died violent deaths) and rebellions – notably in the great revolt of the peasants in 1381. Intellectual historians point to the growing strains in the unity of Christendom – to the Papal Schism, or to those developments in philosophy which caused argument and led to a separation of reason and faith, or to the growth of heresy. Sir Richard Southern sees the end of 'medieval humanism' in the early 14th century:

> Europe then entered a period when the optimism which had buoyed up the efforts of the previous two centuries was abruptly destroyed: the flow of new intellectual materials came to an end; the forward movement in settlement and expansion came to a halt; the area of disorder in the world was everywhere increasing; everything began to seem insecure.[2]

He draws attention to the disillusionment expressed by Petrarch, 'who above all stood for a new kind of humanism in the mid-14th century'. The interpretation of the disruption of the age given by historians varies. On the one hand, some follow Huizinga in seeing it as a 'waning' (or rather as an 'autumn'),[3] a period decaying and dying, and, consequently, stress elements of death and decay. Others see a dissolution of an intellectual order (especial-

---

1 Charles Muscatine, *Poetry and Crisis in the Age of Chaucer* (Notre Dame, 1972); Barbara Tuchman, *A Distant Mirror. The Calamitous 14th Century* (London, 1979).
2 R. W. Southern, *Medieval Humanism and Other Studies* (Oxford, 1970), pp.58-9.
3 J. Huizinga, *Herfstij der Middeleeuwen*, tr. as *The Waning of the Middle Ages* (London, 1924).

ly if their 'idea' of medieval culture is based on Northern Europe, on Paris, Oxford and the 'schools'). On the other hand, some, especially those who look to the developments in Italy in this period,[4] where a new humanism was developing within older intellectual traditions, would say that something new and vital was emerging in the fourteenth century to bear fruit later.

These are very large questions, to which a lecture on the humble English songs and lyrics of the period cannot hope to offer a solution. However, the songs and lyrics are part of late medieval culture and literature, and they may help to illuminate the whole 'picture', or at least give us pause in our generalizations. A discussion of them will, I think, certainly show that the 'picture' of fourteenth-century English literature is a complicated one.

We are instantly confronted with problems, both large and small. Literary historians tend to like neat patterns. They like to be able to speak of authorship, of schools of poets, of the development of forms, of geographical areas of literary production. In the case of fourteenth-century lyrics it is often not possible to do this. It would be very interesting to know how many came originally from East Anglia, which we know was rich and a great artistic centre, or from the equally rich West Midlands, or from London, the growing metropolis. In most cases we cannot say. Questions of 'development' are equally difficult. I am not sure that one can certainly detect a more sombre or more macabre mood in lyrics which seem to come after the Black Death, or that one can say that there is a new attention to the subject of the Nativity about the middle of the 14th century, stimulated by the mystery plays.[5]

It is possible to isolate some reasons for these difficulties, and probably in doing so, we learn something about our lyrics. Firstly, there is the problem of survival. Our evidence is incomplete, because manuscripts have been lost or destroyed, or because many songs were never written down in the first place. Probably religious poetry was most likely to be written down. Secular songs are sometimes found scribbled on fly-leaves. There are references to fugitive songs and poems like the 'Com hider love to me' which Chaucer's Pardoner sings, or the 'Rymes of Robyn Hood and Randolf Erle of Chestre' mentioned in *Piers Plowman*.[6] From such references, we can say with some certainty that there must have been a considerable body of lyrics and songs which has not survived.

Even when lyrics do survive in manuscripts, we do not know as much about their context as we would like to. The majority are anonymous.

---

4 Cf. W. Ullmann, *Medieval Foundations of Renaissance Humanism* (London, 1977)
5 Rosemary Woolf, *The English Religious Lyric in the Middle Ages* (Oxford, 1968), p. 148.
6 Langland, *Piers Plowman I-VII*, ed. J.A.W.Bennett (Oxford, 1972), V. 402. Cf. R.M.Wilson, *The Lost Literature of Medieval England* (London, 1952).

They cannot be fitted into the pattern of the development of a known individual poet. Nor can they (with a few exceptions) be fitted into 'schools' of poetry. It seems that in 13th and 14th century literature in English there are not those distinctive and dominant lyric poets with imitators or followers who are characteristic of France and Italy. (One reason for this is to be found in the status of the English language itself, which throughout the earlier Middle Ages had definitely not been the language of sophisticated, courtly literature. Its growing importance throughout the 14th century is clearly one of the most significant cultural developments of the period.) It is also very difficult to date the lyrics. If there are no internal references to datable historical events, and no certain linguistic evidence, the best one can do is to date, more or less approximately, the manuscript in which they are recorded. But, of course, it is usually impossible to say whether the lyrics in the manuscript are contemporary with it, or if they have been handed down from an earlier time.

Another problem is that the material of the lyrics is itself highly traditional in nature: there are traditional formulae, phrases, images. This is especially the case with religious lyrics, which will contain echoes of the Bible, the liturgy, the hymns of the church, or may even be translations of earlier Latin originals. The poets will use familiar, traditional devotional topics: the uncertainty of death's coming, the Five Joys of the Virgin, and other such topics are repeated in lyric after lyric, and in generation after generation. This is the case not only with religious lyrics; it is true even of some 'political' poems. Some of these are, as one might expect, anchored in the contemporary events they refer to, but by no means all. There is, for example, a rather impressive alliterative lyric, beginning 'Opon a somer Soneday I se the sonne' — it is a vision of Fortune's wheel, from which a king is thrown down. One of its editors confidently gave it the title 'A Lament for Edward II (1327)',[7] but in fact there is no clear or certain evidence to connect it with the fall of that particular king. It seems more likely to be a general poem on Fortune (like the pattern familiar in iconography of figures aspiring to rule, ruling, falling, with the words *regnabo, regno, regnavi*). There are many poems of this kind on the mutability of Fortune, reflections on the falls of princes or the wickedness of the present age (in these, the list of vices is the same for the early 14th century as for the early 16th). The general, proverbial tone of these works seems to have been popular. This is not simply an example of 'medieval moralizing', but rather of a liking for general 'wisdom' — for wise sayings which can explain events, and bring consolation by putting them into a traditional pattern of belief (in the manner of proverbs — of which there are many in the lyrics).

---

7   R.H. Robbins, *Historical Poems of the XIVth and XVth Centuries* (New York, 1959), No. 38.

I suspect that sometimes these very general statements could be read or written by individuals as a kind of reflection of their own particular circumstances. This is perhaps more typical of medieval lyric than that immediacy, that sense of a poem arising directly and individually out of crisis or conflict which is often found in later lyrics.

This brings us to a further point which we need to remember, that these are not Romantic lyrics, that they are not (typically) the distillation of a unique individual experience. Indeed they often are not striving for any consciously aesthetic effect. They are often very practical: they are meant to be *used*. Professor John Stevens has argued convincingly that later – in the 15th and early 16th centuries – many 'courtly' lyrics should be seen as part of a social context, that they are almost 'moves' in an elaborate 'game of love', being used as compliments, persuasions, to accompany gifts to the lady, and so on.[8] It can be argued that some kinds of religious lyric equally were used – and may have been written to be used – in a similar practical way, as part of devotional life. The prayers in verse would be an obvious group, as would the meditations, one of which has a rubric implying just this: 'in saying of this orison, stop and wait at every cross and think [on] what you have said'.[9] The same must have sometimes been true of more popular songs also. We hear of laments, and of lullabies – a sermon refers to women 'that lulle the child wyth thair fote and sinnges an hauld song, *sic dicens:*

Wake wel, Annot,
    Thi mayden boure;
And get the fra Walterot,
    For he is lichure.'[10]

(it is a pleasingly human touch that this 'lullaby' is far from edifying). We know that there were dance-songs – especially the *caroles,* of which one has the burden 'hand by hand we shall us take'. There were probably also work-songs, like the mariners' songs described by a 15th-century German pilgrim in a Venetian galley: they 'sing when work is going on, because work at sea is very heavy, and is only carried on by a concert between one who sings out orders and the labourers who sing in response. So these men stand by those who are at work and sing to them, encourage them and threaten to spur them on with blows.' In fact, in a taunting song which is supposed to have been sung by Scottish girls after the defeat of the English at Bannockburn:

---

8   J. Stevens, *Music and Poetry in the Early Tudor Court* (London, 1961), ch. 9.
9   Carleton Brown, *Religious Lyrics of the XIVth Century*, rev. G.V. Smithers (Oxford, 1952), p. 114.
10 R.H. Robbins, *Secular Lyrics of the XIVth and XVth Centuries* (Oxford, 1952), p. xxxix.

> Maydenes of Englelande, sare may ye morne,
> For tynt ye have lost youre lemmans at Bannokesburn

there are in the refrain what seem to be snatches of sailors' or watermen's songs — 'with hevalogh', 'with rombylogh' — and it has been suggested that these may be satirical allusions to King Edward's predilection for water travel.[11]

It will be obvious that by isolating 'difficulties' such as these — the apparent lack of individuality, 'authorship' and so on — we have already learnt something about the cultural context of the songs and lyrics: that they were often not 'literary' in a self-conscious way, but were close to, and indeed part of, the fabric of ordinary life. I suppose that the moral of my introduction is twofold. Firstly, a negative warning — to beware of over-neat patterns, easy generalizations or generalized categories. Indeed, I should even question two that I have been using — for convenience, in the manner of literary historians. I have been speaking of 'secular' and 'religious' lyrics — but though these terms may serve as convenient 'poles', the categories some-times overlap: there are a number of high-minded, but not specifically religious, 'moral' poems, there are parodies, and in the manuscript collections 'religious' lyrics quite frequently are mixed together with 'secular' ones. I have also used the terms 'courtly' and 'popular', associated with a distinction which is a very revered one: 'there are the two big sub-divisions of Middle English poetry, the courtly and the popular — reflecting the stratification of medieval society' writes a famous scholar.[12] This is probably too neat. Medieval society was certainly stratified, but not in this absolute or simple binary way. Different classes often met and mingled in daily life, and especially in entertainment and worship (and we might ponder on the rôles played in literary contact and dissemination by such groups as nurses, squires, minstrels, or 'clerks'). If we have to have two 'poles', of 'courtly' and 'popular', it is important to stress that there must have been constant interaction. A scholar writing on French lyrics[13] has suggested that there we should rather think of a 'popularising' register (e.g. lyrics with refrains, with generalized personages) and an 'aristocratising' register (e.g. 'pure' lyric, with elaborate form, with a *tornada* instead of a refrain). Secondly, a more posi-tive moral: that we need to understand fully the traditional nature of medi-eval English lyrics. If we are to discover individuality, we need to be aware of the traditional material out of which the poetic works were formed, and the possibilities it offered to the poets. The lyrics are profoundly traditional — in form, language, and imagery. In love lyrics, for instance, we find again

---

11 Robbins, *Historical Poems*, p. 262.
12 Robbins, *Secular Lyrics*, p. xxxiii.
13 P. Bec, 'Quelques réflexions sur la poésie lyrique mediévale', *Mélanges offerts à Rita Lejeune* (Gembloux, 1969), pp. 1309-29.

88

and again the beautiful (and sometimes 'daungerous') beloved and the languishing lover, simple oppositions (e.g. of joy and sorrow), and a series of 'key terms' (*termes-clé*) with special overtones (developing, perhaps, because of the constant repetition) — 'eyes', 'heart', 'service', 'longing', etc. At nearly all levels this is a formal poetry,[14] delighting in rhetorical talent, in the construction of a poem as a literary object (and sometimes in the element of 'game' in its composition) — a delight which is sometimes elegant and self-conscious, sometimes more robust and hearty.

Now let us turn to some examples, which may serve to illustrate something of the variety of 14th-century lyric. My first example is a very well-known love lyric:[15]

> BETWENE March and Averil,
> When spray biginneth to springe,
> The litel fowl hath hire wil
>> On hire lud to singe.
> Ich libbe in love-longinge
> For semlokest of alle thinge;
> Heo may me blisse bringe —
>> Ich am in hire baundòun.
>>> An hendy hap ich habbe y-hent;
>>> Ich'ot from hevene it is me sent;
>>> From alle wimmen my love is lent,
>>>> And light on Alysoun.
>
> On hew hire her is fair ynough,
>> Hire browe browne, hire eye blake;
> With lofsom chere heo on me lough,
>> With middel smal and wel y-make.
> Bute heo me wille to hire take
>> For to been hire owen make,
>> Longe to liven ich'ille forsake,
>>> And feye fallen adown.
>>>> An hendy hap, *etc.*
>
> Nightes when I wende and wake —
> Forthy myn wonges waxeth won —
> Levedy, al for thine sake
>> Longing is y-lent me on.
> In world n'is non so witer mon
> That al hire bounté telle con:
> Hire swire is whitere than the swon,
>> And fairest may in town.
>>> An hendy hap, *etc.*

---

14 Cf. R. Guiette, 'D'une poésie formelle en France au moyen âge', *Questions de littérature* (Gent, 1960).

15 *The Oxford Book of Medieval English Verse*, ed. C. and K. Sisam (Oxford, 1970), No. 43.

Ich am for wowing al forwake,
  Wery so water in wore,
Lest any reve me my make
Ich habbe y-yirned yore.
Betere is tholien while sore
Than mournen evermore.
Gainest under gore,
  Herkne to my roun.
    An hendy hap, *etc.*

The vigour and liveliness of this comes partly from its rather breathless syntax, and partly from the insistent alliterative patterns (probably coming to the poet from earlier times — like a later poet of the 'alliterative revival', the author of *Pearl,* he blends alliterative patterns with a fairly intricate rhymed stanza). 'Alysoun' is particularly interesting in its own distinctive use of traditions. The 'spring-opening' so common in French — and English — love lyrics is given a thoroughly 'English' expression: 'when spray biginneth to springe'. The language is usually highly formulaic (e.g. 'semlokest of alle thinge', 'whitere than the swon') — though there is one striking and surprising simile in 'wery so water in wore (? = turbulent pool)' — but such is the vigour and the confidence that there is no sense of flatness or stiltedness. Notice the boldness with which the poet uses an alliterative formula 'gainest under gore' (37) in the final direct address to his lady. We also find traditional themes and ideas — 'grace' in love is sent as a gift from heaven. We can see one or two of the 'key words' of the love lyric — 'ich libbe in *love-longinge'* (5), a theme which is repeated again when the poet gives us a description of that state in the second to last stanza: *'longing* is ylent me on' (25) (*cf.* the words *yyirned . . . tholien . . . mournen* clustered around it). It uses the simple oppositions of the traditional love-lyric. The lover is 'longing', the lady has him 'in hire baundoun' (this is not a completely 'static' opposition, of course: *longing* is an unsatisfied, a 'potential' state, and *baundoun* suggests the complex of feelings associated with the 'yoke of love', which is both happy and sorrowful). On the one hand there is joy and life (*blisse, hendy hap,* etc.), on the other sorrow and death (*longe to liven ich'ille forsake*). The poet's alternations of mood are successfully done. The doubts and sorrows of 'longing' break in upon the happy, almost jaunty movement of the verses; the joyous notes of the repeated refrain are sometimes played off against a note of sorrow.

'Alysoun' is a rhetorical poem, but not in any mannered way. There is a formal *descriptio* of the lady in stanzas 2 and 3, enlivened by what is almost a flash of a dramatic 'scene' in the words 'with lofsom chere heo on me lough'. The progress is characteristically abrupt, almost jerky. The *descriptio* is broken up by exclamation (it is especially noticeable in stanza 3, where a direct exclamation to the lady — 'al for *thine* sake' — is quickly followed by a return to the description of *'hire* bounte'). One result of this (deliberately ?) uneven progress is to create a direct and emotional effect. Characteristic too is the way in which an intricate 'decoration', both rhetorical and metrical (with insistent alliteration and elaborate rhyme) is applied to a basically simple syntactic structure (consisting largely of statements, comparisons or exclamations). The alternating moods seem to be brought to a restful conclusion in the proverbial-sounding consolatory lines:

> Betere is tholien while sore
> Than mournen evermore.

'Alysoun' comes from a very attractive collection of English lyrics in MS. Harley 2253 in the British Library. The Harley lyrics contain religious as well as secular songs, and some which defy categorization — like the odd 'Man in the Moon' which seems closer to folklore than to any 'courtly' tradition. It is important to remember that these English lyrics, pleasing and attractive though they are, are only a part of the material which the manuscript contains.[16] It seems to be a cultural and a linguistic 'mirror' of at least one part of England in the earlier 14th century. Besides the English lyrics, it contains an English romance (*King Horn*), and much material (saints' lives and fabliaux) in Anglo-Norman, and in Latin. The manuscript was probably written in the fourth decade of the 14th century, and was certainly produced in the West of England, probably in Herefordshire (the latest research suggests Ludlow),[17] near the Welsh border. The scribe is known to have also copied another manuscript, now in the British Library, which contains a couple of Anglo-Norman romances. It seems as if the tastes of the Harley scribe's patrons or patron were varied and catholic. Indeed, if I may recall my opening remarks for a moment, I would be inclined to say that neither the lyric 'Alysoun' nor the Harley anthology as a whole suggest or reflect any kind of 'crisis' or extreme tensions, but show rather a delight in exploiting a variety of linguistic and literary traditions — English, French, and Latin —, a delight in the possibilities and the challenges of form and style, and a delight in that mingling of 'earnest' and 'game' which we tend to associate with literary works from the latter part of the century. It is perhaps worth recalling that the manuscript containing the works of the 'Gawain poet' — who was certainly interested in this delicate intermingling — also comes from an area which, like this, was far away from the metropolitan centre of London. Perhaps it too reflects the cultivated and distinctive taste of local patrons.

My second example comes from a lyric by Laurence Minot. We know his

---

16   See the facsimile, ed. N.R. Ker, EETS 255 (1964).
17   Professor Carter Revard (private communication).

name because he puts it in one of his political/historical poems on the achievement of Edward III:

> Minot with mowth had menid to make
> Suth sawes and sad for sum mens sake . . .

His poem on the English victory over the Scots at Halidon Hill (1333), which he celebrates as a revenge for Bannockburn, opens thus:

> SCOTTES out of Berwik and of Abirdene,
> At the Bannokburn were ye to kene;
> There slogh ye many sakless, as it was sene,
> And now has King Edward wroken it, I wene.
> It is wroken, I wene, well wurth the while!
> Ware yet with the Scottes, for they ar full of gile!
>
> Where ar ye Scottes of Saint Johnes town?
> The boste of youre baner is beten all down.
> When ye bosting will bede, Sir Edward is bown
> For to kindel you care and crak youre crown.
> He has crakked youre crowne, well warth the while!
> Shame betide the Scottes, for they ar full of gile![18]

You will notice again that the forceful alliterative formulae — 'the boste of youre baner is beten all down', 'he has crakked youre crowne' —, again combined with rhyme, are obvious and insistent. The battle is seen in personal terms, as a personal revenge by 'king Edward' on the Scots (the phrase 'crakked youre crowne' suggests that he is a kind of popular champion). Dr. Dianella Savoia, in her fine study of Minot,[19] rightly says that this is characteristic of the poet, and that it is not quite true to describe him — as has been done — as 'nationalistic' in the full modern sense of the word. She draws attention to his singularity. He is certainly an author who does not fit easily into any one category. His political and historical songs sometimes sound like romances (they have a very noticeable narrative element), but (as she says) he interprets history for poetic ends and does not write verse chronicles. He seems close to popular verse and feeling, and yet he does not sound quite like a simple minstrel. His poetry does not seem consciously 'ecclesiastical' or 'clerical', but he treats religious motifs exactly. The kind of political/historical poem, of which this is a very distinctive example, continues through the 15th century to the time of Skelton.

So large is the number of surviving religious lyrics that it is difficult to choose one or two examples which may be regarded as 'typical'. I have already remarked on the fact that they were often used in a decidedly

---

18 *OBMEV*, No. 71.
19 'Poesia e Storia nei Versi di Laurence Minot', *Studi Medievali* 3a Serie XIX, I (1978), pp. 339-362.

'practical' way, as prayers and meditations. Another way they were used was as quotations in sermons. Medieval preachers often inveighed against 'lascivious' songs, and it is not surprising to find religious adaptations of them. A Franciscan bishop of Ossory, in Ireland, wrote sixty Latin lyrics for his clergy to sing, and in some cases in the MS. they are found together with scraps of vernacular love-songs (presumably to indicate the tunes).[20] Sometimes secular verses are quoted in sermons and given a moral or allegorical meaning, as in the famous case where in

> Atte wrastlinge mi lemman I ches
> And atte ston-kasting I him forles

'wrestling' is explained as fighting like a good champion against the world, the flesh and the devil.[21] Other verses, both secular and moral, are collected in a number of 'preaching books', such as that of John Grimestone, or the *Fasciculus Morum,* or the MS. containing the sermons of Bishop Sheppey. Such verses in sermons have recently been discussed in an excellent book by Professor Siegfried Wenzel.[22] They are often mnemonic aids — to the preacher in his exposition, and to the congregation for recollection in day-to-day living. In Grimestone's book, for instance, we find:

> *Respiciamus:*
> *oculis*   The rede stremes renning
> *auribus* The Jewes orible criying
> *gustu*   Of Cristis drink the bitternesse
> *ractu*   Of Cristis wondis the s[h]arpnesse[23]

giving us four 'topics' of the Crucifixion, and four ways of considering them. Sometimes such verses are proverbial encapsulations of 'wisdom' which may be applied to situations in everyday life (in this period, verse still had a distinctly mnemonic function, and was regularly used for didactic and educational purposes). Here too we find a mixture of 'earnest' and 'game'. I would agree with Professor Wenzel (in his charming article on the 'joyous art of preaching')[24] that the reason some preachers included merry tales or verses in their sermons was not always a simply didactic one, but rather because they enjoyed them, and expected their hearers to enjoy them also.

The religious lyrics are also rooted in a tradition of intensely personal and 'affective' devotion, which characteristically stresses the humanity of

20 Cf. *The Lyrics of the Red Book of Ossory,* ed. R.L. Greene (Medium AEvum Monographs NS V, Oxford, 1974).
21 Woolf. pp. 191-2. Cf. T. Stemmler, *Anglia* 93 (1975), p. 9
22 *Verses in Sermons* (Cambridge, Mass., 1978). Cf. E. Wilson, *A Descriptive Index of the English lyrics in John of Grimestones's Preaching Book* (Medium AEvum Monographs, NS II, Oxford, 1973).
23 Wilson, No. 191.
24 *Anglia* 97 (1979).

Christ and the grim reality of his sufferings, and attempts to make the
audience visualize them (cf. the Grimestone lyric just quoted) and react to
them in a strongly emotional way. Sometimes Christ's sufferings are treated
in an expansive or indeed an exaggerated way, sometimes with a kind of
intense austerity:

> Whit was His nakede brest and red of blod His side
> Bleik [pale] was His fair andled [face], His wounde deep and wide;
> And His armes ystreight hy upon the rode
> On fif stedes [places] on His body the stremes ran o blode.[25]

Here the sharpness of the visual effect crystallizes the whole complex of
emotions associated with this archetype of suffering into a single moment.

The following two examples were chosen because it seemed to me that
they were ones in which a cultural historian *might* find significant evidence
for that sense of disillusionment sometimes supposed to be characteristic
of the fourteenth century (although I would want to point out that they
belong to a long-standing tradition of *Contemptus Mundi,* which often
dwells gloomily on the vanity of this world). They both come from very
interesting poems:

> Lollay, lollay, litel child! Why wepest thou so sore?
> Nedes most thou wepe; it was y-yarked thee yore
> Ever to lib in sorow and sich, and mourne evermore,
> As thyn eldren did er this, whil hi alives wore.
> Lollay, lollay, litel child! child, lollay, lullow!
> In to uncouth world y-comen so art thou . . .[26]

This is the beginning of a lullaby, but not like that of Annot and the lecher
Walterot, nor indeed like the lullabies commonly put in the mouth of the
Virgin Mary. It seems to be spoken by an ordinary mother over her weeping
child, and it is a singularly bleak statement of the human condition. The
child is born only to suffer and to die, which is the destiny of Adam's
wretched seed. Later in the poem, even the usual image of man as a pilgrim
in this world is rejected — 'child, thou nert a pilgrim bot an uncuthe geste'.
It is, as I said, in a tradition which sees man's life as a vale of tears, but in
the last line of our stanza the adjective *uncouth* gives extraordinary expression to a profound human sorrow. It is a remarkable example of a poet
using a tradition to create something new.

The next example:

---

25 *OBMEV,* No. 4.
26 *OBMEV,* No. 61.

Which is man who wot, and what,
    Whether that he be ought or nought?
Of erthe and air groweth up a gnat,
    And so doth man, when al is sought;
Though man be waxen gret and fat,
    Man melteth away so deth a mought.
Mannes might n'is worth a mat,
    But noyeth himself and turneth to nought.
Who wot, save He that al hath wrought,
    Wher man bicometh when he shal dye?
Who knoweth by dede ought but by thought?
    For this world fareth as a fantasye.

Dyeth man, and beestes dye,
    And al is on occasioun;
And alle o deth bos bothe drye,
    And han one incarnacioun;
Save that men beeth more slye,
    Al is o comparisoun . . .[27]

is part of a long reflective poem in the Vernon MS. (from the end of the century) with the refrain 'for this world fareth as a fantasye'. It is based on passages from the Old Testament book of *Ecclesiastes* (itself a sceptical and deeply melancholy work) and it stresses the smallness of man's reason, which cannot comprehend the mysteries of the creation. Man is of no account; he turns to nothing, and dies as beasts die. Since reason is inadequate, he can only rely on faith (a hint of the anti-intellectualism sometimes found in late medieval devotion and theology).

We notice again the alliterative patterns (though not so insistent as in the earlier examples), the intricate stanza form, and the pervasively proverbial ring (most obviously in the recurring refrain). Other poems in the collection have similar combinations of elaborate metrical form and alliteration with proverbial refrains: 'each man ought himself to know', 'think on yesterday', 'whoso saith the sooth he shall be shent', 'fy on a faint friend', etc. The MS. is a vast collection, which includes not only religious and moral verses, but visions and romances, and much more didactic material (e.g. on 'how to hear Mass'), collections of proverbs (such as the school-text 'Cato') and of other 'wisdom' literature (advising the reader, for instance, 'if you take gifts, you lose your freedom' or 'think before you speak'). In the religious and moral poems, there is a constant stress on the uncertainty of life and the coming of death. Sometimes such poems adapt the traditions of *Contemptus Mundi* to actual events, as in the poem on the earthquake of 1382. They are full of vivid phrases like those of the preachers (with alliteration often

---

27   *OBMEV*, No. 134.

reinforcing the proverbial matter): 'the laste bour schal ben a bere', 'our bag hangeth on a slipper pin'. In one ('Think on Yesterday') the world is likened to a shadow cast on the wall by candlelight, which children attempt to catch. The collection is full of warnings of death, but it is only fair to say that some of the poems contain an element of consolation through self-knowledge or penitence. Anxieties are both excited and assuaged.

It would be easy to continue for pages illustrating the variety of lyrics in the period, but I must conclude now with Chaucer, whose lyric poetry in some ways is very different, yet in some ways may sum up the heterogeneous tendencies in the work of his predecessors and contemporaries. It is important to remind ourselves that he was not only a distinguished lyric poet, but, apparently, a prolific one. According to Alceste in the Prologue to *The Legend of Good Women,* Chaucer has made

> Many an ympne for Loves halidayes
> That highte balades, roundels, virelayes.

His lyrics that have survived include not only those which are now printed in editions as 'Short Poems' but songs in longer works like *The Legend of Good Women,* or *The Parlement of Foules,* at the end of which a roundel is sung by the birds:

> Now welcome, somer, with thy sonne softe,
> That hast this wintres wedres overshake,
> And driven away the longe nyghtes blake!
>
> Saynt Valentyn, that art ful hy on-lofte,
> Thus syngen smale foules for thy sake:
> Now welcome, somer, with thy sonne softe,
> That hast this wintres wedres overshake,
>
> Wel han they cause for to gladen ofte,
> Sith ech of hem recovered hath hys make,
> Ful blissful mowe they synge when they wake:
> Now welcome, somer, with thy sonne softe
> That hast this wintres wedres overshake,
> And driven away the longe nyghtes blake!

This excellent lyric, so smoothly eloquent and so full of vitality, at once suggests a number of points relevant to our inquiry. It is, firstly, worlds away from crisis, disillusionment, and calamities. In fact, it is a song of praise to the Goddess Nature, the progenitor of all living species, and comes at the climax of a poem in which, as Professor Bennett said,[28] Chaucer presents 'a view of the place of love in human life which is balanced, harmonious, and satisfying, yet which does not ignore the paradoxes and

---

28   *The Parlement of Foules* (Oxford, 1957), p. 186.

dilemmas that are as old as human society'. It also shows Chaucer handling with ease and fluency one of the newer (at least in England) French forms. His syntax is obviously more relaxed and more 'literary' than that of the Harley lyrics (though there is still a hint of the old emphatic alliteration). Possibly his undoubted success helped to ensure the continued popularity of this form throughout the following century. Chaucer provides us with other examples of courtly French forms, gracefully turned (as the *Complaint of Pite*), and sometimes enlivened by his characteristic wit — as in the ballade *To Rosemounde:*

> Nas never pyk walwed in galauntyne
> As I in love am walwed and ywounde

(it is in this poem that he refers to himself as 'trewe Tristram the secounde'). He also provides us with satirical and comic verses — as the poem to the scribe Adam, or the complaint to his purse (a form which also becomes popular in the 15th century). And he writes religious lyrics, like the elegant *ABC* or the Prologue to *The Prioress's Tale,* and references — 'my lief is faren in lande' etc. — show a knowledge of popular song. There are 'philo- sophical' lyrics on general moral topics such as 'Fortune' or 'Gentilesse'. In some ways, these may perhaps be comparable to the Vernon poems, but essentially, I think, they are rather more 'secular' or 'humanist' (again, this kind of 'Boethian' moral lyric continues to be popular in the 15th century). There are also some interesting verse epistles. Professor Norton-Smith, in his excellent discussion of the *Envoi a Scogan* and the *Envoi a Bukton*, argues that in style these are Horatian, with a self-consciously urbane and conver- sational effect: 'in the *Envoi a Scogan* the command of urbane conversa- tional syntax and style, of sly and playful use of mythology, of structural indirection, together with the Horatian borrowing, marks Chaucer out as the first English poet to master the essentials of the Augustan verse epistle'.[29] I think that there is no doubt that Chaucer's work can be related to the older traditions of 'medieval humanism', whether or not he was in touch with the newer humanism of 14th-century Italy. These 'Horatian epistles' seem to be a very individual development, not followed up by his successors in the fifteenth century (who did imitate his more 'realistic' verse letters[30] in *Troilus and Criseyde*).

My final example is another example of 'discontinuity', of a new start which was not immediately pursued, and yet is a marvellous achievement in its own right. At various climactic points in *Troilus and Criseyde,* Chaucer

29 'Chaucer's Epistolary Style' in *Essays on Style and Language* ed. R. Fowler (Lon- don, 1966), pp. 157-65.
30 Cf. N. Davis, 'The *Litera Troili* and English Letters', *RES* NS XVI (1965), 233-44.

uses lyrics or songs. When Troilus returns from the temple (in Book I),
where he has seen and fallen in love with Criseyde, he sings:

> If no love is, O God, what fele I so?
> And if love is, what thing and which is he?
> If love be good, from whennes cometh my woo?
> If it be wikke, a wonder thynketh me,
> When every torment and adversite
> That cometh of hym, may to me savory thinke,
> For a thurst I, the more that ich it drynke.
>
> And if that at myn owen lust I brenne,
> From whennes cometh my waillynge and my pleynte?
> If harm agree me, wherto pleyne I thenne?
> I noot, ne whi unwery that I feynte.
> O quike deth, O swete harm so queynte,
> How may of the in me swich quantite,
> But if that I consente that it be?
>
> And if that I consente, I wrongfully
> Compleyne, iwis. Thus possed to and fro,
> Al sterelees withinne a boot am I
> Amydde the see, bitwixen wyndes two,
> That in contrarie stonden evere mo.
> Allas! what is this wondre maladie?
> For hete of cold, for cold of hete, I dye.

This is a splendidly eloquent version of a Petrarch sonnet (and Chaucer
seems to have been aware of the form, since he gives two rhyme royal
stanzas to the octave, one to the sestet). He adapts it into a more general
statement about love, and yet fits it very appropriately to the particular
case of his hero, for his Troilus is a profoundly Petrarchan lover, an intellectual with a 'divided soul', who argues out the paradoxes of love in a
philosophical way, suffused with intense emotion.[31] For a literary historian,
this is a great moment: it is, as far as we know, the first time an Italian
sonnet of Petrarch's was ever turned into English. With our knowledge of
the rich Petrarchan tradition in the sixteenth-century English lyric, we are
naturally tempted to make a 'connection'. This would be rash. As far as we
know, no one in 15th-century England followed this lead. Chaucer's knowledge of Italian vernacular literature seems to have been quite exceptional,
and we have to wait for the different intellectual 'climate' of the Tudor
court (and for an Italian revival of interest in Petrarch) for the English
Petrarchan tradition to flourish. But the literary historian should return to
the *Canticus Troili*. It is time now to look back to 'Alysoun'. A comparison

---

31 Cf. Patricia Thomson, *Sir Thomas Wyatt and his Background* (London, 1964),
pp. 152ff. It seems just possible to me that the shorter 'Canticus' of Troilus in
IV, 638-44 may echo Petrarch's 'Passa la nave mia colma d'oblio'.

is almost unfair to the earlier poem, so great is the difference in the eloquence and the flexibility and ease of Chaucer's writing. There is nothing of the enthusiastic, almost jerky movement of syntax so noticeable in the earlier poem; Chaucer's syntax is smooth and fully sophisticated. Chaucer has made the courtly and European tradition totally his, and brought it into an English language itself now a vehicle for sophisticated poetry. The vivid word 'possed' illustrates the confidence of his control of the resources of the vernacular. The simple oppositions of 'Alysoun' have become more complicated emotional paradoxes. It is an excellent poem, but poetry of this kind is finely poised. This sort of writing itself can early become simply formulaic and mechanical. Troilus's song springs from a dramatic situation, and it means something; is has therefore that quality which Sidney later (in his fight against a decadent lyric tradition) called *energeia,* a kind of dynamic force.

Our conclusion must be that our 'picture' of 14th-century lyric is complicated, and not totally clear (largely because of the gaps in our knowledge). It is certainly not a neat picture. We can see different literary traditions at work — English, Anglo-Norman, Latin, contemporary French, and even Italian — and very different ways of treating inherited material. Variety is surely the most obvious characteristic. We can see some continuities with the past, and some with future fashions and traditions. There is often a delight in the mingling of 'earnest' and 'game'. There are examples of 'disillusionment', and sometimes we may sense strains and tensions, but this is hardly characteristic of the corpus as a whole. We certainly do not get a sense of the 'waning' or the end of an era. The 'cumulative' nature of the English tradition, the way in which old patterns and new experiments coexist, might rather suggest a period in which something new and vital was emerging. Our lyrics are the product of an era which was both unsettled and creative.

NARRATIVE AND DIALOGUE IN MEDIEVAL SECULAR DRAMA*

PETER DRONKE

In several languages, a feature of some of the earliest surviving texts which pertain to secular drama is that they include narrative elements as well as dialogue. This has led many scholars to cast doubt on whether such texts were actually performed as plays. Perhaps they were simply read aloud, it is often claimed, by a single reciter; perhaps, again, they were mimed as well, but by a solo performer, who differentiated characters by changes of voice and gesture.

The problem of how such medieval texts were performed is a many-sided one, not susceptible of a simple generalized answer. At the same time, it is a problem that I believe is best broached comparatively: if we ascertain what was possible in one language and tradition, this can help us to a sounder basis for assessing evidence in others. Here I shall focus particularly on five profane texts — two Latin, two English, and one Spanish — and suggest how, in the question of performance, they illuminate one another.

The Latin comedy that achieved the greatest diffusion throughout Europe — from Spain to Iceland — was *Pamphilus*.[1] Some 170 manuscripts are known, and at least 20 incunabular printings. Its popularity with early printers was such that the name *Pamphilus* was transformed into a common noun: a pamphlet was, in the first place, a little *Pamphilus*. In a recent study[2] I tried to show why *Pamphilus* must be dated around 1100, no later, and analysed the earliest information as to how it was performed. In the second half of the twelfth century a scholar from Orléans, commenting on Ovid's passage about how over-exciting theatres are for those who are in love, amplifies Ovid's words as follows:

there, in the theatre, fictive lovers are mimed — like Pamphilus and the others who are brought on in a comedy as characters (*persone*); people

---

*   I hope to return before long to the problems adumbrated in this lecture, and to give more detailed textual evidence for some of my suggestions. Here notes have had to be kept to an essential minimum, and texts cited in translation only. Translations are my own throughout.

1   Ed. S. Pittaluga, *Commedie latine del XII e XIII secolo*, III (Genova, Istituto di filologia classica e medievale, 1980) 11-137

2   'A Note on *Pamphilus*', *Journal of the Warburg and Courtauld Institute* XLII (1979) 225-30

become inflamed . . . aroused by the love-making of the characters. These are mimed — represented by means of leaping (*saltationes*) and gesturing. He adds that 'zithers and lyres' are 'the instruments which plays in the theatre demand'.

This scholar, called Arnulf, would seem to have been familiar with a daring and colourfully dramatic performance of *Pamphilus*. The play — 780 verses, in elegiac couplets — was not long by modern standards: as the lines were spoken, not sung, it suggests about an hour's playing-time, or perhaps a little longer if there were musical interludes, or if the dialogue was marked by passages of musical accompaniment. What is most important in Arnulf's observations is that there was more than one actor, and that the actors impersonated the characters by use of mime and gesture — even, if we recall his word *saltationes,* by movements of a dance-like kind.

At the opening of the comedy, the lovelorn hero, Pamphilus, pines for Galatea. He prays to Venus for help, and pictures the goddess giving him an emboldening reply. Even this, however, leaves him tongue-tied and helpless when the lovely Galatea suddenly appears. He accosts and woos her by a series of comically inept ploys, which she wards off, humorously though not unkindly or with total firmness. Just as Galatea begins to show that she too has erotic thoughts in mind, she sees her parents coming out of the temple — we are in a vaguely antique, not Christian, world — and so has to dash back home.

Pamphilus now seeks the help of an old bawd (*anus*) to bring about Galatea's surrender. The bawd persuades him this will be difficult ('Another man's in love with your beloved'), and so she gains from Pamphilus a promise of rewards if she succeeds. She goes to walk outside Galatea's house, pretending not to know the young woman is there, and sings Pamphilus' praises. When Galatea comes out, she redoubles her efforts on the young man's behalf. Returning to Pamphilus, she torments him with fibs about Galatea's wedding-preparations — again to make her task seem difficult and deservedly well-paid. But she at last persuades the girl, filled with desire as much as with inner fears, to come and visit her house. Pamphilus takes his cue to enter, and on a pretext the bawd leaves the young couple alone. Then follows the scene that Arnulf recalled as inflammatory, especially for the lovers in the audience. As Galatea cries out:

> Pamphilus, let go! You're trying in vain . . .
> It's no use at all — what you seek cannot be.
> Pamphilus, let go! Now you're making me angry!
> The old woman will be back now — Pamphilus, let go!
> Stop, or I'll shout! . . . It's wrong of you to undress me!
> Oh God, when will that wretched old woman be back?   (681-90)

the performance that Arnulf recalled showed the erotic encounter in mime — *per saltationes et gesticulationes.*

Admittedly there is a faint possibility that Arnulf's reference to 'Pamphilus' was not to the medieval comedy but rather to one of the ancient plays by Terence in which a young lover (also named Pamphilus) appears. Yet this is unlikely, because the Terentian plays never show the characters making love in so explicit a way as to arouse the spectators. That comment must, I believe, refer to the scene in which the medieval Pamphilus overcomes Galatea's resistance. Yet even if Arnulf's comment did refer to Terence, and meant 'That's how lasciviously Roman plays were performed in Ovid's day', he would not have vouched this simply as a piece of archaeological information. The point of such allusions in medieval commentaries is far more likely to be topical than antiquarian. Already in eleventh-century commentaries, as Bernhard Bischoff showed in a fine essay, 'Living with the Satirists',[3] the satiric vignettes in Horace and Persius were made vivid and 'relevant' by being interpreted in terms of situations familiar from the commentator's own world.

At all events it is beyond doubt that, in the scholastic world of later twelfth-century France, at least one scholar thinking of comedies thought not of a solo reciter or performer, but of several actors, who take on diverse *persone,* and who use gesture and even dance-movements to make their performance vivid. He also felt that such performances demanded musical accompaniment.

What of a narrator? In this *Pamphilus* is a rather special case among the Latin profane comedies. In the past, it was thought to have one moment of narrative transition — a half-line consisting of the words 'Then Venus says' (*Tunc Venus hec inquit*), which introduced a speech by Venus. On the other hand, as the earliest description of *Pamphilus* (from southern Germany, c. 1150) says that it has only three characters — Pamphilus, Galatea, and the bawd — I have argued that this implies that Venus is not a fourth character in the action, but rather an aspect of Pamphilus' own thoughts in his first soliloquy.[4] That is, the words 'Then Venus says' are not spoken by a narrator so as to introduce Venus on stage, but are spoken by Pamphilus himself: in the midst of his tormented fantasies he says, 'I'll speak to Venus then . . .', and, having poured out his heart, he goes on to imagine what Venus says in answer.

If this is correct — and essentially that turns on whether our oldest account of the play is correct — then *Pamphilus* consisted of pure dialogue. One other outstanding comedy, *Babio,* from the mid-twelfth century, clear-

---

3   *Classical Influences on European Culture A.D. 500-1500,* ed. R.R. Bolgar (Cambridge, 1971), pp. 83-94

4   Cf. also S. Pittaluga, ed. cit., pp. 34, 66f.

ly contains dialogue only.[5] Yet the great majority of the Latin comedies have not only a number of narrative passages but also transitions of the 'he said', 'she said' type. That is, we cannot generalize from Arnulf's testimony, cannot infer from it that all the Latin comedies were given dramatic performance with a different actor for each part. On the contrary, in those pieces where narrative transitions are the rule, this would be — in default of specific evidence — a far-fetched assumption. There it seems natural to assume a single narrator-performer. To what extent he mimed as well as read or recited, or changed voice so as to give the impression of different roles, is undiscoverable: it will no doubt have varied with the reciter's inclination and gifts.

The problem becomes truly complex and fascinating when we turn to the earliest of the extant Latin comedies, known as 'The shrewd messenger' (*De nuntio sagaci*) or as 'The girls' Ovid' (*Ovidius puellarum*).[6] This — the title in the manuscripts — is the one I shall adopt. I take 'Ovid' to be a metonymy for 'lover' here — we might translate the title a little freely as 'the ladies' man'. *Ovidius puellarum* was known to the author of *Pamphilus,* and was composed perhaps not very much earlier — I would tentatively assign it to around 1080. It did not become as widely famous as *Pamphilus:* still, there are seventeen manuscripts and three incunabula. Unfortunately in none of these does the text survive complete: it breaks off in mid-action, and even in the fullest version we possess the fragment is only half as long as *Pamphilus.*

In its distribution of narrative and dialogue, *The girls' Ovid* is remarkable. The poet, who introduces the text, is also the protagonist, the lover *malgré lui.* He had hoped, he tells the audience, to have done with love, yet Amor is assailing him again. And no wonder — for he is so handsome and desirable! In his extravagant burst of self-praise we are not far from the boasting-songs (*gaps*) that the troubadour William IX was to compose two or three decades later. —

> Venus herself insists on doing it with me,
> Helen cares no more for Paris, when she sees what I am like ... (21-22)

Yet the rodomontade ends in an admission of weakness: a supremely radiant beauty has just smitten the poet with new desire. He continues (and here the dramatic problems begin to be engrossing):

---

5 Ed. A. Dessì Fulgheri, *Commedie* (n 1), II (1980) 129-301.
6 *De nuntio sagaci,* ed. G. Rossetti, *Commedie* II (1980) 11-125. I have also consulted the edition by G. Lieberz, that appeared the same year under the title *Ovidius puellarum* (Frankfurt a.M.,1980), and have collated the earliest extant MS of the piece, London B.L. Add. 49368, s. XIII[1], which was used as the basis of an edition by H. Alton, *Hermathena* XLVI (1931) 67-79.

What did I do then? I began to send gifts of mine,
greeting her and offering my heart, if she please, and my gifts.
She took these, saw, wondered, and secretly laughed —
her face went red, then suddenly grew pale . . .
She was at a loss, and could not say a word;
what I had sent fell from her trembling hands.
Seeing this, she sighed and said:
'Who is this boy? . . . When has he met me?
Tell me! Met? I don't even know who he is . . .
The rumour goes, no one is handsomer,
no one more courtly or adept than he.
I don't know if it's true.' 'It is', the messenger said . . .   (54-66)

The last words show we are still in the midst of narrative, yet precisely in terms of narrative the abruptness with which the messenger is here — for the first time — mentioned would seem artistically careless. If the performance included an element of mime, on the other hand, all would be in order. The poet-lover, after the words 'What did I do?', would gesture to summon the messenger and dispatch him; he would observe the girl's reactions to the gifts. In that case, would she and the messenger have spoken their own words? Or would they simply have mimed, while the lover continued his tale? For the moment this, and even whether there was mime at all, must be left open.

What is certain is that, a few lines later, the girl and the messenger engage in a conversation of nearly a hundred lines that are pure dialogue, without a trace of narrative or of 'he said', 'she said'. Adroitly and wittily the messenger pleads his master's cause, and she again and again swiftly challenges his sophistries. Their exchanges, sparkling with wordplay, have a quality that foreshadows *Love's Labour's Lost:*

'What did I say? Let's see him? If I said that, I'm sorry.'
'Did someone hear aright? Did I hear "sorry"?'
'I don't know what I said. If I said it, I'd be dead.'
'It would have been well said, if proved in deed . . .
Look how you deny what you'd praise, were it begun.'
'I'd praise what's done? What's "done"? I know not one
usage of "done" that's seemly — tell me one!'   (117-124)

The whole of such a dialogue could in principle be made intelligible and entertaining by a single performer — and yet the comedy of mishearing is easier to envisage if there are two.

At the close of this exchange the girl agrees to meet the poet, provided the messenger swears he won't leave her alone with him. Here the poet takes up the tale: he tries to make the girl yield, but in the midst of his efforts she cries out, resisting, and her words of protest — some fourteen lines — stand out sharply from the narrative. They could have been reported by the poet;

yet the effect if she spoke them herself, as it were breaking into his erotic daydream, would have been more striking.

Venus helped him, the poet tells, to persuade the girl to a nearby bed. Then at once, as narrator, he announces a scene-change: 'When this was done, a new play (*ludus novus*) followed.' The 'new play' is in fact a dialogue (65 lines) between the ironic, perjured messenger and the aggrieved girl. This scene is once more wholly free of narrative. So, too, a complex episode in the final surviving scene has 59 lines of pure dialogue (311-69). When dawn comes, the girl insists on the messenger's accompanying her home, through the woods. There they are discovered and seized by kinsmen of hers, who threaten the messenger. He outwits them by claiming he has just found the girl in the forest and saved her from suicide. She at first seems to play up to his ruse, then, as the fragment ends, it looks as if she is both pining for the poet and trying to devise a revenge on the treacherous messenger.

What is so unusual in *The girls' Ovid* is that three quarters of the surviving text consists of dialogue,[7] which *prima facie* one would take to be dramatic dialogue, were it not for the narrative moments in the rest. Even so, that there are some narrative passages, and especially some narrative bridge-phrases, might lead one to conclude that the piece was performed by a single reciter or actor, with whatever amount of miming and impersonation he fancied to enhance the occasion. This would certainly seem the simplest solution, and yet I believe it may be too facile. A number of points make me somewhat uneasy.

The earliest extant manuscript of *Ovidius puellarum*, though it is more than a century younger than the comedy itself, has indications in the margin when the girl or the messenger speak: P for Puella, N for Nuncius. The copyist occasionally puts these letters a line earlier or later than required, and occasionally forgets them where the context demands; in the last third of the text they are omitted altogether.[8] Yet it seems that the exemplar from which he was copying must have been designed with a view to distinguishing these two roles from that of the poet-protagonist. Evidently this is not decisive: the letters may have been meant as indications for a single performer when to change voice and bearing. But it is certain that, before our earliest written transmission of this text, the differentiation of the characters was important to somebody. That it was not just a matter of clarifying for reading purposes can be seen from the fact that P and N are placed not only in the passages of pure dialogue, where they would be a real help to a reader, but just as frequently alongside those parts where a narrative transition leaves readers in no doubt as to who is speaking.

---

7 This is reckoning the lover's opening soliloquy with the 'dramatic' part.
8 The last 'P' occurs at B.L. Add. 49368 fol. 49r, beside line 257. (It is not supplied by Alton, as his edition indicates, but appears in the MS).

Secondly, it has not been noted that this earliest manuscript contains, as well as the signs for Puella and Nuncius, a series of arrows in the left-hand margin, pointing at various verses. (These are probably in a different ink from the main text.) The first of these arrows occurs at the moment the protagonist mentions sending gifts (55). The next is at the girl's first words (61); then at the narrative bridge, 'the messenger is silent, but the girl importunes him' (69); then there are two as she says: 'Why should he send a girl gifts? . . . Tell me, tell me!' (75-6). And two more as the messenger says: 'Do take the gifts . . . he is longing to know you' (80-2). The last arrow occurs much later, as the messenger is about to escort the girl home at dawn, and boasts that with him she is safe, even if 'Hector and Achilles, Ajax and mightiest Hercules should threaten me' (291).

I cannot believe that these arrows are capricious decoration. On the contrary, each place where they occur seems to me to be one that would particularly demand stage-business or gestures if the piece were being acted. Then the first arrow, at the mention of sending gifts, would be a cue for the lover to summon his messenger, the second, a cue for the girl to enter; the next — at the words 'she importunes him' — a sign that she must convey her importunacy by miming. Those that follow might again indicate that insistence and eagerness, both on the girl's part and the messenger's, must be conveyed by movement as well as words. Possibly the arrow where the false messenger says 'he is longing to know you' was a cue for giving a broad wink to the audience, and the last, as he declares himself unafraid of Hector and Achilles, a sign for him to give some comic or bravura display of strength. At all events, the arrows in this first surviving manuscript seem to be purposefully placed, to indicate where certain dramatic effects were required.

Again these effects would not necessarily imply more than one performer. And yet there is another consideration that speaks — even if not decisively — in favour of this. It is the relation between *Pamphilus* — which was performed by three actors — and *Ovidius puellarum*. The author of *Pamphilus* drew on the earlier piece considerably in language, technique, and even in plot-details: the young lover seducing the girl with the help of a go-between, the girl's mixture of warmth for her lover and anger at the go-between. It is not easy to imagine that *The girls' Ovid* was performed in a radically different way from its renowned offspring, *Pamphilus*.

And yet the problem of the narrative moments remains. Here one or two parallels from the sphere of religious drama may shed further light. A play that is contemporary with *The girls' Ovid*, and is likewise preserved incomplete, the later eleventh century Magi play from Freising, opens with words that might be thought a set of stage-directions:

> The king shall mount and sit upon his throne;
> he shall hear his advisers' opinion;
> he shall take counsel inwardly.
> Then an edict shall be promulgated
> that any who detract from his sovereignty
> shall perish instantly.[9]

We know, however, that these words were not mere stage-directions, because they have musical notation over them. That is, they were intended to be sung by a narrator, and no doubt each musical phrase — Herod's ascent of his throne, his audition of counsellors, his reflection, his edict, and its diffusion — was accompanied by appropriate mime. The next words in the play are sung by an angel: 'Shepherds, to you I herald a great joy'. That is, the play has already moved into a different scene. The first scene consisted entirely of a mime of Herod and his counsellors, in which a narrator sang to announce and explain what was taking place.

The Freising play was undoubtedly performed by a sizeable group of actors: there are solo parts for Herod and two of his retainers, for the angel and the three magi, as well as parts for shepherds, midwives, scribes, soldiers, and the pages in Herod's palace. Again, the complex *Carmina Burana* Passion-play,[10] composed towards 1200 and demanding an extensive cast, is interspersed with numerous passages of sung narrative. At times these are chanted as responsories by a choir, giving a hieratic frame, as it were, to the more naturalistically conceived episodes. Even the scenes that are boldest in conception and farthest from the bible text — Mary Magdalen's joyous songs tempting her lovers, her three dreams in which an angel and a demon appear to her, and her impassioned grieving — are counter-balanced by scenes where the clergy sing words based on biblical narrative, against which the dialogue, sung by the soloists, stands out. Thus after Mary Magdalen's and Martha's words [John 11, 21. 32]:

> Lord, if you had been here, our brother would not have died
> *the clergy shall sing:*
> The Lord, seeing Lazarus' sisters weeping, wept beside the monument in the presence of the Jews, and shouted:
> *then Jesus shall sing* [John 11, 43]:
> Lazarus, come forth!
> *And the clergy:*
> And he came forth, hands and feet bound, having been four days dead.

---

9   *Ordo Stellae,* in K. Young, *The Drama of the Medieval Church* (2 vols., Oxford, 1933) II 92-97; there is a fine discussion of all the eleventh-century versions of the *Ordo Stellae,* with much new textual material, in J. Drumbl, *Quem quaeritis. Teatro sacro dell' alto medioevo* (Roma, 1981), pp. 304ff.

10   Ed. B. Bischoff, *Carmina Burana* I 3 (Heidelberg, 1970), no. 16*.

Meanwhile Judas shall hurry on stage saying:
Oh high priests, men of great counsel, I want to betray Jesus to
you.   (168-172)

While the words of Mary and Martha, and those of Jesus, are directly
biblical, the moments of narrative, sung by the clergy, are not. That is, it is
not as though these passages had been deemed necessary and immutable
because they were part of the sacred text. Rather, a play that ranges from
the freely developed scenes of the Magdalen's love-life to the Virgin's long
arias of lament, both Latin and German, could also take moments of 'epic
theatre' in its course.

I believe there is something even more closely akin to 'epic theatre', in
Brecht's sense of the term, in the late twelfth or early thirteenth century
French play *Courtois d'Arras*.[11] The lad Courtois, a native of Arras, is the
Prodigal Son in modern garb: the text is a vivacious transformation of the
biblical parable into contemporary citizens' comedy. More than half the
play (which approaches 700 lines) takes place in a tavern, where the naive
Courtois is gulled by two call-girls, Manchevaire and Pourette, and by the
barman, Lequet. The moments of narrative are deliberate demarcations: as
Courtois leaves his father's house, there are five lines:

Now Courtois takes to the road,
alive with joy as he leaves home;
he brings a swelling purse with him —
it is huge, filled to the brim:
he thinks it never will run dry.   (91-95)

The verses deftly signal the change of scene, and at the same time sound
an ominous hint — for Courtois will indeed lose all his money at the tavern
he is approaching. Ironically they underscore the next lines, where Courtois
begins a soliloquy:

God, what these shillings and pence can buy!
When ever shall I have spent all this?

The function of these brief narrative moments (here and in other early
French plays) has been much debated.[12] Yet I think it is clear that in this
example at least they are integral to the play, because the last of the five
narrative lines rhymes with the first of Courtois's next speech. So too, the

---

11   Ed. E. Faral (2nd ed., Paris, 1922).
12   See esp. W. Noomen, 'Passages narratifs dans les drames médiévaux français',
     Revue belge de philologie et d'histoire XXXVI (1958) 761-85; W.H. Lyons,
     'Narrative and the Drama in Medieval France', *Fs. H.W. Lawton* (Manchester,
     1968),pp. 203-22.

next narrative line, which follows that speech, and introduces the world of the tavern — 'Then Courtois hears a pot-boy calling out' — rhymes with Courtois's closing words.[13] That, among the couplets which are the play's principal form, the hero should have been given two defective couplets within a few lines, seems inconceivable.

The next group of narrative verses introduces the two call-girls:

> While the host has the wine drawn,
> Pourette and Manchevaire come on.
> They sit down beside each other
> and say to Courtois: 'Drink, young master!' (147-50, MS A)

The girls, that is, begin to speak right in the middle of the narrative line. Thus — at least in the manuscript that preserves the scene in this form — the narrative bridge is again inseparable from the drama. In another manuscript there are two further places where a narrative couplet occurs — one marking Courtois's sudden return, at a moment when the girls and the host are scheming how to fleece him, the other again introducing a new scene and a new character: the burgher who gives the destitute Courtois work as a swineherd.[14] As these two narrative bridges are self-contained couplets, not rhyming with lines of the dialogue, one cannot prove that they too must be retained in the play-text; and yet I cannot see any good reason for excluding them. The first serves to make the audience aware that the plot against Courtois is almost overheard by him, the second once more to demarcate a scene. And the point of such demarcations is, I would suggest, to make a certain detachment possible, which will let the audience think about the events within the scenes: it is a didactic point, in much the way that in our day Brecht has recommended:[15]

The spectator of epic theatre says: I'd never have thought this would happen. One shouldn't act in that way . . . This must not be. The suffering of this person moves me, because he could find a way out.

The narrator in *Courtois,* I submit, has a function very similar to that of his modern counterpart in such plays as Brecht's *Caucasian Chalk Circle.*

Even if this analogy seems over-daring, it should by now be clear that for a variety of purposes narrative moments were acceptable — were, one might say, acclimatized — in medieval plays. There is absolutely no evidence that they were regarded as making plays less dramatic, or that the presence of

---

13 *Courtois,* ed. Faral 91-96 (the narrative line 'ne cuide que ja mais li faille' rhyming with 'Dieus ! tant escot de sols e maille !'); 101-2 (Courtois's line 'se fesist ja trop bon mucier !' rhyming with 'Atant ot un garchon hucier').

14 See Faral's textual apparatus p. 27, the couplet after 278, and p. 28, the couplet after 450.

15 B. Brecht, 'Das Epische Theater', *Gesammelte Werke* (20 vols., Frankfurt a.M., 1967) XV 265.

such narration precluded a play from having more than one actor or reciter. Thus, while we cannot rule out the possibility that in *Ovidius puellarum* the narrative moments and the dialogue may have been left in the hands of a single performer, I think on balance it is more likely that this piece was performed in the same way as *Pamphilus* – using three actors, not one. If this is correct, the question of how much of the verse was spoken by the protagonist-cum-narrator remains delicate. It would not have been possible to disguise the fact that one of the three performers was both metteur-en-scène and participant in the scenes. On the contrary, this could itself have become the source of some arresting dramatic effects. The poet-protagonist would be almost a kind of Prospero *avant la lettre*, one whose figments – the messenger, the girl, the captors – at times take on independent life in the action, at others subside again into his own reflections. We cannot prove that this is what the author had in mind, yet his artistry is such that we can credit him with subtleties of this order.

Such considerations allow a new look at the two earliest medieval English texts in the sphere of profane drama. These are *Dame Sirith* and the fragmentary *Interlude of the clerk and the girl* (*Interludium de clerico et puella*). They are thirteenth-century texts, surviving in copies – not autographs – of around 1300. (In the case of the *Interlude*, 'survived' might be more appropriate, as this manuscript was lost by the British Museum in 1971 and has not come to light since)[16]. The received opinion is that *Dame Sirith* is a verse fabliau and not a play-text, even though it contains a lot of dialogue; it is also universally held that the *Interlude* is a dramatic version of the plot which in *Dame Sirith* is told as fabliau. I should like to propose, by contrast, that *Dame Sirith* is itself a fully-fledged play, with three characters and a narrator; and secondly, that the *Interlude*, while it echoes the language of *Dame Sirith*, much as *Pamphilus* echoes *The girls' Ovid*, was developing an intrigue of a wholly different kind – up to the close of verse 84, where the sheet of parchment broke off. I think one can even make a well-founded guess as to how that intrigue unfolded.

---

16 *Dame Sirith* and the *Interludium* are most conveniently accessible in G.V. Smithers' edition: *Early Middle English Verse and Prose*, ed. J.A.W. Bennett and G.V. Smithers (2nd ed., Oxford,1968), nos. VI and XV. For *Dame Sirith*, I have also collated the unique MS (Oxford Bodl. Digby 86); for the *Interludium*, the British Library kindly made me a copy of an excellent ultra-violet photograph, still in their possession, of the lost MS (Add. 23986). I have also compared the older editions of the *Interludium* by W. Heuser, *Anglia* XXX (1907) 306-19, and by E.K. Chambers, *The Medieval Stage* (2 vols., Oxford, 1903) II 324-6. These differ in a number of minor details from Smithers and from one another. Below, however, I mention only two palaeographic points relevant to the meaning of the verses cited in translation.

The plot of *Dame Sirith* belongs in a special way to world literature. Sanskrit in origin, it is preserved in the vast poem of the eleventh-century Kashmir brahmin Somadeva, the 'Ocean of Rivers of the Great Romance', itself the adaptation of a lost earlier romance of the first centuries of our era. There are versions in Arabic and Hebrew, and the story reaches western Europe for the first time in 1106, in the collection made by the converted Spanish Jew Petrus Alfonsi. From then on its success as an *exemplum* in Latin and in European vernaculars was huge. By the thirteenth century at least half a dozen versions were current in Europe.[17] These show a number of variations in detail, and one cannot say for certain that any one of the twelfth or thirteenth century recorded versions is *Dame Sirith*'s source. The general mechanism of the story, however, is this. —

A beautiful and virtuous married woman, whose husband was abroad, was asked for love by a young man. But she rejected him. He, in despair, sought help from an old bawd, who promised him she would make the woman yield. She fed her little dog with mustard-covered bread, and took it on a visit to the beautiful wife. 'Why is your little dog weeping?' With a griefstricken air the bawd replied: 'This poor creature was my daughter once. A young man sought her love, but she was so pure that she denied him. He, sick with love, had recourse to black magic, and turned my daughter into this little dog. She is still weeping that she did not yield to him in time.' 'But I too have a young wooer whom I sent away', said the virtuous wife. 'What might he do to me? I must get him back and say yes, before he takes revenge. Can you help me?' 'I'll try and find him for you', said the bawd.

The thirteenth-century English version of this plot, *Dame Sirith,* has six-line strophes alternating with rhymed couplets — 450 verses in all. The bawd's name, Sirith, is the Nordic Sigrīth, the young lover is called Willekin (a name imported from the Netherlands), the wife is 'dame Margeri'. In the unique manuscript, however, these three characters, when they speak, are indicated by letters: Sirith is F (probably Femina), Willekin is C (Clericus), and Margeri V (Vxor). As with the first manuscript of *The girls' Ovid,* the copyist does not continue this lettering to the end of the text, and once, in the part he completed, a letter is left out. He also uses a fourth initial, T, for the narrator's part. This T has baffled scholars, but a guess seems to me possible. A word that occurs very frequently in the contexts where church-men express their disapproval of mime-players, clowns and actors — *mimi, scurrae, histriones* — is *thymelici.* While according to Isidore of Seville a *thymelicus* was a theatre-musician,[18] in many later references it is clear that the word was also extended to actors. Yet if my conjecture, that in this

---

17   See the valuable conspectus in H. Osterley's edition of the *Gesta Romanorum* (Berlin, 1872), pp. 716 f.

18   *Etym.* XVIII, xlvii *(De Thymelicis).*

manuscript the narrator's T stood for *thymelicus,* is right, then I should be very happy to imagine him with an instrument, such as a lute — that is, not only introducing the proceedings, bridging scenes and speeches, and once (as we shall see) commenting on the scene like a chorus, but also perhaps underlining and enhancing the action here and there with phrases of melody.

The narrator introduces Willekin, about to visit and woo Margeri, whose husband is away on a business trip. Margeri, unaware of what is afoot, answers his greeting with eager friendliness: 'Welcome, as ever I hope for joy!' At that moment, with the words 'Quod this wif' (27), the narrator takes his leave. These three words are the only narrative intervention within dialogue in the entire text. There follows an extended wooing-scene, Willekin's hotheaded pleas alternating with Margeri's protestations of loving loyalty to her husband. More than a hundred lines later, the narrator, T, returns for two strophes. In these he bridges the first and the second scene: Willekin, he tells, went away gloomy at being refused, and a friend advised him to consult Dame Sirith. The next scene, again more than a hundred lines of pure dialogue, is the encounter between Sirith and Willekin. At first she is all injured innocence — 'I'm a good woman, I am' — but soon she is both swayed by a promised bribe and touched at the vehemence of Willekin's love. He gives her twenty shillings, and she sets to work. Here she has two strophes, which the manuscript gives without any indication of transition, and which I think are particularly revealing for how this text will have been used:

> Never were pence better spent
>   than these ones shall be!
> For there's a trick I shall try out,
> a masterpiece, a cunning feat,
>   as you soon shall see.
>
> Pepper's what you've got to eat,
> this mustard shall be your meat,
>   and cause your eyes to stream . . .   (274-281)

The reader of the manuscript, if he did not know the story in advance, would here be totally at a loss. It is only if the text is not just read but in some measure acted — only if we see Sirith turn from Willekin to her dog to give it pepper and mustard — that her words make sense. That she says 'this mustard' does not necessarily mean that mustard was one of the stage-properties; even her dog may be imagined rather than physically present. But the less there was in the way of props, the greater would have been the demands of acting and miming to make the point of the passage intelligible.

The narrator reappears for six lines to make the transition to the next scene, bringing Sirith to Margeri's house.[19] Sirith begins with laments about

---

19   Here (303), in Sirith's first line, we once more have the intervention of 'she says': 'Louerd', hoe seiþ, 'wo is holde wiues'.

her poverty, and Margeri welcomes her with warm compassion, plying her with food and drink. Then, just as Sirith is about to try out her lie and shed crocodile tears for her metamorphosed daughter, the narrator intervenes once more. This time it is to express his own taking of sides, to alert the audience and make them think about the implications of what is happening. It is a mere two lines:

> Thereupon the old woman — may
> Christ curse her life! — began to say . . .　　　　　　(331-2)

— but the effect, as the detached narrator suddenly reveals his passionate concern, is startling.

He still reappears to bridge the two small final scenes — guiding Sirith back to Willekin, and then both of them back to Margeri. But it is Sirith who is given the epilogue: one strophe ribaldly urging Willekin to make the most of his erotic escapade — 'see that you plough her well, stretch out her thighs, may God damn you if you spare her' — the other addressed to the audience, offering her services, for a fee, to any who find their sweethearts totally unyielding.

Here, then, we have a piece for three characters and a narrator — a narrator who only once breaks into the conversation of the characters (capping Margeri's opening words with 'quod this wif'). We have accurate and virtually complete indications of who is speaking for nearly two thirds of the text. And we have at least one moment — where Sirith turns from addressing Willekin to addressing her dog — which, if the piece were not acted but purely read, would be incomprehensible. Nonetheless the last editor of the text, G.V. Smithers, says 'Dame Sirith is evidently not a full-blown drama: the dialogue lacks the very brief replies appropriate to a play'.[20] In fact the dialogue includes three one-line speeches, two two-line and five three-line ones. I should have thought these would count as 'very brief'; at the same time I do not know by what criterion Smithers rules only 'very brief' replies appropriate to a play'. Would he seriously wish to disqualify, say, Poliziano's

---

Yet this time I believe it is a matter of a copyist's intrusion: it is significant that, if the words 'hoe seiþ' are retained, this verse — uniquely among the 450 in the composition — would have five stresses instead of the usual four or three. ('Louerd', incidentally, is disyllabic throughout this text: cf. 17, 31, etc.). It seems likely that the scribe, or whoever copied the exemplar of this MS, inserted 'hoe seiþ' under the influence of 'hoe bigon' in the previous line.

20　Ed. cit., p. 78. Smithers published Dame Sirith under the heading Fabliau (p. v), and indeed the word fablel occurs in the rubric that the Anglo-Norman copyist set over the piece. Yet it should perhaps be noted that there are at least four verse fabliaux in French in the same MS, of the traditional narrative kind, and that, when someone speaks in the course of these fabliaux, there is never any question of indicating speakers by means of letters in the margin.

Orfeo or the *York Harrowing of Hell*, Goethe's *Tasso* or Eliot's *Murder in the Cathedral*, from being plays, because in these replies tend to be rather long?

The problem was similar with the distinguished older editor of the Latin comedy *Babio*, Edmond Faral. *Babio* consists entirely of dialogue; it has numerous indications in the manuscripts of where asides are intended; it makes use of sophisticated theatre-devices such as eavesdropping. And yet Faral gave *Babio* the fighting subtitle 'Poème comique du XIIe siècle'. It could not be a play, he argued, for various reasons, such as that the text requires too many scene-changes.[21] (One wonders what he would have made of, say, Act IV of *Antony and Cleopatra*.) Faral postulates for *Babio* a single performer, miming the five principal parts and changing his voice. He has no evidence for this, and in view of the evidence we do have about *Pamphilus'* performance it seems implausible. In any case it is not clear to me why a play, even with a single performer, should cease to be called a play and be rechristened 'poème comique'. Should one, for instance, disqualify Cocteau's *La voix humaine* because it must be played by a single actress? Or Beckett's *Oh les beaux jours* because there is only one speaker?

But there was another reason why Faral and many scholars were so keen on the idea of a single actor miming a variety of roles: this hypothesis was always supported by a reference to the epitaph of a mime-player called Vitalis.[22] All historians of drama whom I have read suggest that Vitalis flourished at some time between the ninth and thirteenth centuries. Yet not long ago an archaeologist, Ferrua, published a salutary reminder:[23] four fragments of the epitaph of Vitalis were found beneath the basilica of San Sebastiano in Rome; the discovery was published in 1915. The basilica was built over the cemetery where Vitalis lay buried in the first half of the fourth century. So Vitalis' epitaph can tell us something about Latin miming in the time before or around 300; it gives us no indications of what Latin mime-players did in the period that concerns us. Besides, it is not even evident from the wording of Vitalis' epitaph that he acted *plays*: he tells of mimicking well-known men and women, who were also often among his audience, and were amazed − or embarrassed − at how he captured them to the life. That is, Vitalis' performances will probably have been a kind of satiric cabaret, rather than drama.

As for the fragmentary *Interlude of the clerk and the girl*, no one seems to have felt any qualms about its being drama. Yet there is an equal − and in my view alarming − consensus, that the story of this play was identical

21 *De Babione* (Paris, 1948), esp. pp. xliv-l.
22 'Quid tibi, Mors, faciam, quae nulli parcere nosti' (*Minor Latin Poets*, ed. J.W. and A.M. Duff, Loeb Classics, pp. 636-9).
23 *Rendiconti della pontificia accademia di archeologia* XXXIX (1966/7) 145-52.

with that of *Dame Sirith*. The *Interlude* playwright evidently knew *Dame Sirith:* he uses a number of tag-phrases and tag-rhymes that his predecessor had used, and he draws on him more specifically for his *vetula*'s reaction of mock-horror when she is first approached for help. Here there is deliberate adaptation of a comic routine — though quite possibly from memory of *Dame Sirith* rather than from a written text. But the *Interlude* breaks off with the *vetula*'s patter about how holy she is. We have no indication how she helped the clerk, or even *if* she helped him: it is at least possible that she duped him — as for instance the poet (allegedly Ovid himself) is duped in the pseudo-Ovidian *De vetula*. Again, there is no reason to imagine that a little dog featured in the *Interlude*. That is why I have been amazed at the certainty with which scholars have taken the *Interlude* to be the dramatization of *Dame Sirith*, which they call 'the fabliau'. Thus for instance Heuser wrote:

It is universally recognized that the *Interlude* and the fabliau treat essentially the same material . . .
He went on to say that while

all versions of the story, eastern as well as western, make the victim of the deception a married woman, in the *Interlude*. . . an unmarried girl is substituted.[24]

This sounds to me rather like saying of a play: 'The plot is essentially the same as *Hamlet*, except that the hero's father is alive and well.' That is, I think the fact that the *puella* in the *Interlude* is a maiden is no trifling difference but a fundamental one. It entails a different imaginative situation. This is clear, for instance, if we recall *Pamphilus*, where the complete plot survives. The married woman Margeri, in *Dame Sirith*, refuses Willekin because she loves her husband so much and is determined to be loyal to him. Galatea wards off Pamphilus because she is afraid — of her own feelings, of her parents, of her possible dishonour. To get the unmarried Galatea to bed, the bawd has to allay her fears; to achieve this with the steadfast wife Margeri, she has to undermine her, she has to inspire fear — the fear of being transformed by sorcery.

In the medieval erotic stories known to me, it is not at all common for a lover to employ a *vetula* in order to win the love of a girl whose love is not yet bound. The few examples I can recall clearly reveal their debt to the immensely influential *Pamphilus*, though the finest — the *Libro de Buen Amor* and *La Celestina* — also go far beyond the Latin comedy. The hypothesis I should like to propose is that, notwithstanding some real debts to *Dame Sirith*, the dramatist of the *Interlude* was making his own modest but spirited attempt at adapting *Pamphilus* in his vernacular. Because from the

24 Heuser, ed. cit. pp. 312, 317.

Interlude a mere 84 verses survive, a definitive demonstration of this is hardly possible. Nonetheless, the parallels in the language, as in the sequence of exchanges among the three characters, in *Pamphilus* and the *Interludium,* render it extremely probable.

At the opening of the *Interlude,* Clericus asks Puella where her parents are, and she admits that neither of them is at home. He takes advantage of their being away to woo her. This absence of parents was crucial, too, to Pamphilus' wooing of Galatea: the moment Galatea catches sight of her parents returning, she says 'I must go home, so that I don't get scolded'. In both pieces the girl's first words of rebuff to the young man show her thinking she'll be deceived by him. Where Galatea begins:

> That's how many men cheat girls, by many a ruse . . .
> Go look for wenches who don't mind your wantonness —
> perhaps they'll fall for your fickleness and guile!　　　　(187-192)

The *puella* (whose name, we later learn, is Malkyn) begins:

> Go along on your way, good sir,
> for you've lost[25] all your chances here!　　　　(11-12)

Pamphilus counters by swearing fidelity:

> I call the god of heaven, the gods of the earth to witness,
> I don't say this in deceit or craft.
> No girl lives in this world whom I find lovelier . . .　　　　(197-9)

This is particularly close to the English clerk's rejoinder:

> Now, now! By Christ and by Saint John,
> in all this land I know of none,[26]
> Maiden, whom I love more than you.　　　　(13-15)

Both men then have a moment of self-pity — Pamphilus 'And yet I speak in vain', the clerk 'I can say alas, alack' — followed by renewed urgings. At these the thoughts of the two girls turn to the fear of public shame: Galatea, in the course of her next reply, says:

> You want us to be together — but not alone together:
> that I refuse. It's not right for us to be
> in a solitary spot — for it brings harm
> and loss of reputation.　　　　(223-5)

---

25 *losye* MS (but Smithers' *losyt* could be accepted as an emendation).
26 *In al þis land ne wis hi none* MS (*ne . . . Hi none* Smithers).

And Malkyn:

> I don't want any clerk from the schools,
> for to many good women they bring shame.
> You should have stayed home, in Christ's name! (28-30)

Yet Galatea, by the end of her first scene with Pamphilus, has given him far more signs of encouragement than Malkyn has to her clerk; so Pamphilus goes off more buoyantly.

Both lovers then seek out their *vetula*. In the *Interlude* she is given the intriguing name Helwis, that is, Heloise. What connotations might this name have had? If we assign the *Interlude,* as most scholars do, to the years shortly before 1300, it is at least possible that the name was chosen with deliberate irony, because the poet (and some of his audience) knew Jean de Meun's portrayal of Abelard's Heloise, as the woman incomparably wise in matters of love and marriage.[27] It is also just possible that a Breton popular tradition already existed which made Heloise into a mighty and evil sorceress — yet the famous Breton ballad which presents her thus[28] was collected only in relatively recent times, and it is hard to tell whether it has ancient roots.

The parallels between Pamphilus' approach to the Anus and the clerk's to 'Aunt Helwis' might be determined simply by the similar situation: both the young lovers politely ask for advice (*consilium, cunsayle*); both ask for mediation — Pamphilus, 'let your words go between us', the clerk, 'You shall be my errand-bearer'; both promise their helper rich rewards if she agrees. Aunt Helwis's shocked refusal is different from the Anus's first reply (and far closer to *Dame Sirith* in language). Yet it is significant that the Anus too ends her speech with a 'no' to Pamphilus:

> I won't go on talking to you; I have other pressing business.
> People should go their own ways and help themselves. (311-12)

Thus everything in the surviving part of the *Interlude* is compatible with its being adapted from *Pamphilus,* and several moments in the wording and design seem to betray the English playwright's acquaintance with the Latin text. While he also knew *Dame Sirith,* I can find no sign in his text that he was planning to follow the *Sirith* plot: rather the contrary, since winning the love of a girl who is free to love implies a radically different kind of plot from winning a married woman's favours. Thus our earliest English material suggests to me traces of two distinct thirteenth-century plays, and not a fabliau version and a dramatized one of the same story.

---

27 *Le roman de la Rose* (ed. D. Poirion, Paris, 1974), 8759-8832; cf. my *Abelard and Heloise in Medieval Testimonies* (Glasgow, 1976), pp. 28f.

28 H. de la Villemarqué, *Barzaz-Breiz. Chants populaires de la Bretagne* (Paris, 1867), no. XVI (pp. 135-40).

I should like to conclude with a singularly beautiful example of a text that combines narrative and dialogue, from late medieval Spain. There we do not have evidence for secular drama as early as in northern Europe. And with our earliest Spanish evidence, as so often at the beginnings elsewhere, much remains uncertain about the extent of dramatic realization.[29] In the *cancioneros* of the late fifteenth and sixteenth centuries a number of pieces in the form of verse dialogues are preserved, but with little or no indication of their mode of performance. As Fernando Lázaro Carreter has cogently argued, certain indirect testimonies suggest that some at least of these pieces were destined to be acted rather than just recited. In particular, the piece called 'Dispute before the god of Love' (*Querella ante el dios de Amor*)[30] may be identifiable with what a fifteenth-century romance calls an *auto de amores,* a name that, Lázaro claims, would indicate a 'rigorously theatrical' conception.[31]

The *Querella* is by a Valencian poet, Juan Escrivá, who was Spanish ambassador at Rome in 1497. It brings together narrative and dialogue, prose and poetry. As in *The girls' Ovid,* the poet is both narrator and lover. He becomes as it were the projectionist through whose presentation the other characters emerge. Yet Escrivá is more refined than his eleventh-century predecessor both in technique and content. He takes advantage of the transitions between narrative and dialogue to give his composition an oneiric quality. The lover here is not successful seducer but victim – victim of hopeless love, and, in terms of the composition, victim of his own dreams. We have moved from the world of fabliau motifs to that of a rarefied love: this unhappy lover, in his quest among the phantasmagoria of his desires, never attains the goal of possession.

Despite this, the *Querella* remains in many respects close to medieval Latin traditions. The 'mixed' form, alternating prose and verse, was characteristically revived in the learned world of the twelfth century – Alan of Lille's *De planctu Naturae,* still extant in more than 130 manuscripts, was the most famous example from that time. There too the poet-narrator is a dreamer, who begins with a lament and passes imperceptibly into a dream-realm, where he encounters allegorical beings. Yet in content and movement the lament of the poet in the *Querella* is closer to the first speech of Pamphilus: like Pamphilus, he too is complaining of lack of success in his love. The

---

29 See especially the recent study of the early Spanish texts by R.A. Surtz, *The Birth of a Theater* (Princeton-Madrid, 1979); Surtz does not, however, discuss the Comendador Escrivá.

30 Ed. D. Fernando Lázaro Carreter, *Teatro medieval* (3rd ed., Madrid, 1970), pp. 207-225; ed. D. Antonio Rodríguez-Moñino, *Suplemento al Cancionero general* (Madrid, 1959), no. 150 (pp. 86-93). The piece was added to the *Cancionero* in the second edition (Valencia, 1514).

31 Lázaro, p. 70.

lament, again like that of Pamphilus, is full of poetic conceits, especially in
its lyric passages: the poet's eyes tell him why they are weeping, and his
tongue, why he is right to weep. But where Pamphilus in his melancholy
prays to Venus for aid, this poet-lover curses Amor:

> Who gave him the name Love,
> this cruel, loveless one,
> this cunningest deceiver?
> Who ever trusted what he won
> to this thievish wolf, this traitor?

As the poet sings these maledictions, playing his lute, he hears a knocking.
The next moments read (Lázaro, pp. 209-10):
I ceased playing, and, in a voice so sweet that it lulled my senses, I heard:

> Will you open? Shall I enter in?
> I answered: What is it that you ask?
> Who are you that is calling thus?

> Open and I shall tell you.
> You shall open for him of whom you speak —
> Amor.

The passage into waking dream has been accomplished. First Amor speaks
in his own voice, breaking into the poet's railing. After his 'I answered'
(*Respondí*), he and Amor engage in direct altercation. With a conscious,
subtle effect the poet has allowed the dramatic exchange to grow sponta-
neously out of his own turbulent reflections. He has conjured up the god of
whom he had sung so harshly. Unlike Venus in *Pamphilus,* who has only a
single speech, that remains essentially a part of Pamphilus' meditation,
Amor here emerges detached from the poet's thoughts, to become an active
participant in the rest of the piece.

Each of the characters who next speak is introduced into the action by
words of the poet. It is he who projects Amor's messenger, sent to the cruel
beloved; he, likewise, who makes the bridge to her reply. Only then does the
messenger speak to the lady direct. So too, drawn to the stream that bars
him from a paradisal spot, the poet evokes the voice of the boatman Care
(Cuidado), who ferries him across, and the song of the lovely girl Esperanza,
who meets him there. Then his encounter with Esperanza grows once more
out of narrative into pure dialogue. She leads the poet to the dais of Amor,
and again he introduces new voices — a choir of Love's courtiers, who sing
the praises of the god. Thus the poet-lover heralds each new turn in the
action by his narrative continuo, and each time the characters evoked by
him go on to take up their own parts. They have direct exchanges not only
with the poet but with one another — as when the lady challenges Amor:

What evil have I done, my lord,
that you command me here as a prisoner?
   Amor
You are causing a lover's death,
one who's filled with as loyal a love
as ever any person had.
   La Dama
And will you not hear my side
before judging me?

This leads to the contention between the poet and the lady, sixty verses of pure dialogue, in which he pleads the justice of his love and she cruelly answers that his sorrows are self-induced: 'Es vuestra la culpa, amigo'. Esperanza, the poet's advocate, makes a final plea to Amor in her client's name. Then the poet, narrating, brings on one more personage, a herald who proclaims Amor's sentence: this loveless lady shall henceforth live bitterly, quite unloved. From here till the epilogue the piece is again pure dialogue. The poet asks Amor, 'But how will you reward my service?' — 'By freeing you of your passion for her.' — 'No, that's impossible! Command her to love me!' The lady breaks in: 'Amor can kill me, but he can never force me to love you.' — 'I shall make you unlove her', says Amor to the poet. 'No, rather let me die.' Amor confesses that he can do no more for his devotee, who, in a prose epilogue, bids farewell to Esperanza, and tells that he was ferried back by Cuidado to the other shore, where he waits for death.

If in *The girls' Ovid* one had a certain sense of still hesitant experiment with narrative and dialogue, in the *Querella* they are interwoven with complete assurance. In the *Cancionero General* of 1514, where Escrivá's text was printed, the speakers of the lines are given flawlessly throughout. Lázaro, in his edition, has added to the text his own imaginative stage-directions. If we accept his sensitive interpretation, and envisage the words not only as spoken by diverse characters but as enhanced by lute-music and mime, the *Querella* will have been a courtly entertainment of exceptional artistry and élan. The poet who projects, and becomes fatally caught up in, his fantasies of love is a more complex creation than the boastful narrator-seducer in *Ovidius puellarum:* in some ways one might almost see Escrivá's Poeta as the ancestor of Lorca's Don Perlimplín, another illusionist and victim of love for whom the fabricating of illusion ends in death.

The conclusions that this brief discussion may suggest are twofold. One, that the use of narrative elements interspersed in dialogue need not militate against drama, but can, on the contrary, extend the range of dramatic possibilities in unusual, and at times beautiful and exciting, ways. The other, that the evidence for early profane drama, both in Latin and in several vernaculars, may be richer than is commonly supposed. That is, in several languages we are confronted with some crucial texts which we are not certain were performed dramatically. It is naturally right not to be over-credulous, not simply to assume without close investigation that any piece containing substantial dialogue must have been presented as a play. Yet at times it has seemed in the past as if scholarly agnosticism had turned aggressive, as if what mattered was to try und prove that even something which bore every mark of being a play — *Babio,* for instance, or *Pamphilus* — was not a play after all. I think it is excessive to take agnosticism to the point where nothing short of a medieval Customs declaration — 'unsolicited dramatic gift' — would satisfy the doubter. Naturally external evidence about performance of profane drama is rare in the earliest period — which is why the testimony about how *Pamphilus* was performed is particularly precious. It compels us to look again open-mindedly at a whole range of other texts where only internal evidence is available. And with these a little scepticism of a converse kind may also be in order. Perhaps with some texts we would do well to ask: 'Could this dialogue really be meant for only one reader?' — Just as Dame Margeri might have done well to ask: 'Could this little dog really be Sirith's daughter?'

ENGLISH MEDIEVAL DRAMA

AGOSTINO LOMBARDO

English drama, similar in this to the entire Western theatrical tradition in the modern age, has its immediate origins in religious ritual and liturgical drama rather than in the Classical authors. The determined efforts of the Church to suppress theatrical performances, their condemnation (taken up, centuries after, by the Puritans as sinful and devilish manifestations – in this respect, it is sufficient to recall how Tertullian, in *De Spectaculis,* urges his readers to stay 'far from the theatre, inasmuch as it is the dwelling place of lechery' –), the destruction and transformation of theatrical buildings: all these factors contribute to the dissolution of the tradition of Classical Drama (in the Middle Ages the very idea of 'comedy' and 'tragedy' is confused and in any case far from its original meaning) yet are unable to stifle that theatrical instinct which is a living and inalienable element of the human mind. In fact, this instinct draws life and substance from the very institution which wished to suppress it: banished from social life, drama is reborn in the very heart of the Church. The Mass was of course already dramatic, as Tertullian perhaps sensed when he advised Christians to seek *spectacula* in religious functions, and as De Sanctis, among others, clearly realized in his *Storia:* 'The Mass is nothing if not absolute, if unintentional, drama', while T.S. Eliot noted that 'the Mass is a small drama, which observes all the unities'. All the Church's functions are, at least potentially, dramatic, truly sacred dramas *ante litteram,* and the same applies to sermons, processions and at times even to prayers.

What could be more natural, then, than that drama, after this long interruption, should have the liturgy as starting point for its further development? The process has by now been closely analysed: in the ninth or tenth century, a cantor (perhaps Tutilo) of the abbey of St. Gall introduced a personal element into the Easter service, thereby violating an age-old norm of the ritual. A dialogue takes place, fleeting, yet a dialogue. The angel asks the Maries, who are seeking Christ, the object of their search: 'Quem quaeritis in sepulchro, o Christicolae?'; the Maries answer, 'Jesum Nazarenum crucifixum, o caelicolae' and the angel informs them that Christ has risen, inviting them to spread the news: 'Non est hic; surrexit, sicut praedixerat. Ite, nuntiate quia surrexit de sepulchro'. This is all, yet no dialogue ever had such importance or was more prolific. This trope, this personal gloss on the authorized text of the liturgy, these 'versiculi ante, inter vel post alios ecclesiasticos cantus appositi' are the basis of medieval drama, of medieval man's effort to regain and transmit to the modern age a lost expressive medium. To trace the working out of this dialogue, its development from dialogue to scene and then to veritable performance, is in fact to trace the awakening consciousness, the development and the maturation of theatre itself.

This process was not confined to one country or region but, on the contrary, given the unity of the Church and the consequent unity of medieval culture, knew no national boundaries and involved the whole of Europe. It can be closely followed in England. Thus the Winchester trope is very like that of St. Gall but has already added to the dialogue. Here, the angel's answer is followed by a new phrase from the Maries, exalting Christ: 'Alleluja! Resurrexit Dominus hodie, – Leo fortis, Christus filius Dei! – Deo Gratias dicite, eia!' which in turn evokes a further utterance from the angel, calling on the Maries themselves to verify that Christ is gone and to spread the news among His disciples: 'Venite et videte locum ubi – positus erat Dominus, alleluja! – Cito euntes dicite discipulis quia surrexit Dominus, alleluja, alleluja!' To close the trope, the Maries, following the 'instructions' which accompany the text, 'sing jubilantly in unison': 'Surrexit Dominus de sepulchro – Qui pro nobis pependit in ligno, alleluja!' The tenth century *sepulchrum* contained in the famous *Regularis Concordia* of a Benedictine saint, Ethelwold, based on French models, shows this vague presentiment of the theatre in a clearer form. The instructions to the celebrant recall a dramatist's: the garments he must wear, the tone of voice he must use and even the gestures and the poses to adopt are indicated. For example, one of the four monks the performance calls for must, 'dressed in white', 'enter as if doing something else' and sit down, motionless, beside the tomb, while the others, with heads covered, must approach the tomb 'in the fashion of a person searching for something', so that the angel, seeing them 'as if lost', may ask them 'quem quaeritis?'. Here we may note the powerful sense of an action to be represented and justified in its details, even its psychological details, and how the ritual and symbolic elements are combined with realistic and dramatic elements of no less importance.

Clear evidence of this dramatic awareness is to be found in the further development of the 'trope'. A second episode, the running of John and Peter, is added to the original one. This is the case (one could quote from many texts) of a fourteenth-century Dublin *sepulchrum*. In the preceding text the dramatic tension of the Maries' encounter with the angel was dependent on the faithful's awareness of the foregoing situation, and, obviously on the mood to which this 'memory' gave rise. Whereas here, the task of preparing the spectators psychologically, although it presupposes a knowledge of the events of the Passion, allows the stage a measure of autonomy. The angel's appearance is preceded by the song of the Maries, whose mode of entrance clearly reveals the desire to create a damatic 'atmosphere': they do not appear together, but one at a time, and each sings her own lament. In the words they use, Christ, generally just an ideal and abstract name, becomes a figure with full and solid contours. The terms habitually used to define him are vitalized and as it were renewed in the crude grief of the three women who pronounce a diatribe against the 'cruel people of Judaea', against the 'execrable mob' that has killed Christ. Thus the Passion theme, instead of being degraded to a static exposition of events, becomes a drama of human feeling: on the one hand, hatred for the 'harsh folly' of the populace, on the other, love for the goodness of the 'shepherd' who has been killed. In this way the three Maries become three-dimensional, not just mere symbols, and acquire human and feminine characteristics. This is what makes the meeting with the angel, and the discovery that Christ has risen, so dramatic. The women's 'alleluja!' draws strength from the grief that went before, as from a background of suffering that makes the joy more complete. The dramatic effect is thus the result of an internal process. The 'representation' is largely self-sufficient, due to an interior logic of character and action, and does not lean excessively on a preceding knowledge of the events and of their causes.

In a text such as the Dublin *sepulchrum* liturgical drama reaches a notable degree of perfection. Nevertheless, here, as in other of the best examples of liturgical drama (which represents not only the 'tomb', but also the 'crib', then goes beyond the two fundamental episodes of the Christian story, the Nativity and the Passion, to take as its subjects the Resurrection of Lazarus, the Conversion of St. Paul, the story of the Virgin Mary, and then episodes from the Old Testament, from the Sacrifice of Isaac to the story of Joseph and his brothers or of Daniel, the lives of the Saints and in particular of St. Nicholas, or the theme of Antichrist), nevertheless, one factor prevents them from reaching full dramatic expression: their language. The Latin form, however enlivened by the dramatic qualities of the situation, has no connection with the surrounding reality: it is inert, and the genuine power of feeling is as it were crystallized in an eloquence that merely draws on religious tradition. This precisely is the aesthetical shortcoming of liturgical drama: however close it may come to art, it contains an antithesis which can be attenuated but not overcome. Losing many aspects of ritual, it is drawn back to it by a language whose origin and strongest tradition lies in the ritual. For authentic drama to be possible, the Latin of the liturgy must give way to a language capable of coming closer to reality, even if crude and elementary.

The truth of this observation is demonstrated by *The Sepulchre,* a *sepulchrum* which may be looked on as the first vernacular drama in England. The form of the vernacular is dubious, almost a paraphrase of the Latin version: in fact, the characters, having spoken in Latin, repeat their 'part' in the vernacular, in verses rhyming alternately. Rough, primitive, this idiom nevertheless gives action and characters a solidity and mobility of which liturgical Latin could only achieve a shadow. Precisely because it is contemporary, the vernacular is alone qualified to depict the truth of feeling, is its essential medium. The appearance of vernacular drama is therefore necessary and inevitable, not accidental or arbitrary or a question of 'technique', but the natural answer to the unresolved contradiction inherent in liturgical drama which by its very existence was clear proof that the aspiration to theatre which is a constant in human history still persisted, yet could express it only in vacuous, shadowed form.

Other elements at work, in England and throughout Europe, and tending to change the nature of liturgical drama, made the advent of drama in the vernacular all the more inevitable. At the beginning of this lecture it was noted that drama was reborn within the Church. This is the moment to add that, through these centuries, other forms of drama and spectacle exist alongside liturgical drama. So, although the Classical tradition has broken up, some residues are still preserved. If not the Greeks, certain Latin authors, at least, continue to be read: Seneca, Plautus, Terence. While the nun Rosvita of Gandersheim, born around 935, is inspired by the work of Terence and attempts to use Terentian elements for the purposes of edification in her naive, delightful plays, never acted, Albertino Mussato, in his *Ecerinide* (composed in 1314-15) gives Europe modern drama's first attempt to imitate Seneca in a tragedy. Nor must we pass over the so-called 'elegiac comedies' of the twelfth century in silence: learned works for the most part, products of the schools, narrative rather than dramatic, some of them nonetheless contain dramatic elements worthy of note, as for example the renowned *Il Babbeo,* written in the second half of the twelfth century. Forms such as the 'laments' (*planctus*), 'funeral laments' (*fabulae funeraticiae*), and 'disputes' (*altercationes, conflictus*), while basically literary, have a certain dramatic content, while the survival of the mime tradition is an even more important factor. The Church might have a free hand in suppressing the formal theatre but was powerless (in spite of St. Ambrose's violent attacks) against the types of performance linked with the independent activity of *mimes* and *pantomimes.* Although no text has come down to us which could throw a light on the precise nature of the mime aimed at the lower classes (we have some examples of the more educated kind of mime, acting out and satirizing some religious or cultural subject), it very likely consisted of pantomime and farcical dialogues, of scurrilous scenes, in other words, of the very elements the Church had criticized most violently (the more so in that they had succeeded in infiltrating the sacred representations themselves).

There exists therefore, both within and external to liturgical drama (it would be wrong not to recall the survival and insertion in Christian festivities of motives linked to pagan rites, namely of the dances, processions and symbolical representations which the populace used to propitiate the forces of nature) a ferment, an impulse driving it towards transformation, to come nearer reality and become a form of theatre still sacred, yet freed, above all by means of the vernacular, from its subjection to ritual. This transformation certainly did not take place all at once. One could say that throughout the whole of the thirteenth century liturgical drama tends to overshadow the sacrificial, devout ritual it was originally meant to adorn (E.K. Chambers), while vernacular expressions appear alongside the original Latin. This development is accompanied by a gradual shifting of the acting area from the choir to the nave, from the nave to the atrium and thence to the public square, with obvious consequences. The texts and the information that have reached us do not permit us to follow this process with the precision possible for the various phases in the development of the liturgical drama: but we may state with certainty that during the fourteenth century liturgical drama reaches the end of its road and, we may add, exhausts its purpose. In the minds of the populace and in everyday practice, its place is taken, in England, by the *miracle play*, a term which, in modern use, implies all scared representations in the vernacular. In fact, the distinction between *miracle play* (inspired by the lives of the Saints) and *mystery play* (drawn from the Old and the New Testament) is not valid, as has by now been thoroughly proved, for English drama.

The great number of miracle plays of which we have direct or indirect knowledge, and the wide range of places in which we know them to have been performed in the fourteenth and fifteenth centuries (they continued to be performed in the sixteenth and early seventeenth centuries, and Shakespeare himself appears to have been present at them) form an initial, implicit indication of the impossibility of establishing fixed rules for their structure, organization and mode of performance. True, most miracle plays were acted in the open, either in the church square or along the streets, but there are also cases where they were acted inside the church, after the fashion of liturgical drama. Similarly, while the guilds, art and trade corporations, were generally responsible for the performances, in a number of cases the clergy itself organized them. In fact, each region, each town, each village even sets on the miracle play the imprint of its own character, its own socio-economic structure, its own principal features and spiritual needs: this emerges in the choice of the subject to be acted, the greater or lesser importance given to spectacular elements, the number of actors, the type of language. An art aimed principally at the people will naturally be conditioned, more than 'high' art, by the environment that moulds it: this is eminently true of the miracle play. Without forgetting this variety, however, it must be said that from 1311, when a Papal decree ordered that Corpus Domini be solemnly celebrated, the miracle plays tended to be performed especially on that feast day (this is in fact true for the whole of Europe); moreover, they tended to be grouped in organic 'cycles' where each single episode, generally assigned to a particular 'corporation' by reason of some affinity (for example, the Noah episode was put on by the carpenters' guild), found a place. These cycles were generally performed in processions, stopping at various 'stations' in each part of the city, so that a sort of mobile stage (*pageant*) became necessary.

It is perhaps superfluous to note that the 'cycle' is feasible only in towns sufficiently rich and sufficiently advanced, socially and economically, to affront the considerable expense involved in organization, and with a large enough population to furnish the often considerable number of actors and extras which the performance needed. Thus it is hardly surprising that the miracle play reaches the cyclical form in only some of the many localities practising it: poorer towns and villages simply represented individual episodes from the Bible, or, at even less expense, the life of a saint, usually the local patron. We have records of cycles in only about ten English towns, mostly in the North and the Midlands: the only southern city where we hear of miracle plays being acted is London where, moreover, the clergy and not the corporations were responsible for the performances. Thus (and the popular nature of the miracle play is a confirmation) centres such as York, Wakefield, Coventry, Chester, Beverley, Newcastle-upon-Tyne, Norwich are more important than London. And it is from these towns that complete, or almost complete cycles have come down to us.

This is the case, first of all, with the Chester cycle, probably the oldest and which can be dated round about 1325, comprising twenty-five plays, some added at a later date, covering the whole Christian and pre-Christian history. Thus a first group contains, among other episodes, the Fall of Lucifer, the Creation, Noah, Abraham and Isaac; a second, which could be titled 'the Nativity', contains the Annunciation, the Nativity, Herod, the Massacre of the Innocents; while a third, representing the story of Christ and naturally centred on the Passion, concludes with the Last Judgement. Precisely because it is so old, this cycle, more than the others, bears the traces of the specifically ritualistic origin of medieval drama; the Chester texts frequently lack the vivid human interest, the leaning towards realism, that characterize the miracle play: the dramatic nature of the various situations is rarely grasped, and they are rather seen as mere illustrations of Scripture; psychological interest is absolutely secondary, as is the creation of 'personages' or 'characters': the very monotony and uniformity of the versification reveal a minimal interest in drama. As Baugh has remarked, the original, anonymous author was a man of cosmopolitan tastes, cultivated but not profound, more learned than popular, with little or no sense of humour and scarcely capable of entering into his characters. The principal merit of the cycle lies in its being an archetype, inasmuch as it introduced in England, most likely following the example of the French, a form which, as we have seen, was to meet with great fortune there; but, if we set aside this archetypal quality, the work seems mediocre, undramatic, edifying much more than theatrical or poetic.

The York cycle, next in order of time, datable in part to 1350 and comprising forty-eight plays, is much more significant in this sense. The general outline is basically the same as in the Chester cycle, but further episodes have been introduced – or rather, the episodes of the preceding cycle have been extended and subdivided, clearly with the idea of drawing from them the maximum dramatic content. Thus it is interesting to note how the York dramatist treats the story of Adam and Eve in four parts: creation, prohibition, sin and punishment, where the single episodes of the Chester dramatist had been rather long and colourless. This search for the centre, the dramatic nucleus of each Biblical event, occurs throughout the York texts and makes of the whole cycle a notable example of dramatic art. This is all the more true because we may discern in many of these plays the masterly hand of one who has been defined the greatest metricist of medieval drama. According to Greg's convincing analysis, the cycle may be divided into a first group (datable around 1350 and the work of only one author or school), close, in inspiration and in metre, to the Chester cycle, whose didactic and moralistic bent, and monotony of metre, it conserves; a second group, the work of various schools, characterized by a heightened realism and comic sense and by the presence of a 'master of metre'; and finally, a third, which may be attributed to one single artist, 'in no sense a skilled metricist', who writes 'forceful, but slovenly and crude' alliterative verse, but is, nonetheless, a 'true dramatist'. Thus the York cycle is both a vigorous step forward as regards technique and a complete expression, even if only on the level of popular consciousness, of the spiritual life of the English Middle Ages, so much so that Purvis has defined it 'a national monument of medieval thought', yet also an oustanding example of true dramatic poetry. It is no accident that, in recent years, some productions of this cycle have encountered extraordinary success.

The same applies, with greater justification, to the cycle following the York cycle: that of Wakefield (previously known as the Towneley cycle), which can be dated around 1425 and comprises thirty-two plays. The York experience is resumed here, but refined and transfigured by an artist who, though anonymous, stands out as the foremost and most recognizable personality of the miracle plays. The presence of this master – the Master of Wakefield – is clear here and there throughout the cycle, but with certainty in five plays: the Noah episode, two plays devoted to the shepherds (known as the *Prima* and *Secunda Pastorum*), the Massacre of the Innocents and the Last Judgement. It is thanks to these five plays that the Wakefield cycle occupies such an outstanding position in the history of English drama: as Pollard has written, the difference between the other plays and those of the Wakefield Master is the difference between 'respectability' and 'genius'. Using in general a nine-line stanza, the Master in fact combines the talent for realism characteristic of the miracle plays' authors with a very marked sense of drama, a vigorous grasp of his material, an exceptional skill in depicting character, and that ability to blend comedy and tragedy which is a constant in all English drama. These qualities emerge in all the works attributed to him: one need only think, in the *Noah* play, of Noah's wife, a Chaucerian figure who refuses to enter the ark and finally is dragged in by force by her husband and sons; yet in the *Secunda Pastorum* they seem to find their richest and most intense expression. This lively, refreshing work, rich in both humour and poetry, might even be called the first English comedy, could one not distinguish, alongside the comic vein and equally rich and vibrant, a sensibility ever ready to catch the tragic or at any rate dolorous aspects of reality — as at the beginning:

> Lord, what these weders ar cold!
> And I am yll happyd.
> I am nere hande dold
> So long haue I nappyd;
> My legys thay fold
> My fyngers ar chappyd,
> It is not as I wold
> For I am al lappyd
> In sorow.
> In stormes and tempest,
> Now in the eest, now in the west,
> Wo is hym has neuer rest
> Myd day nor morow!

The truth is that here, as often with English drama, classifications can only limit the significance of the dramatic experience being described. The dramatist is interested in reality *tout court* and, just as reality is not only comical or only tragic but both at once, so the flexibility of the drama gives a complete image of it (and this is the great lesson the medieval drama in England transmits to subsequent drama, along with a sense of absolute spatial and temporal freedom). Moreover, here the very 'sacred performance' seems to fall into second place. More than by the annunciation to the shepherds or their visit to the Child, the mind of the artist is attracted by the character, the life, the reality of the shepherds as human beings. Thus he dwells on their pathetic and at the same time comic lamentations (behind which we can, however, clearly detect a powerful and even violent social protest, not unlike Langland's or that voiced, in Italy, in the celebrated Umbrian dispute between 'The Poor Man and the Rich Man'); thus too he dwells on the figure of Mak, the sheep thief, and on the undisguised parody of the Nativity when he tries to pass off the stolen sheep as a newborn child. Moreover, precisely the lively humanity of this sort of 'play within the play' makes the last scene so truly and profoundly religious, and renders the force of the Christian message it seeks to transmit more intense.

Little of this force, this dramatic quality, this still crude but lofty and vibrant poetry is to be found in the fourth cycle which has reached us in a good state of preservation, the so-called *Ludus Coventriae*, of whose origin we know for certain only that it did not come from Coventry. This cycle of forty-two plays is collected in a manuscript dated 1468 (probably the date of transcription from a previous text, reworked and reordered); some of the dramas it contains (the Shepherds, the Magi, the Resurrection) have elements worthy of praise, but all in all, the cycle is inferior, not only to the Wakefield cycle, but also to the York cycle, and marks an unmistakable decadence within the form as a whole. Moreover, the evident hand of a later revisor makes it nearly impossible to estimate the real merits of the original text. This difficulty is even more noteworthy in the case of the true Coventry cycle, of which we have only two plays, in quite deplorable state; while, as regards the other cycles of which we have news, nothing has remained which would allow us to declare anything more than that they existed (Newcastle, Norwich).

And so, at this point, whoever wishes to trace the contribution made to drama by the English Middle Ages must look in other directions. For example, to those texts where one of the fundamental themes of the English Ballad, the tale of Robin Hood, is worked over dramatically — texts which are not only incomplete, but also very hard to date. Or to those folk performances, or rather dances, which revolve around St. George, and where, as in the Robin Hood plays, one may discern the awakening of an interest in history which foreshadows the *chronicle play* of subsequent drama. Or to the late fifteenth century plays based on the lives of the saints, such as the 'Conversion of St. Paul'. Or to a 'lay' work such as the play, unfortunately fragmentary, from the fourteenth century which relates the story of 'Duk Moraud'. The life of the miracle play is not, in fact, limited to the cycles, even if these are its richest and most complex expression. Thus in a text based on the Bible but not inserted into a cycle we may encounter one of the English medieval drama's highest achievements: the fourteenth century 'Sacrifice of Isaac', discovered at Brome Manor. Nor should we forget complex, tense, dramatic plays such as the 'Sacrament' from the second half of the fifteenth century, or the 'Mary Magdalene', of the same period. This latter is important, not only for its intrinsic qualities, but also because it clearly illustrates a formal transition. Here, in fact, the lineaments of the miracle play begin to alter; the play has a realistic and popular vein, but another emerges clearly alongside it. The artist is not content to follow tradition, to relate the story of Mary Magdalene in the simple and direct manner of the miracle play: a different kind of sensibility urges him to go deeper, to seek the motives for sin rather than just describing it. And in this way, a spiritual action moves parallel to what we might call the earthly action, and the drama of Mary Magdalene, without ceasing to be the story of a woman, becomes also the story of a soul's moral conflict. Allegorical figures join the realistic characters, symbols of the conscience throng the stage. TheWorld and the Flesh, Sins and Devils, the Good Angel and the Bad Angel appear: Mary Magdalene's fall is shown as the result of moral weakness, of a temptation which has a real form: the Sins besiege her house and induce her to evil. The entire psychological process of a soul struggling between two opposite principles takes on plastic form: Mary Magdalene's interior drama is projected outside her. And this changed idea of drama is nothing isolated or momentary: on the contrary, the importance of 'Mary Magdalene' (and of the 'Sacrament') lies in its offering the lieveliest possible illustration of how, at the beginning of the fifteenth century, the miracle play is replaced by another form, that of the *morality play*.

As I have tried to suggest, the miracle play, in English drama, is that moment in which the dramatic intuition of reality, alive already within the forms of the liturgy and even more so in liturgical drama, reaches, through the use of a more authentic and more real language, individual expression. Christian history becomes reason and pretext for performance; a taste, a sensibility is formed which perceives the conflicts, the collisions, the oppositions of reality, so that life is seen as a stage and, at the same time, as protagonist in a perennial drama; the personages of the Bible become *dramatis personae*, whose gestures and actions are followed, explained, interpreted, and the episodes of Scripture become both illustration of religion and a human experience that must be transfigured in a play; the very words, for all the great immaturity of the language, begin to be dramatic, poetic.

Through the very fact of being a 'representation' of traditional episodes (only partially, never substantially modified) the miracle play has a precise limit, the impossibility of going beyond the exposition and interpretation which tradition gives of those events. An artist like the Wakefield Master tries, often with success, to delve deep into the matter he has received and inject into it his own feeling for life, thus creating his own imaginative world, yet many of the contours of this world have been marked out *a priori*. Therefore the miracle play lacks the kind of full and independent feeling for reality that derives from a genuine freedom of expression. Whereas the morality play, though it too has its limits, comes nearer this kind of independence, related to the miracle play in many of its aspects, and flourishing alongside it, yet following a quite distinct path. While here too we must speak of a religious drama, since religion is central to the search here made, and gives the dramatist not only a linguistic model, but also a cultural and thematic source, a well-defined vision of life, nevertheless the artist is allowed greater freedom of structure, in the organisation of his material, in developing the 'plot', in characterization, in psychological investigation. All this because the performance has as its object, not a particular episode from Scripture, but the struggle between good and evil for possession of the human soul; and the characters are not Biblical figures, or saints, but man, 'Everyman', sins, virtues and vices, good and evil, God and Satan.

This transformation is once more, as with the transition from liturgical drama to miracle play, not extrinsic but natural, necessary, internal. The miracle play — and this is a vital distinction between it and continental drama, which introduces the 'miracle' to medieval culture and literature — discusses and interprets a world that is still elementary, expression, at times extremely forceful, of a folk world, a society whose existence revolves around a few primary feelings and passions, follows a few essential, indecorate lines (and the principal merit of the miracle play is in having discovered them and marked them out with such power) but in which meditation, thought, moral awareness are still immature if not embryonic. In the morality play, on the other hand, a more complex world comes to the surface, where these feelings and passions have grown more mature, those lines richer and more numerous; where moral awareness has acquired clarity and authority, and where intuition and reflection are not severed. We encounter a more restless, more inquiring mind, which discerns not only the most immediate side but also and especially the less visible aspects of reality. Form and language of the miracle play, its immediate, direct, 'visual' realism, are no longer sufficient for this mind, this sensibility, which therefore seek for and mould a more suitable instrument, a more adequate idiom. The prime origin of the morality play as dramatic form is to be found precisely in this new spirit, this new moral preoccupation. While we must take into account the opinions of those who consider the morality play a derivation of the sermon — which had become, with the resurgence of preaching at the hands of the Franciscans and the Dominicans in the twelfth and thirteenth centuries, an 'element of considerable importance in English religious life' (Chambers) — and cannot neglect the opinions of those who see in it primarily a dramatic elaboration of the *danse macabre* (Craig), nevertheless, to limit its appearance to causes of this order would in fact be to restrict an aesthetic problem within the limits of a genetic law which is irreconcilable with art. Sermon and *danse macabre* are among the elements which make up the morality play: to ignore them would preclude the possibility of perceiving this form in all its fullness. However, they are not its prime movers, rather to be found in the emergence of an intellectual attitude which the miracle play was insufficient to express.

The most concrete proof of this is in the appearance of allegory, pointing towards a more complex, reflective and intellectual attitude, yet at the same time towards another important fact, that the morality play has a different, and much tighter link to contemporary literature, than the miracle play. Here again, one cannot fully accept the idea of those who see in the morality play a derivation of the 'love for allegory': as 'Mary Magdalene' clearly demonstrates, the use of allegory is the effect and not the cause of the attempt of theatre to depict the drama of conscience. There can, moreover, be no doubt that the dramatist of the morality play gets the allegorical form from the literary tradition — the whole of fourteenth-fifteenth century literature is dominated by allegory, and one need only cite, for England, certain of Chaucer's works, or of Lydgate's, or Hoccleve's; John Gower's *Confessio Amantis;* and that extraordinary work, in so many ways not unlike the morality play, *Piers Plowman* by William Langland. This is proof that the morality play, while it preserves some characteristics of the miracle play, is not a popular but an educated production, rooted not only in the life, but also in the culture, the taste of the Middle Ages. The miracle play is clearly set apart from contemporary literature, so much so that the particularly authoritative presence even of Chaucer had not the slightest influence on this form. This cannot be said of the morality play, where a livelier and more active contact with literature can be seen, and which marks the beginning of that exchange of forms and motives between drama and literature which culminates in the Elizabethan drama, in particular in that perfect fusion of poetic and dramatic form which is its most fecund aspect. Moreover, the religion which informs the morality play is more 'educated', less primitive and direct than that which inspires the miracle play, not ignorant of philosophical studies, of religious experience or of the distinctions and definitions of the Scholastic philosophers.

This is obviously the explanation of the powerful echo we find in the morality play of the characteristic feeling and subject-matter of medieval literature and, more broadly, of medieval culture; thus the idea of death which, as Huizinga writes, no epoch cultivated with greater 'regularity' and 'insistence' than did the Middle Ages, dominates the morality play, too; the same applies to the *vanitas vanitatum,* the frailty and fleetingness of humanity, melancholy and regret; these feelings, which we encounter in Petrarch, in Boccaccio and in Villon, are present also in the morality play, giving substance to its moral search, its religious aspiration, the passionate attempt to place man's anxious and fragile existence within the order of a superior and eternal harmony. Thanks to their presence the morality play is able to reach the level of art, notwithstanding the serious aesthetic risks to which its very subject matter and the type of approach expose it: didacticism (the more so inasmuch as a by no means negligible link with preaching upholds and intensifies it), abstraction, thinking in schemes.

The first morality play of which we have any news is a *Pater Noster* from York; the first text we have (incomplete) is *The Pride of Life,* its theme the struggle between life and death for the soul of the hero, 'Rex Vivus'. The oldest morality play whose complete text we have is *The Castle of Perseverance,* dating from the early fifteenth century. The most interesting element, here, is constituted by the 'staging' instructions in the manuscript (which bears the date 1429), evidence that the stage is fixed and no longer mobile, as for the miracle play: there is a drawing of a circle surrounded by two rings, and we read that the space between them is to contain water; within the circle the 'castle of perseverance' is depicted; there are also instructions as to the placing of the characters, who must position themselves according to the four points of the compass. But this play is also a precious document for the study of the elements which go to make up the form. In fact, thanks to the technical and aesthetic immaturity of the work, one can discern with particular clarity how dramatic, rhetorical, didactic and poetic motives are superimposed, each with its own importance and physiognomy, and rarely combined so as to create a unified structure. As with all morality plays, the theme is the struggle between good and evil for possession of the human soul: Mankind yields to the invitation of the Bad Angel and, rejecting the advice and warnings of the Good Angel, enters the service of World, who consigns him to sins, to be introduced to evil. However, the Good Angel turns to Shrift and Penance, who manage to persuade Mankind to return to the path of right; to keep him safe from evil they lead him to the Castle of Perseverance, protected by the Virtues, who repulse the attacks of World and of the Sins; but, once more, Mankind is seduced by the wiles of evil. Death overtakes him, and Mankind in vain seeks help from World: at the moment of death the Bad Angel takes possession of his soul; at the last, Mercy intervenes, begs divine pardon for him and saves him.

The dramatic substance which emerges from this outline of the plot only intermittently succeeds in assuming plausible form, in acquiring harmonious expression. Often the drama is only an embryo, still at the stage of intention; generally the *dramatis personae* are limited to mere allegorical figurations, without reaching the status of 'characters'; nor can the dialogue be described as dramatic, largely a matter of exhortations or sermons cast in dialogue form. However, in opposition to this moralistic, ritualistic tendency, which continually stifles drama and poetry and, robbing the language of almost any expressive power, degrades it to a rigid scheme, we find some moments — all concentrated on the figure of 'Mankind' — where a vivid and poignant sense of the human condition manages to free the hero, and his drama, from the bonds of oratory and religious casuistry, so that art and feeling may prevail:

> Whereto I was to þis werld browth,
> I ne wot, but to woo and wepynge
> I am born and haue ryth nowth
> To helpe myself in no doynge.
> I stonde and stodye al ful of þowth,
> Bare and pore is my clothynge.
> A sely crysme myn hed hath cawth
> Þat I tok at myn crystenynge.
> Certys I haue no more . . .   (287-296)

Just as, in the miracle play, the artist was able to give himself free rein particularly in the depiction of characters who were not precisely and canonically characterised in Scripture, so in the morality play he may be most original in dealing not so much with the Vices and Virtues as with the hero, Man: an allegorical figure, too, but more intimately linked to the 'specific' experience from which art always originates. This is what happens with the figure of Mankind in *The Castle of Perseverance:* while the other figures are monotonous and schematic, in Mankind human nature begins to emerge with the richness, the fluidity of attitudes, feelings and thoughts which are to find their greatest interpreter in Shakespeare:

> Whom to folwe wetyn I ne may.
> I stone in stodye and gynne to raue.
> I wolde be ryche in gret aray
> And fayn I wolde my sowle saue.
> As wynde in watyr I wave.   (375-379)

The Castle of Perseverance shows the morality play still at an uncertain stage, in every sense: *The Summoning of Everyman* is, on the other hand, a perfect example of how, in the hands of an artist of greater talent and more delicate sensibility, the morality play can serve the ends, not only of edification and religious and moral mastery, but also of independent dramatic enactment. *Everyman* too (which dates from the end of the fifteenth century – while it has an evident relationship to a similar Dutch work, today there is still controversy as to which of the two came first) is a religious, allegorical work: but, unlike *The Castle,* it subordinates this end to the creation of human figures, placed in a universal situation nonetheless perceived in all its actuality, reality and particularity. The feelings stirring, in *The Castle*, in the figure of Mankind yet seeming inert and crystallized in the other characters are here vigorous and living sap, continually nourishing the drama, its actions and its personages. While *The Castle* depicts the whole of man's life, seen as a conflict between good and evil which accompanies man from birth to youth, from maturity to old age and death, *Everyman* catches this conflict at a precise and specific moment, the approach of death: less grandiose in conception, the drama gains notably in intensity, concision and, most of all, in dramatic power:

DEATH I am dethe that no man dredeth
     For euery man I rest and none spareth
     For it is goddes commaundement
     That all to me sholde be obedyent

EVERYMAN O deth thou cũmest what I had ỹ leest in mynde
     In thy power it lyeth me to saue
     Yet of my good wyll I gyue ye yf ye wyll be kynde
     Ye a thousande pounde shalte thou haue
     And dyfferre this mater tyll another daye... (115-123)

Nor is the moral feeling of *The Castle* lost or lessened, but rather strengthened, made deeper and more active by the humanity of the predicament, the intense, tragic light in which it moves and appears to us, the high relief with which its outlines are drawn. In the first morality play man's weakness and fragility, his yielding to evil, are enounced and criticized directly: in *Everyman* the consequences are shown, above all loneliness:

EVERYMAN Alas I may well wepe with syghes depe
     Now haue I no maner of cumpany
     To helpe me in my iourney & me to kepe
     And also my wrytynge is full vnredy . . .
     The tyme passeth lorde helpe that all wrought
     For though I mourne it aualeth nought
     The day passeth and is almost ago
     I wote not well what to do . . .   (184-195)

The infinite misery of this solitude indicates the choice to be made, underlines the need for a moral standard. Thus the drama reaches its exemplary form, moral, yes, but entirely transmuted into dramatic terms: characters, dialogue and action. What was an exception in *The Castle* is here the rule, diapason of the entire play.

Undoubtedly, *Everyman* is not supreme art, nor are the more significant and important miracle plays or morality plays (this is the moment to recall another, *Mankind,* of 1475). What is lacking is perhaps the mark of genius; and indeed medieval drama has no Marlowe, no Shakespeare, no Webster to give their individual stamp to the production of a period. The complexity and totality of experience, the multiplicity of life which great poetry expresses are missing; there is still too rigorous a dependence on religion and its form, too tenuous and uncertain is often the link with literary culture. Yet even within these limits, *Everyman* is poetry, authentic drama; not only this, it is also an admirable conclusion to the search that runs through all of

English medieval drama, a search for moral reality and for its dramatic image. This, above all, would seem to be the significance of the miracle play and of the morality play, even in their most rhetorical and didactic moments: and it is medieval drama's greatest lesson to the Elizabethans. Wishing to fix, even empirically, points of reference, one might say that in the miracle play the artist uncovers the dramatic core of reality and represents it in 'particular' terms; in the morality play, as *The Castle of Perseverance* presents it, he uncovers the moral struggle which moves that reality and represents it in 'universal' terms; in *Everyman* both tendencies, both experiences, meet: the representation of the universal and of the particular are blended together. The tragedy of *Everyman* is a valid symbol of human tragedy because its individual features are represented: it is human history because above all it is the story of one man.

(translated by CHRISTOPHER WHYTE)

THE MIDDLE ENGLISH ARTHURIAN ROMANCE: THE POPULAR TRADITION IN THE FOURTEENTH CENTURY

JÖRG O. FICHTE

In comparison with continental literary developments, Arthurian romance written in English makes a relatively late appearance owing to the general cultural and linguistic conditions prevailing in England after the Norman conquest. Arthurian material independent of the historiographic tradition based on the *Historia Regum Britanniae* by Geoffrey of Monmouth is treated for the first time in English in the second half of the 13th century, that is, approximately 100 years after Chrétien set out to create a new literary genre which was to captivate the imagination of the courtly writers and the aristocratic audiences during the High Middle Ages. Moreover, the first so-called English Arthurian romance, *Arthour and Merlin,* originating in Kent, does not take its inspiration from the classical Arthurian verse novel — I use this term to designate the genre employed by Chrétien and his followers, such as Hartmann, Gottfried and Wolfram — ;rather, the work is an adaptation of the Merlin story as we find it treated in the Vulgate *Merlin* and in the chronicle tradition before Robert de Boron. These sources and the author's conception of his material combine to produce a work with a decidedly historiographic bent. We are presented with an account of the emergence of an Arthurian realm which is firmly anchored in the historical process and located in a recognizable geography. As a matter of fact, the English author endeavors to remove any geographical vaguenesses he may have found in his sources in order to increase the degree of verisimilitude.[1] Furthermore, Arthur becomes a true English King[2] with whom an audience consisting probably of members of the gentry and the bourgeoisie could easily identify. The work purposes to be a history tracing the development of England from a relatively unimportant country to a European superpower under the strong leadership of a great national hero. Emblematic of this rise from humble origins to prominence is Arthur's victory over the forces of all the rebels and invaders trying to challenge his position and possessions in England as well as on the Continent. This expansion of English domination, however, which started already during the

---

1 Elizabeth S. Sklar, *'Arthour and Merlin:* The Englishing of Arthur', *MichA* 8 (1975) 49-57.
2 Karl Heinz Göller, *König Arthur in der englischen Literatur des späten Mittelalters* (Göttingen, 1963), p. 57.

reign of Arthur's father Uther, has a particular topicality in the second half of the 13th century. At that time, England, under the leadership of Edward I, an "Arthurian enthusiast",[3] who was compared by contemporary historians with Arthur himself,[4] not only became a unified national state but also one interested in subduing its neighbors on the British Isles, the Welsh and the Scots, and in consolidating its French dominions, especially in Gascony.

Arthour and Merlin, therefore, reflects political ideas and interests current in the 13th century. It is a document which recalls a former high point in English history, thereby promoting the formation of a distinctive English national consciousness and bolstering English claims to both the adjacent territories and the crown's possessions in France.[5] Consequently, the object of this work which calls itself a romance is not the creation of a fictional social ideal embodied in the society of the Round Table; rather, it purposes to be a national history which occasionally contains features we associate with romance writings. For this reason, I would assign *Arthour and Merlin* to the category of historiography rather than designate it an Arthurian romance, a genre distinguished from historical writings by its different relationship to reality.

The hallmark of Arthurian romance, however, is fictionality; this genre as its precursor, the classical Arthurian verse novel, is characterized by an almost total divorce from the process of history. The action originates at some specified time, most often Pentecost or Easter, to run a year or longer without partaking in the general course of history. Consequently, time is suspended in Arthurian romance: neither do the characters age, nor does society move towards a certain destinal point in history. Though following a historical

3 Roger S. Loomis, 'Edward I, Arthurian Enthusiast,' *Speculum* 28 (1953)114-27.
4 *The Chronicle of Pierre de Langtoft,* Vol. II, ed. Thomas Wright (London, 1868), p. 381.
5 English claims to the dominion of Scotland, for instance, are supported by references to historical precedence set by King Arthur himself, as they are contained in a letter allegedly written by Edward I to Boniface IX: 'Item Arthurus rex Brictonum, princeps famosissimus, Scotiam sibi rebellem subjecit, et pæne totam gentem delevit, et postea quemdam nomine Anguselum in regem Scotiæ præfecit. Et cum postea idem rex Arthurus, apud civitatem Legionum, festum faceret celeberrimum, interfuerunt ibidem omnes reges sibi subjecti, inter quos Angusellus rex Scotiæ, servitium pro regno Scotiæ exhibens debitum, gladium regis Arthuri detulit ante ipsum, et successive omnes reges Scotiæ omnibus regibus Brictonum fuere subjecti'. *Annales Londonienses,* in *Chronicles of the Reigns of Edward I and Edward II,* Vol. I, ed. William Stubbs (London, 1882), pp. 113-14. See also the MS. B text of *The Chronicle of Pierre de Langtoft,* Vol. II, pp. 404-06: 'E li rei Arthur, prince renomé,/Destrueit Albanie pur lour adversité./A sire Augusele Escoce après doneit/E qe les services au rei Arthur feseit. / A Kerlion après Arthur tint sa feste, / Où tretouz ses reis lour services aveit presté; / Le rei Auguisele l'espeie Arthur porteit, / Pur le service d'Escoce, qe à li deveit. / Puis cel houre en sceà le reis deAlbanie / Unt touz esté suget au reis de Bretanie.' Yet not only does historiography testify to employment of Arthurian fiction in the pursuit of real political goals; rather, these goals could determine the plot of the Arthurian verse novel itself as Beate Schmolke-Hasselmann, *Der arthurische Versroman von*

progression, the movement of Arthurian romance is historically antiteleo-logical, a fast which differentiates it markedly from the development of Christian history moving inevitably towards a conclusion of all time. Man, living in the seventh age, is entrapped in an eschatological movement hurry-ing him forward to the end of the world, judgment day, and the beginning of timelessness. In Arthurian romance, on the other hand, the movement takes place entirely on the level of story time, which is transformed into action time. Moreover, the movement is circular, not sequential: the action issuing initially from the court of King Arthur also ends there after passing through two distinct stages, often, but not necessarily, connected by an intermediary scene placed at Arthur's court.

This extrinsic structural pattern found in both the classical Arthurian verse novel and the Arthurian romance is paralleled by an intrinsic structure underlying the composition of all of Chrétien's Arthurian novels. This intrinsic structure is controlled by two elements: *aventure* and quest. These combine to comprise an action consisting of two movements. The story proper, if not preceded by a prehistory, begins with a challenge to the Arthurian court by a representative of the counterworld who forces the Round Table into action. The chosen or challenged knight then sets out in pursuit of knight errantry, a journey always accompanied by the "bride winning" pattern. The end of the first movement leaves the protagonist believing he has reached his goal, which also includes the winning of a bride. His success, however, proves to be illusory. The hero is shaken by a deep, personal crisis which causes him either to resume his knight errantry or to engage in a quest. The structure of the second movement, often arranged in incremental patterns, reflects the personal development of the protagonist who must prove his excellence of character by overcoming the obstacles facing him. His redemptive progress concludes with the attainment of his goal and the restoration of internal and external harmony, i.e., the resolution of the protagonist's personal crisis and the elimination of the external danger from Arthurian society.[6]

Chrestien bis Froissart: Zur Geschichte einer Gattung (Tübingen,1980),pp. 222-28 has demonstrated convincingly for *Escanor* (between 1279 and 1282), a work reflecting Edward's marital policy in regard to Scotland.

6   For differently accentuated structural models see Wilhelm Kellermann, *Aufbaustil und Weltbild Chrestiens von Troyes im Percevalroman* (Halle, 1936), pp. 11-13; William S. Woods, 'The Plot Structure in Four Romances of Chrestien de Troyes', *SP* 50 (1953), 4; Erich Köhler, *Ideal und Wirklichkeit in der höfischen Epik* (Tü-bingen, 1956), p. 243; Paul Zumthor, 'Le Roman courtois: essai de definition', *Études literaires* 4 (1971) 82-83; G.J. Brogyanyi, 'Plot structure and Motivation in Chretien's Romances', *Vox Romanica* 31 (1972), 272; Christoph Cormeau, *'Wigalois'* und *'Diu Crône' Zwei Kapitel zur Gattungsgeschichte des nachklassi-schen Aventiureromans* (Zürich und München, 1977), p. 18; Walter Haug *'Das Land, von welchem niemand wiederkehrt': Mythos, Fiktion und Wahrheit in Chretiens Chevalier de la charrete; im Lancelot Ulrichs von Zatzikhoven und im*

The intrinsic structure of the classical Arthurian verse novel generates a meaning quite distinct from that of the historiographical Arthurian works with their additive structure. While these latter works try to illustrate a fluctuating historical development, preferably paralleling contemporary events, Chrétien's fictional treatments attempt to present an unchanging ideal. Arthurian society in these novels represents a state of perfection. It is a model exemplar of the chivalric way of life; it cannot develop into something else or something more perfect. Moreover, neither can the protagonist as a member of the perfect court become more perfect, although he undergoes a process of education. How are we to understand this apparent paradox? And more important, how are we to reconcile it with the intrinsic structural pattern just outlined? If a potentially perfect protagonist leaves a perfect society in order to confront a challenge from a representative of the counterworld and to win a bride in the process, he may have difficulties in accomplishing his task, but he should not experience a severe, personal crisis after he has obviously achieved his objective. And yet, all protagonists have just such a crisis. They are incapable of reconciling their personal love relationship with the demands made upon them by Arthurian society. Erec fails because he places his love for Enite above society; Yvain fails because he places his love for society above Laudine; and Lancelot fails because by loving Guinevere he entangles himself in an insoluble situation of conflicting loyalties. The second movement, therefore, is designed to show that the personal relationship can be harmonized with the standards and ethical requirements of Arthurian society. Consequently, the protagonist has to undergo a learning process which does not make him a more nearly perfect knightly individual, but which reveals to him the whole spectrum of the meaning of knightly existence before he is ready to take his place again within Arthurian society. The great number of Arthurian novels treating this theme shows that the process of self-realization is a repetitive one. The individual always experiences a personal crisis which he overcomes by accomplishing a number of tasks – a process that not only brings about his personal maturation, but also adds to the collective renown of Arthurian society. Thus, both the individual and society profit from the feats accomplished by the protagonist, without, however, improving upon their postulated ideality which has simply been confirmed through actualization.

In England the continuation of the classical type of Arthurian verse novel is difficult to trace. As a matter of fact, only one romance, *Ywain and Gawain,* dating from the first half of the 14th century, is clearly a translation

Lancelot-Prosaroman (Tübingen, 1978), p.5 and Rainer Warning. 'Formen narrativer Identitätskonstitution im höfischen Roman', *Grundriß der romanischen Literaturen des Mittelalters,* Vol. IV/I, ed. Jean Frappier & Reinhold Grimm (Heidelberg, 1978), pp.33-39.

and adaptation of a French source, Chrétien's *Yvain*. Though the English author reduces the volume of the original by two-fifths, he does not alter the incidents of the plot substantially. Consequently, the prerequisites for the possible retention of the instrinsic structure do exist here. The English author, however, narrows the theme of composition. While Chrétien focused thematically on love, the English author omits any reference to it, and instead he substitutes troth.[7] On the one hand, Ywain demonstrates his "troth" to society, when he takes over the unfinished *aventure* from Calo-grevance,[8] and on the other, he breaks his personal troth plighted to Alun-dyne when he does not return in time. Consequently, he has to restore his personal troth by keeping all his commitments and promises during the quest which takes place in the second movement of the romance. Once he has demonstrated his faith and reliability, a reconciliation with Alundyne can be effected — an achievement that repeats Ywain's public success on a personal level.

To sum up then, the classical pattern is still recognizable in the English adaptation of Chrétien's *Yvain*, even though the announced shift in thematic focus serves to reduce the complexity of the French source. By de-emphasiz-ing the theme of love, the analysis of which is essential to Chrétien's *Yvain*, the English poet simplifies the personal relationship between the hero and his lady. Consequently, the complex interrelationship between following one's personal inclination and satisfying a public need is also simplified. Still, the pattern used by the English author reproduces something of the original meaning of the genre, even though the profundity and ultimate complexity of Chrétien's version is not attained.

As I have indicated above, *Ywain and Gawain* is the only extant Arthurian romance based directly on a work by Chrétien. All other English Arthurian romances are either redactions of well known stories or adaptations of traditional motives to the Arthurian milieu. Moreover, the adaptations be-long to a particular group of popular romances, many of which are collected and preserved in the Auchinleck Ms. dating from approximately 1340. Thus, the question naturally arises of whether we can also prove the existence of the classical Arthurian structural pattern underlying the composition of the Middle English *Ywain and Gawain* for these adaptations. To help us answer this question we shall have to analyze the two representatives of this category

---

7 *Ywain and Gawain*, ed. Albert B. Friedman and Norman T. Harrington, *EETS O.S.* 254 (London, 1964), 11. 33-40. See also Dieter Mehl, *The Middle English Romances of the Thirteenth and Fourteenth Centuries* (London, 1968), p. 138 and Gayle K. Hamilton, 'The Breaking of the Troth in *Ywain and Gawain*', *Mediaevalia* 2 (1976) 111-35.

8 *Ywain and Gawain*, 11. 544-49.

dating from the 14th century, *Lybeaus Desconus* and *Sir Perceval of Galles.* Such an analysis, of course, presupposes a heuristic model which serves as the poetological touchstone by which variations can be tested. Since such a model will consist of a catalogue of criteria suitable to the investigation of the available material, I propose the following paradigmatic schema of four major categories: first, form divided into internal and external form; second, authorship and presentation; third, content and meaning; and fourth, authorial intent and reception. These four major headings are subdivided into a number of subordinate constituent parts, for this will facilitate a more detailed analysis of the two works under discussion.

Let me begin with *Sir Perceval of Galles,* since it is probably the earlier of the two romances and a treatment of a story already told by Chrétien. We can, however, say for certain that the author of *Sir Perceval of Galles* had no first hand knowledge of either Chrétien's *Perceval* or of any later French adaptation of the Perceval story, such as the *Perlesvaus* or the *Queste Saint Graal* of the Vulgate cycle.[9] It seems more likely that he knew the material from oral sources of uncertain origin — the external form which features the tail rhyme stanza unlike *Ywain and Gawain* composed in the classical meter of four stressed, octosyllabic couplets is a sure indication of the work's close ties to the popular romances indebted to an oral tradition. A brief comparison with Chrétien's classical treatment shows that the English author followed the sequence of events roughly until the Belrepeire episode, and that he took two scenes from the remainder of the story, the fight with Orilous and the encounter with Gawain. The central theme of Chrétien's *Perceval,* the history of the grail, is not mentioned in the English romance. In spite of this radical reduction of the Perceval story, the English author still follows the structural pattern of the classical Arthurian verse novel. He even includes a prehistory, delineating the events leading up to the mother's selfchosen exile in the woods and describing the education of the young Perceval before he sets out to seek knighthood at the court of King Arthur. In the presence of Perceval, the king and his knights are challenged by the Red Knight who receives now for the fifth time his annual tribute, a golden cup, without being contested. The Red Knight, however, is not only the declared enemy of the Arthurian court, he is also the slayer of Perceval's father. After the Red Knight has departed with the golden cup, he is confronted by Perceval who kills his opponent, appropriately enough, with his

9   See Robert W. Ackermann, English Rimed and Prose Romances, *Arthurian Literature in the Middle Ages,* ed. R.S. Loomis (Oxford, 1959), pp.510-11. For recent views on the relationship between the English and Chrétien's Perceval see David C. Fowler, '*Le Conte du Graal* and *Sir Perceval of Galles*', *CLS* 12 (1975) 5-20 and Keith Busby, '*Sir Perceval of Galles, Le Conte du Graal,* and *La Continuation-Gauvain:* The Methods of an English Adaptor', *EA* 31 (1978), 198-202.

heirloom, a Scottish spear. Perceval's stay at his uncle's castle is related next — the counterpart of the Gornemant de Goort episode. There is then Perceval's hasty departure to aid Queen Lufamour who is besieged by the forces of a pagan sultan; this is followed by the hero's victory over his adversary, a triumph which provides for him both bride and realm. Thus, the first movement ends. The personal crisis occurs twelve months later, when Perceval suddenly starts up out of his sleep vexed by the memory of his mother left behind in the woods. He immediately starts out in search of her, a quest which consists of a series of adventures: the fight against the Black Knight, whose *amie* he had forced to exchange rings on his way to King Arthur's court; the destruction of the giant who had taken Perceval's ring and shown it to his mother; and finally the finding and recovery of his mother who had lost her sanity grieving over the supposed death of her son. After Perceval returns to his own realm with his mother, he lives happily until at last he ends his life gloriously as a crusader in the Holy Land.

This digest shows that the important features associated with the structural pattern of the classical Arthurian verse novel are still recognizable. On the surface, the progress of the hero bears some resemblance to that of his classical counterpart; the original meaning, however, has been obscured almost completely. The classical story attempts to describe the education of a young, untested knight who discovers his own identity after the bitter experience of personal guilt and atonement; it depicts what it means to a knight in general to have to confront the dangers posed by earthly existence. None of these important questions are asked in *Sir Perceval of Galles*. Unassailed by the painful experience of public ostracism from the Round Table, an experience which demonstrates to the French Perceval the sad insufficiency of his education and precipitates his personal crisis, the English Perceval reaches his final goal — which remains the recovery of his mother — an objective illustrating the differently accentuated circular pattern of this romance. The author obviously avails himself of the popular "separation-restoration" episode pattern identified by Susan Wittig[10] as one of the two type episode sequences frequently employed in the composition of what Kathryn Hume calls the type A romance, "the amorclad folk tale."[11] Through his easy victory over the pagan sultan, which gives him both bride and mastery, the 'fole one þe filde', as Perceval is repeatedly called,[12] becomes suddenly King Perceval, who seems to acquire the wisdom and maturity

10. Susan Wittig, *Stylistic and Narrative Structures in the Middle English Romances* (Austin and London, 1978), pp. 175-78.
11 Kathryn Hume, 'The Formal Nature of Middle English Romance', *PQ* 53 (1974), 162.
12 *Sir Perceval of Gales,* ed. J. Campion and F. Holthausen (Heidelberg, 1913), 1. 289, 1.505, and 1.1498.

144

necessary for his high office by virtue of his title. The minutely graduated process of education spanning the two movements of Chrétien's *Perceval* is distorted almost beyond recognition in the English version since it treats the educational theme only in rudimentary form.[13] This nondevelopment of the essential theme explains the different nature of the hero's personal crisis, and the overlay of the 'separation-restoration' episode pattern accounts for the different objectives of the ensuing quest. Of the original structural pattern there remains only a mutated shell.

The other popular treatment of a classical source is found in *Lybeaus Desconus* which is ultimately indebted to *Le Bel Inconnu* probably composed during the last decade of the 12th century by Renaut de Beaujeu.[14] The story of the Beautiful Unknown enjoyed great popularity in the Middle Ages: aside from treatments in France and in England, we find versions of it in Germany, the *Wigalois* by Wirnt von Grafenberg[15] and in Italy, the *Carduino*.[16] Both treatments were unknown to the English poet, nor did he have the French original before him when he composed his romance, though it is possible that he knew it. He may have read it or, what is more likely, he may have heard it, for the general outline of Renaut's story is retained in the English version. The English author, however, made some changes and reduced the extent of the narrative seen in Beaujeu's treatment by two-thirds, from 6226 lines to roughly 2200 lines depending on which of the six manuscripts one uses. Like *Sir Perceval of Galles, Lybeaus Desconus* also features the tail rhyme stanza of the popular romance tradition – a fact which seems to substantiate further my thesis of the relationship between the English and the French versions, i.e. that the English is an adaptation, not a direct translation, of its French source.[17]

In order to abstract the structural pattern underlying the composition of the story, let me again provide a brief digest of the events recounted in the English romance. Unlike the French courtly novel, the English version begins

13 See also Madelaine P. Cosman's chapter 'The Education of Perceval' in *The Education of the Hero in Arthurian Romance* (Chapel Hill, 1965), p. 50-100.
14 It is very difficult to date Renaut's *Le Bel Inconnu* precisely. Thus, suggestions range from 1190 – a date given by Urban T. Holmes, *History of Old French Literature* (New York, 1962), p. 178 – to 'à la fin du XIIe siècle ou au début du XIIIe' – an approximation given by G. Perrie Williams, the editor of Renaut de Beaujeu, *Le Bel Inconnu* (Paris, 1929), p. VIII, while Claude Luttrell, *The Creation of the First Arthurian Romance* (Evanston, 1974) p. 83 opts for c. 1200 as probable date of composition.
15 Wirnt von Gravenberc, *Wigalois,* ed. J.M.N. Kapteyn (Bonn, 1926).
16 *Carduino,* in *Poemetti Cavallereschi,* ed. P. Rajna (Bologna, 1873).
17 I emphasize this point because earlier scholarship, notably the source study made by Max Kaluza, the editor of *Libeaus Desconus. Die Mittelenglische Romanze vom Schönen Unbekannten* (Leipzig, 1890), pp. CXXXI-CXLV, has come out in favour of direct translation: 'Der Bel Inconnu des Renauld de Beaujeu ist die Vorlage des englischen Libeaus Desconus gewesen'. p. CXXXXI.

with a prehistory obviously modelled on the Perceval story. Here, too, a young man educated solely by his mother in ignorance of his knightly origin desires one day to go to King Arthur's court to be knighted there. Since he does not know his name, he is called Lybeaus Desconus, the Beautiful Unknown, by Arthur. At this moment the action proper starts with the traditional challenge to Arthurian society. A messenger from Synadoun accompanied by a dwarf arrives at the court asking for the services of Arthur's most excellent knight because her lady has been captured and imprisoned. Lybeaus volunteers, but the damsel rejects him, demanding a better qualified man such as Perceval or Gawain. Since Arthur refuses to accomodate her, she has to make do with Lybeaus. She, rather disgruntled, the dwarf and Lybeaus set out for Synadoun. Their departure initiates the first movement, which consists entirely of adventures. Once the hero has successfully completed his first encounter with the defender of the Poynt Perylous, Sir William Delaraunche, he is fully accepted by the damsel and her companion, who have ample opportunity to watch the display of Lybeaus' martial prowess in five more fights. First, Lybeaus overcomes Sir William's three companions; second, he kills two giants who have abducted a young damsel; third, he defeats Sir Geffron in a gerfalcon contest; fourth, he overcomes Sir Otis de Lile, whose dog Lybeaus had misappropriated; and fifth, he kills the giant knight Maugys who importunes the mistress of the Golden Isle. The first movement ends when Dame Amour in gratitude for her liberation offers her love to the hero. This event, of course, corresponds to the bride-winning motif found in this position in the classical model. After a twelve months' sojourn with Dame Amour, Lybeaus is severely criticized by his guide, the messenger from Synadoun, for forgetting his mission: the liberation of her mistress. Her reproach causes Lybeaus to repent — a reaction somewhat akin to an internal crisis — and to resume his journey. After three days, they arrive at their proper destination, the city of Synadoun. Here, they are opposed by the steward, Sir Lambert, who challenges Lybeaus to a final encounter. Lybeaus has no difficulty in overcoming the steward, who rejoices in his defeat since he now knows that Lybeaus is the long awaited saviour of his imprisoned mistress. Lybeaus will be able to defeat in battle the two warlocks holding her captive. Once this has been accomplished, he is approached by a serpent which has the head of a damsel, and when it kisses him, the enchantment is broken. In gratitude for her liberation, the mistress of Synadoun offers herself in marriage. Lybeaus accepts. After a seven days' stay with Sir Lambert, the two return to Arthur's court, where their wedding is lavishly celebrated. Finally, the young couple is taken back to Synadoun by Arthur himself, and the romance ends.

As my interspersed comments have already indicated, the classical pattern becomes transparent in this English romance, too. It contains a challenge, adventure, and the "bride winning" motif in the first movement, all of which is followed by a momentary rest at the court of Dame Amour, where the motif of uxuriousness known to us from *Erec* is introduced. A personal crisis triggers the second movement in the form of a quest for the original goal. Once this is attained the action returns to Arthur's court, the symbolic center of social and personal harmony. As in *Sir Perceval of Galles*, however, the meaning of the pattern has also been largely obscured. This is partially due to the fact that the "bride winning" motif is doubled — a feature already apparent in the Fench version of the story — and that it is combined with the "love-marriage" episode sequence, identified by Susan Wittig as the other dominant, structural and thematic pattern in Middle English popular romance.[18] The last movement of the English romance clearly features the familiar type episodes of love, threatened marriage, rescue, and finally marriage, a pattern which Susan Wittig has shown to exist in 19 Middle English romances.[19] Moreover, this popular pattern is not present in analogous form in Renaut's treatment of the Lybeaus story, which itself deviates from the classical pattern found in Chrétien's courtly novel. Renaut adopts Chrétien's structure rather playfully to make it fit his own personal situation and objectives. The *sens*, that is the meaning of the story, Renaut claims was given to him by his lady for whom he undertook to write the work.[20] The romance is, consequently, not just a tale of love and adventure, but it mirrors partially the situation of its author. Renaut frequently draws general lessons from concrete situations which he, in turn, personalizes, that is, applies to his own case. Consequently, we have an authorial involvement in the French version which is totally absent from the English adaptation.

Let me illustrate this by commenting briefly on the Ile d'Or episode. Once Libiaus has defeated Malgiers le Gris, the mistress of the realm, the Fay "aux blanches mains" offers herself and her dominions to the victor. Libiaus declines and departs on the next morning, even though the lovely lady has come privily to his bedchamber displaying all of her charms. Then follows the liberation of the Queen of Senaudon just as it happens in the English version. But instead of now accepting this Queen's offer of marriage and kingship, Libiaus defers the decision to Arthur, while he, deeply in love with the Fay "aux blanches mains", returns to the Golden Isle. The account of the second stay there covers over 1100 lines and becomes the central episode of the romance. We are treated to a detailed anatomy of love in which this interesting phenomenon is analysed clinically and psychologically. Libiaus, who once rejected the Fay's offer of love, must now earn her good graces by undergoing some trials as a test of his ardour. He is finally pardoned and restored to the role of the Fay's lover. They both live together happily,

---

18   Susan Wittig, pp. 175-78.
19   Ibid., pp.146-51
20   *Le Bel Inconnu*, 11.1-5.

while, on the other hand, the Queen of Senaudon must appeal to Arthur to help her regain Libiaus. In order to draw him out of hiding, the King announces a great tournament. Libiaus cannot withstand this temptation. In spite of the appeals by the Fay to stay with her on the Golden Isle, he returns, wins the tournament, and is married immediately to the Queen of Senaudon. With the return to Senaudon the story proper ends, to be concluded by an epilogue in which Renaut addresses himself once more to his lady and promises a sequel under the following conditions: the hero will find his *amie* again if she shows him "un biau sanblant" – a friendly face.[21] This statement, however, makes it very clear that Renaut regards the Fay "aux blanches mains" as Libiaus' true love, even though he has him marry the Queen of Senaudon.

The bride-winning motif appears twice, as I have indicated before – a fact which explains its dual presence in the English version. And yet it is employed quite differently in both treatments of the Libiaus story, the result being two different structural patterns. In the French version the protagonist's personal crisis occurs after he has attained his original goal, the liberation of the Queen of Senaudon. He now knows that he is really in love with the Fay and thus after a psychomachia he decides to return to the Ile d'Or, where he now has to earn the love of the jilted Fay. Thus, the second movement in Renaut's poem actually begins with the return of Libiaus to the Ile d'Or and not with his departure from there in order to liberate the lady of Senaudon. The English version follows the classical pattern at this point more closely than Renaut's work. Renaut's playful handling of the classical pattern, obviously with the intention to please and impress his lady love, leads to a structural inversion which is rectified again by the English author, though in doing so, he perverts the original *sens* of the French romance. By reducing Lybeaus's two stays at the Ile d'Or to one 12 month sojourn and by making Dame Amour a bewitching enchantress who, with her charms and magical arts, allures the young, inexperienced protagonist, the English author changes the meaning of the French poem into its very opposite. Renaut uses the inherited "bride-winning" motif in order to differentiate between two alternatives: courtly love and marriage. The first possibility is very elaborately treated. All the pains and pleasures of love are described in great detail with a clear indication that initial woe can be turned into incommensurable joy. The second possibility on the other hand, is briefly summarized at the end of the romance and presented exclusively in terms of feudal law. The word *amour* is not mentioned once: rather, the author speaks of the protagonist's coronation and the oath of fealty of the barons who recognize Libiaus as their lord. What is described at the end of

---

21   Ibid., 1.6255.

Beaujeu's work is much closer to quotidian feudal reality than the description of amorous extasy on the Ile d'Or. Yet, it is exactly this description which occupies the central position in Beaujeu's romance which is designed to cajole his lady into granting him her love. It is difficult to say if the English author understood the importance and the meaning of the central episode at all. In any case, like many of his colleagues composing popular romances, he had little interest in describing love; as a matter of fact, he even shows a certain prudishness. Thus, the depiction of the Ile d'Or episode, reduced to little more than fifty lines, is larded with denigrating authorial comments on Dame Amour, who is not only a sorceress, but also unchaste.[22]

Aside from the lack of interest in love typical of the popular romance, there are other features which the English version shares with the popular tradition. Its author, for instance, places little emphasis on the depiction of courtly topoi, such as feasts, tournaments, and the description of interieurs. Thus, the final tournament lovingly described for almost 700 lines by Renaut is dropped completely. Moreover, all descriptions of courtly pomp and ceremony are reduced to a minimum, because the author of the English version, like the authors of popular romance in general, is interested in a plot with a great deal of action. Periods of rest, which Renaut creates by the use of elaborate *descriptiones,* are in this way largely eliminated from the English version. The English poet is much more interested in showing how an underrated young man proves his innate worth in a rapid succession of battles. In order to increase the excellence of his protagonist, the author upgrades one of his opponents. The knight Malgiers le Gris, who defends the access of the Ile d'Or, becomes a giant knight fighting Lybeaus to sheer exhaustion. Moreover, instead of encountering Orguillous de la Lande in single combat, Lybeaus takes on a largely superior force consisting of this antagonist plus his sons and friends. Here, too, the original situation is altered in order to make the battle more difficult for the hero. Finally, the author changes the sequence of the fights so as to produce an incremental pattern. Thus, the initial fight against William Delaraunche is followed immediately by the battle against the three brothers, though the French version had interposed the killing of the two giants. Since giants, however, are more formidable opponents than mere knightly adversaries, the English author changes the sequence of events. From a purely functional point of view, there are only two important encounters: the fight with William Delaraunche which establishes Lybeaus' status as a valiant knight, and the battle with Sir Lambert which reveals that he is Gawain's son and thus

---

22 *Lybeaus Desconus,* ed. Maldwyn Mills, *EETS O.S.* 261 (London, 1969), 11.1476, 1486.

makes it possible for him to be a potential champion on behalf of the Lady of Synadoun. All other fights in the first portion are incidental and their rapid succession in the English version serves the mere purpose of elevating the protagonist's stature to that of the most excellent knight which he is described as being in the prologue. Just as his counterparts, the protagonists in other popular romances, Lybeaus is the best knight and as such his story will be a success story. He is not a kinetic character, that is, he does not undergo a learning process as do the protagonists in the classical Arthurian verse novels; rather, like the heroes of the popular romances, he is perfect and infallible from the very start, even though this fact may not be recognized at first by the other characters.

In addition to the notable shift from description to action and from a kinetic to a static characterization of the hero — both elements of the popular romance — we encounter many stylistic features in the English version that belong to the repertoire of popular poetry. According to Susan Wittig's count, the percentage of lines which contain formulas in *Lybeaus* is 30%.[23] Moreover, the work contains numerous motifemes, scene patterns, and type-episodes common to this type of poetry. The opening of the romance, for instance, follows the set pattern of the exhortation motifeme consisting of prayer, exhortation and synopsis. The French version, on the other hand, follows the pattern of the classical prologue by differentiating between *matière* and *sens,* whereby the authority responsible for the meaning of the poem is identified as Renaut's mistress.

Scene patterns, i.e., a combination of a number of motifemes, are used especially in the description of the numerous combats, which consist of a number of conventional motifemes, such as the bidding-to-battle, the arming-of-the-knight, the tilt and the reward motifeme.

Type-episodes, i.e. combinations of scene patterns, are the largest individual units of composition used by the English author. I have already mentioned that he makes use of the frequently employed type-episode sequence love-threatened marriage-rescue-marriage in order to structure the second movement of his romance, but he also uses the conventional separation-adaptation type-episodes in order to start off his narrative. Here too, he differs from the French version, which does not feature this popular type-episode sequence found in 17 Middle English romances.[24] Incidentally, both type-episode sequences also appear in *Sir Perceval of Galles,* even though this romance de-emphasizes the love-marriage sequence in favor of the separation-restoration sequence, which, together with the classical Arthurian pattern, functions as controlling structural device.

23   Susan Wittig, p. 18
24   Ibid., p.18

In view of the strong formal indebtedness of these two Arthurian romances to the popular romance tradition, I would be inclined to credit professional scribes with their authorship, perhaps writers like the authors of the Auchinleck Ms., to the romances of which both works examined here bear a close resemblance. These, as well as the other popular romances, show many features of oral composition – a fact which does not mean that they were necessarily composed and recited by minstrels, as was often assumed formerly.[25] Their resemblance in composition, diction, and rhyme scheme suggests, rather, a common oral tradition on which their authors drew.[26] The close relationship to the oral tradition also suggests as mode of presentation oral recitation rather than the private reading which would hold true for the classical Arthurian verse novels catering to a reading audience.[27] Oral presentation, of course, conditioned both the structure and the size of the popular romances, since the material to be narrated had to be reduced to a certain number of lines. *Sir Perceval of Galles* comprises roughly 2300 lines and *Lybeaus Desconus* 2200 lines. If one figures approximately 1100 to 1200 lines for a one hour session – neither the reciter's nor the audience's attention span would extend much beyond that – then this time limit would necessitate either that the romance be about that number of lines altogether or that a longer work be subdivided into fits of this length which could be recited in several sessions. Both romances under consideration show such a division. In *Sir Perceval of Galles* the break occurs at line 1124 and in *Lybeaus Desconus* in line 1269.[28] In both cases a critical stage in the narrative development is reached as each respective hero has to face the opponent standing between him and the bride: Perceval gets ready to fight the sultan besieging the castle of Lady Lufamour and Lybeaus prepares himself to do battle with Maugys who is importuning Dame Amour.

---

25 See the discussion by Dieter Mehl, pp. 7-13 and note 18 on p. 264. Mehl dismisses the possible minstrel origin of the Middle English romance summarily. A much more conciliatory view on this matter is taken by Albert C. Baugh, 'The Authorship of the Middle English Romances', *Annual Bulletin of the Modern Humanities Research Association* 22 (1950) 13-28 and 'The Middle English Romance: Some Questions of Creation, Presentation, and Preservation', *Speculum* 42 (1967) 1-31.

26 Cf. especially Susan Wittig's repeatedly cited study, *Stylistic and Narrative Structures in the Middle English Romances*.

27 See Manfred G. Scholz, *Hören und Lesen* (Wiesbaden, 1980), pp. 167-78; 184-91; 198; 202-30, whose careful analysis of the literature on the one hand and of the educational background of the authors and their intended audience on the other suggests a much wider reception of literary texts by means of private reading than had hitherto been acknowledged.

28 See Dieter Mehl, pp. 76-77 for a discussion of the bipartite structure of *Lybeaus Desconus*.

Having analysed the form as well as the authorship and presentation of the popular English Arthurian romance, let us now turn to a consideration of the third category: content and meaning. As I have already indicated in connection with my discussion of the Ile d'Or episode, the author of the English version sets different accents. The treatment of courtly love is consciously de-emphasized in favor of an elaborate description of the various battle scenes, i.e., knightly adventure comprises the core of this romance, as it does likewise in *Sir Perceval of Galles*. Furthermore, the conception of the hero in both romances bears a strong resemblance to that found in other popular romances. He does not embody a specifically Arthurian ethos as do the protagonists in the classical verse novel, even though the Arthurian court occupies a unique position in *Lybeaus*. In this romance, the court retains its function as social and ethical center to a much higher degree than is the case in *Sir Perceval*. Thus, Lybeaus sees himself always in connection with Arthur's court. Initially, he sets out to be knighted there, and at the end he returns to the court in order to celebrate his marriage to the lady of Synadoun. Moreover, our hero is in permanent contact with King Arthur, to whom he sends all vanquished opponents.[29] He regards himself, furthermore, as a member of the Round Table, the fame and honor of which he must defend and increase.[30] Consequently, we can say that even though the author does not endeavor to develop a system of courtly values and to institute chivalric norms which would be superior to the common knightly ethos he does affirm in the person of the hero the validity of the Arthurian honor code as a universally acceptable moral model. The very fact that Lybeaus, regarding himself as representative of Arthurian society, triumphs easily over all external threats by either vanquishing or destroying his antagonists or integrating the defeated opponent into Arthurian society — Sir Otis de Lile is made a member of the Round Table — illustrates the superiority of the chivalric principles in the name of which he fights. In this respect *Lybeaus Desconus* occupies a special position among Middle English Arthurian romances, some of which also more or less tacitly accept the validity of the Arthurian ethos, while others question it occasionally.

A brief look at *Sir Perceval* will suffice to illustrate the differences. In Chrétien's version the relationship between the protagonist and the court is characterized by reciprocity. Not only does Perceval send all defeated knights to Arthur's court, but the court itself leaves Camelot in search of Perceval. No such bond between the hero and Arthurian society exists in the English version. The hero is on his own; he fights for himself, not for the honor of the Round Table. The author of *Lybeaus Desconus*, on the other

---

29   *Lybeaus Desconus,* 11.395-401; 712-17; 1002-05; 1225-32.
30   Ibid., 11. 1348-52; 1572-74; 1989-94.

hand, obviously adheres to the classical concept of mutual esteem and the relationship of interdependence existing between the hero and King Arthur's court as we find it originally in Chrétien's *Perceval*. And finally, the essential element of the hero's self-discovery and self-realization which at last make him an exemplary member of Arthurian society is also handled differently in both romances. In *Sir Perceval*, there is hardly any trace of such a development; rather, the 'fole one be filde' suddenly becomes King Perceval by virtue of his victory over the pagan sultan, giving him both bride and mastery. In *Lybeaus*, on the other hand, there is still an element of initiation present, since the Beautiful Unknown has to establish his knightly valor first. Moreover, three of the eight battles further the progress of the hero's self-realization which extends from initial recognition to the establishment of his identity and, finally, to the attainment of a kingdom. This process, incidentally, differs from that of the French version, which emphasizes Libiaus' role as courtly lover to a much greater extent. Consequently, the hero's self-discovery there is intimately connected with his experiences and education in love.

Closely connected with content and meaning are, lastly, authorial intent and reception. The authorial intent underlying the composition of the classical Arthurian verse novels was probably guided by the traditional concept determining the function of literature: *delectare et docere*. The strong emphasis on knight errantry in both English romances, however, illustrates the preponderance of the aspect of entertainment in the authorial conception — a feature they share with most of the other popular Middle English romances. In spite of the authors' strong engagement for their respective heroes and the likewise strong censure of the actions of their opponents, there is no didactic authorial intent. Even though the members of the audience are asked to symphathize with the fate of the hero, they do not identify with him in order to be themselves initiated into courtly life, as is the case with the audiences of the classical Arthurian verse novels. The progress of Lybeaus, as well as that of Perceval, demonstrates that innate gentility conferred upon an individual by his noble birth will ultimately prevail. Thus, both works are essentially conservative in their affirmation of the existing class structure based on hereditary privileges. Unlike Chaucer, who propagates the humanistic ideal of gentility of the heart in contrast to gentility by ancestry,[31] the authors of the two English romances insist that he who is born nobly will do noble deeds. Lybeaus, Gawain's son, will eventually become the most excellent knight and Perceval, Arthur's nephew, will likewise grow up to be a respectable member of the Round Table.

---

31 *The Works of Geoffrey Chaucer*, ed. F.N. Robinson (Boston, 1957), p. 346, *Boece*, III. Prosa 6 and Metrum 6; p. 87, *WBT*, III, 1109-12, 1146-47, 1113-16, and 1162-64; p. 536, 'Gentilesse'.

Needless to say, under such conditions these two heroes inhabiting the world of popular romance are rarely beset by moral qualms. They experience neither true crisis nor defeat leading to insecurity or doubt. Like the heroes of the other popular romances, they rush from victory to victory and affirm by the example of their success the superiority of the aristocracy implicitly taken for granted by the authors of this genre. That this ideology informing the composition of the popular Arthurian romances was not immune to challenge, however, is shown by the emergence of a different type of Arthurian romance in the second half of the 14th century, one characterized by strong homiletic tendencies. The postulated ideality of Arthurian society is questioned, the validity of its values is scrutinized and they are found wanting. In both respects, the society's eventual demise is an inevitable conclusion as the poems drawing on the *Mort Artu* tradition demonstrate with somber finality.

ARITHMETIC AND THE MENTALITY OF CHAUCER

DEREK BREWER

For some historians the concept 'mentality' implies the collective frame of mind of a whole group, inert, unselfconscious and irrational. While this is a valuable base, it is possible to go beyond this, as Carlo Ginzburg does,[1] to investigate as it were the shape of one individual mind, recognizing in it both its own individuality and what it shares with others in the same historical culture. Only rarely will the necessary evidence for such an investigation into the historical past be available for us, but there are examples, sometimes overlooked by historians. They are provided by major, complex works of art, and especially works of verbal art, where the medium, words, is itself a product of the total cultural mentality as presented through the mind of a single literary genius. When such a writer has composed several works they may be taken themselves as a cultural unity, a model of the historical culture itself, or of some substantial part of it.

We may therefore legitimately investigate the mentality of such a major writer as Chaucer, as we might of his contemporaries or of Shakespeare and Milton. The mention of such diverse geniuses is enough to emphasize the methodological problems of the enterprise. Granted that the author has a large enough mind and *œuvre* to present a sufficient body of evidence, there are many literary questions to be asked about point of view, personal intention, dramatic or ironic modes, the difference between fiction and non-fiction, the status of translation and adaptation, and so forth. Such questions can be only implicitly answered, if at all, in a brief essay such as this. My aim is primarily to introduce the concept of mentality as of real use to those who respond personally to historical works of art but wish to understand literary and historical phenomena as something different from, though interacting with, their own minds. The enterprise is diametrically opposed to that of the 'deconstructionist', whose essential aim is to see the work of art as an extension of his own mind.

There can be no single approach to or method of investigation of Chaucer's mentality. Within the general concept of mentality the present essay will attempt to point out a particular element in Chaucer's work which has

1   Carlo Ginzburg, *Il formaggio e i vermi,* Torino, 1976. Ginzburg gives further references to historians, mainly French, who use the concept of mentality.

been almost totally overlooked, but whose recognition may lead our under-standing further into appreciation of his creative art, and the mind it reflects and communicates. This element is arithmetic, its nature and use.[2]

Arithmetic is never thought of as an intrinsic element in a poet's mentality, and naturally so. The nature of arithmetic is to be impersonal, systematic but empirical, independent of values and feelings. If number is a 'language', as a modern view has it, because it is symbolic, it is not a language in which one can say 'I love you'. To think of arithmetic, and the associated activities of measurement and calculation, as a language is in this case, at least, mis-leading. It is a tool for manipulation and control, without intrinsic purpose or intention.

Before turning to Chaucer a very brief reference to the history and nature of arithmetic is necessary. It is part of the development of rationalism from the tenth century traced by A. Murray, *Reason and Society in the Middle Ages*, Oxford, 1978, in which he frequently illustrates the nature of Chaucer's own rationalism, as Chaucer's life and works would frequently illustrate Murray's own points. To summarize a lengthy and complex history in much simplified terms, arithmetic originates outside the universities in the prag-matic necessities of counting in commercial practices. It is associated with money, with towns, upward social mobility, the vernacular, royal govern-ment and astronomy/astrology: 'the typical late-medieval lay-astrologer was a courtier' (Murray, *op. cit.*, p. 208). It is also associated with chess. All these associations mark Chaucer out particularly, in contrast with Langland, the *Gawain*-poet and Gower. Yet arithmetic was, and is, disliked by religious, literary and uneducated people (see Murray, *op. cit.*, pp. 154, 175, 204; Brewer, *Chaucer and his World*, p. 61). The trouble, from their point of view, is that arithmetic is a complicated skill needing a good education, yet impersonal, reflecting quantities of objects, with little intrinsic life of its own. One number is as good as another, provided each is accurate in its representation of the objects counted. Arithmetic is without reference to values, and counts the bad as easily as the good. The association with money, another impersonal measuring device, allowed it to be associated with the deadly sin of avarice. Chaucer responded both to arithmetic and to the hostility to arithmetic. He came from a mercantile as well as courtly back-ground: in his own life he was an accountant: and there are a remarkably large number of references to arithmetical counting in his writings.

One of the main points of the present essay, therefore, after the emphasis on arithmetic, is that arithmetic in itself, and for what it represents, was in profound conflict with other elements, more traditional but in the end

---

2   A beginning into the study of the history, nature, use and significance in Chaucer's life and works has been made in my *Chaucer and his World*, 1977, pp. 54, 60-2.

stronger, in Chaucer's mind and work, such as desire for personal relationships, interest in feelings and values, religious conviction.

It may be no more than a coincidence that Chaucer's first secular poem, *The Book of the Duchess,* turns on a metaphor from chess, long associated with arithmetic (Murray, *op. cit.,* 204-5). The first clear reference to arithmetic in Chaucer's poetry soon follows, and is very striking, for it is the autobiographical passage in *The House of Fame* in which Chaucer says that he spends all day in the office making his 'reckonings'. To attribute this passage to a purely fictious 'Narrator' who has nothing to do with the 'real' poet would deprive this passage of all sense — which of course is not to say that it must be literally a transcript from life, true in every detail. The concept of the 'Narrator' here, as in many other parts of Chaucer's poetry, can only mislead us. There is no reason to take this passage as pure fiction. It undoubtedly refers to Chaucer's work in the Customs House, and the reckonings which we know from documentary evidence he was supposed to keep with his own hand (1.653). He tells us in the poem that he always spends the whole evening reading, and knows nothing at all about the very neighbours at his doors. In other words he has greatly limited his personal relationships. The poem emphasizes both his possibly unwilling commitment to 'reckoning' and the dissatisfaction he feels at the lack of something in his own life — we may say, at the lack in it of human interest and purpose, evidenced in his craving for stories, which are almost always about personal relationships. There is a dichotomy between arithmetic and the imaginative life. Dissatisfaction also comes out in a curiously indirect, defensive way in Chaucer's reference to his own metre, in which some lines, he says, may fail in a syllable (1098), i.e. be irregular when counted. This might be less remarkable in a French or especially an Italian poet of the time since they were more accustomed to regular syllabic verse. But in English, regular syllabic verse is still something relatively rare even by the late fourteenth century. All the evidence suggests that with certain exceptions a fairly irregular number of syllables even in metrical verse was the custom rather than the exception in medieval English verse. Chaucer's metrical regularity in all his poems after *The House of Fame* deserves note.[3] Chaucer's metrical regularity, so unusual in English, is witness to a new element in English culture of the fourteenth century which is an aspect of numerical skill — regularity in measurement, especially of time. The fourteenth century is the

---

3 This statement is not uncontroversial; there are still scholars who believe that Chaucer's metre is little better than Lydgate's. To examine this problem in detail would exceed the bounds of this essay, but for the latest views on the metre especially of Troilus, with references, see Derek Brewer, 'Observations on the Text of *Troilus', Medieval Studies for* J.A.W. Bennett, ed. P.L. Heyworth (Oxford, 1981) 121-38; and 'The Grain of the Text', *Acts of Interpretation,* ed A. David, Oklahoma (forthcoming).

century in which clockwork develops. Italy led the way, as in practically everything else in Europe in the fourteenth century, and there is no reason to doubt that Chaucer's visit to Italy in 1374 reinforced his natural tendencies in this respect.

Chaucer's next poem, *The Parliament of Fowls,* and the *Troilus,* with his prose translation of Boethius's *Consolation,* all illustrate another major influence connected with arithmetic. That is astronomy. Astronomy is obviously based on numerical skills. Yet for Chaucer, astronomy was part of a larger whole which was in some respects alien to arithmetic, and again we see the dichotomy within his mind and culture. The larger whole of which astronomy is part is made up of many items, but it includes astrology, that is, predictions and evaluations of good and bad destinies; mythology, for the stars were thought to have personalities associated with the names of pagan gods; and theology, for the influence of the stars was part of the mechanisms through which God's love of the world was thought to be mediated. Neither astrology, mythology nor theology have the impersonal regularity and freedom from values that is found in arithmetic, but in so far as they depended on astronomical expertise they had to depend on arithmetic. Astronomy cannot be done without arithmetical calculation of numbers in geometry, the use of angles, of numerical tables, etc., in order to calculate heights and movements. *Troilus* shows particularly clearly Chaucer's interest in astronomy combined with the interest in predestination and providence that makes part of the larger whole.

We also see in *Troilus* a different, plainer interest in arithmetic, which can be emphasized by the contrast with Boccaccio's *Il Filostrato* on which *Troilus* is so closely based. An example is the very careful marking of the passage of time after Criseyde has left the city of Troy to go to the Greeks. Criseyde promises to return in ten days' time. Chaucer emphasizes these ten days much more precisely than does Boccaccio (cf. Book IV, 1. 1320; Book V, 11. 499, 642, 681, 1016-22). It is also worth remarking that the father of Criseyde, Calcas, is a man who is expert in 'calculing', that is, in calculating the position of the stars, in predicting the future and therefore is in a position to know what will happen to Troy. That is why he is a traitor. Calculation destroys values such as loyalty.

It is, however, when we come to the period of Chaucer's full maturity that arithmetic flowers in Chaucer's mind in various ways. I do not wish to over-emphasize the fact; I merely point out that it is a notable element. We may take it perhaps from one of its astronomical bases, the *Treatise on the Astrolabe,* which Chaucer wrote for his own son, little Lewis, aged 10. The astrolabe is a quite complicated instrument for calculating the height of the stars.[4] Chaucer probably wrote the treatise about 1391, that is,

---

4   An illustration will be found in *Chaucer and his World,* p. 62.

when he was at the height of his poetic powers. Why should he spend time on this laborious compilation? Two obvious reasons suggest themselves: first, that he was interested in it for its own sake; and, second, that such a book was not available in English at all, and no one else was available who could write it for him. They indicate both the commitment to and the relative rarity of Chaucer's arithmetical skills, although it should be noticed that astrology was a strong courtly interest in the 1390s in the circle of the beautiful Joan of Kent, the widow of the Black Prince, mother of King Richard II. She was the patroness of a number of Chaucer's friends who had served with the Black Prince, as Chaucer himself may well have done, in Aquitaine in the 1360s.[5] Astronomy is several times referred to in *The Canterbury Tales.* Even the ignorant or, at any rate, the not highly educated Host of the Tabard Inn refers to the height of the sun in astronomical terms (e.g. *CT,* II, 1-15). References to astronomical timing and astronomy generally are scattered throughout the Canterbury Tales. Even Chauntecleer in the *Nun's Priest's Tale* was able by nature to time his crowing according to "each ascension of the equinoctial in the town, and he crew when 15 degrees were ascended" (*CT,* VII, 2857). That is a joke but it is significant of how widely cast are the astronomical references, how deeply they are set in the texture of the poems, and how arithmetical they are. A brief survey of the various sections of *The Canterbury Tales* emphasizes the pervading, though not predominant, references to those matters which depend upon arithmetic, that is to say, on careful pragmatic regular impersonal arithmetical measurement of time and space and money. *The General Prologue* begins with a celebrated opening about spring which in itself is commonplace except for the use of astronomical dating. Arithmetic is connected in Chaucer with money, in a commercial environment. *The Shipman's Tale* is the *locus classicus.* The piratical Shipman is an excellent navigator and can reckon his tides well. The Doctor of Physic is necessarily well 'grounded in astronomy' and does very well out of it. The Manciple is an example to accountants because he manages the account of the Temple of the Law so very well. It is significant that he is called an ignorant man who can do so much better and cheat so easily 'a heap of learned men' (574-5). The pragmatic non-university element in arithmetic is noted. The Reeve is a somewhat similar type. He can manage money far better than his master because he is good at 'reckoning' (*CT,* I, 600) and the word 'reckoning' is always significant in these matters.

When Chaucer sums up the group of pilgrims he says he has told us the rank, the clothing, the *number* of the people who were at the inn, and the cause that they were there in order to go to the shrine of St. Thomas at Canterbury. After supper the host has a cheerful conversation when all the

---

5   *Chaucer and his World,* pp.86-9, 206.

pilgrims have paid their 'reckonings' and suggests that they should tell stories in the course of the journey. Two stories shall be told going and two returning, and although there are other story telling collections in the Middle Ages none seems to have so precise an allocation. Two in this respect is a more significant number than the one story per person per day of, for example, Boccaccio in *The Decameron*, who makes all his stories add up to the round number of 100. Chaucer has few round numbers, and as I shall show, round numbers are different from arithmetic.

The Knight's Tale is based on Boccaccio's poem *Teseida* and again has a vein of numerical detail and accuracy which Boccaccio does not possess. The dates on which the heroes fight, the precise length of time which elapses between their first fight and the elaborate tournament are made much more clear by Chaucer than by Boccaccio. Chaucer likes to fix time and place quite precisely (*CT*, I, 1462). Chaucer gives a much more precise description to the lists in which the tournament is fought (11. 1884ff.). There is a touch of round numbers in this description in the reference to the height of '60 paces' (11. 1890), since 60 is a medieval round number meaning 'a lot', but even so the precision with which the tiers of seats are described is unusual. Chaucer could have designed a theatre or an opera house very much more efficiently than most later architects. He refers to the employment of clever men who understood geometry or ars-metrica. The timing of the visits by the two heroes and the heroine, Emily, to the temples is very exactly given (11. 2209ff.) because this relates to various astronomical or astrological significances. It is upon this quite precise arithmetical basis that all the rich imaginative classicising description of *The Knight's Tale* is founded.

The Miller's Tale, the bawdy counterpart of *The Knight's Tale*, depends on an astronomical joke invented by the student who makes love to the beautiful Alison, and the extraordinary richness of reference in this poem is based on the astrological deceit of the carpenter-husband. *The Reeve's Tale* which accompanies *The Miller's Tale* has a similar joke made by an ignorant man against the learned. Simkin the miller, when he offers to put up the two benighted students in the somewhat restricted space of the bedroom says

> Myn hous is streit, but ye han lerned art.
> Ye konne by argumentes make a place
> A myle brood of twenty foot of space.   *CT*, I, 4122-4.

Simkin refers to 'arguments' and thinks that speech is the characteristic method of such clerks, as indeed it was for the university men. The joke is entirely justified in that he is referring to what would be an arithmetic rather than a verbal exercise, and would be nonsense. But it is also significant that the joke is, after all, on him.

The Man of Law's Tale is about miracles, but there are many clear references to astronomy in this tale. It is unnecessary to mention every instance of arithmetic. Amongst other examples of an arithmetical element in *The Canterbury Tales, The Summoner's Tale* may be singled out because although this is primarily a satire on the Friar, it caps the satire with a gross arithmetical joke. It will be recalled that the Friar in the tale, who has a great fondness for the wife of Thomas, who is ill, is encouraged to grope in Thomas's bed for some money and receives only a fart. Mad with fury he goes to the lord of the manor to complain, in particular because the 'false blasphemer' as he calls Thomas has laid upon the Friar the duty of sharing what cannot be shared. The lord is astonished that a churl has enough imagination to show such a problem to the Friar. No man could find in arithmetic, in ars-metrica, how to divide such a gift between the twelve members of the Friar's convent. The joke lies in the way this unsavoury problem is apparently so seriously considered. The lord of the manor even reflects in scientific manner upon that problem of sound and air-waves which so interests Chaucer in *The House of Fame* (765ff: *CT*, III, 2233-7). But a clever young squire suggests how the Friar can divide this nasty reverberation of air through a cartwheel which has twelve hollow spokes. The whole episode is a parody of arithmetical method, of what Chaucer calls, with an undoubted pun in this case, ars-metrica. Although there are somewhat similar tales found elsewhere, there is no special analogue for this one. As will be seen, the episode may be a parody of an arithmetic handbook. It illuminates very clearly Chaucer's amazing capacity for both a serious and a flippant interest in particular problems.

A similar problem also based on sexual comedy is found in *The Shipman's Tale*. This tale involves a rich merchant, his beautiful wife, and a handsome monk. It is an analogue of a tale by Boccaccio. Chaucer enriches the tale by giving us some detail of the merchant working in his counting house. He gets up early in the morning to labour on his books and his bags of money which he has on his counting board. He works at his accounts in the modern sense of the word. The monk borrows 100 francs and gives them to the wife in return for her favours, and she pays her bills. As to paying her husband she will do it through 'the marriage debt'. The joke here is another arithmetical parody and pun, associating sex with money.

The considerable series of references to arithmetic, to numbering and associated ideas in *The Canterbury Tales* seems to have no parallel in other writings of the period. There is certainly nothing like it in Langland (even though Langland in an autobiographical passage in the B text refers to himself quite precisely as 45 years old). There is, however, another kind of interest in number in the period, of which there is a very clear example in Chaucer's great contemporary, the *Gawain*-poet. The *Gawain*-poet I take to be the same poet who wrote *Pearl*, apparently a meditation on the death of his two-year-old daughter. *Pearl* is a very elaborate work of art, and one aspect of that elaboration is the well-recognized numerical scheme on which the poem is based. The poem culminates in a vision of the hundred and forty-four thousand virgins of the Apocalypse. It is written in 1212 lines. It has 101 stanzas. Such numerical patterning, the theory and practice of which is often called 'numerology' has a long history going back to classical times.[6] The essence of this use of number is to create patterns which have an aesthetic significance. It is not common in medieval English poetry, *Pearl* being the only unequivocal example that I know. It is more common in Latin on the continent. Certain poets found great pleasure in it; it gives a deep aesthetic satisfaction, though of a kind very hard now to recapture. The essential point is that pleasure in numerology is totally different from, indeed at the opposite pole from, an interest in arithmetic. Numerology involves numbers which are always seen as symbolic. Folkloric numbers 3 and 4, 12 and various multiples of them are constantly used. While it is true that almost any number up to, but perhaps not including, 17 can be regarded as symbolic, there are certain obvious favourites, such as I have mentioned, which we can all recognize. The interest in such symbolic numbers is not in the arithmetical operations they can perform, for none such operations are possible in literature. Symbolic numbers create aesthetic patterns and have non-numerical implications beyond themselves. No one has ever been able to show that Chaucer uses such numerological patterning in any of his poems. The contrast between Chaucer and the *Gawain*-poet is as marked here as elsewhere. The *Gawain*-poet was a great poet but the orientation of his 'mentality' was quite different from that of Chaucer.[7]

There is another use of number in poetry which is closely associated with numerological patterning and may indeed be part of it, which needs to be briefly discussed in order to differentiate it from arithmetic proper. This is the use of round numbers, or approximate numbers, common in ordinary speech, often enlivening it with characteristic hyperbole or useful, emotive vagueness. The commonest example in medieval literature is the number 'sixty', meaning a lot, which is presumably very ancient. Romance, and indeed the Bible, use round numbers in this vague way, while close arithmetical counting, as in a census, is traditionally viewed with hostility.

---

6 Cf. E.R. Curtius, *European Literature and the Latin Middle Ages*, transl. W.R. Trask (London, 1953), (German original first published in 1948), pp. 501ff. Of recent years a flourishing numerological industry has grown up in the scholarly literature. There can be no doubt in general that some numerical patterning was intentionally designed in some poems, such as *Pearl*, even if individual examples may be queried.

7 Lack of space forbids the development here of this contrast. My view of the *Gawain*-poet also depends on a non-ironic interpretation of his work which many modern scholars would dispute. For a more extended discussion see my *English Gothic Literature*, London (forthcoming).

Chaucer occasionally uses round numbers, but he uses the round number *dozen,* for example, only once (*CT,* I, 578) and most of his uses of *sixty* are found in the *Astrolabe,* referring to the precise number of degrees in a circle, minutes in an hour, etc. Round numbers are not significant in Chaucer.

Chaucer's interest in arithmetic has been amply demonstrated. There may even be a literary tie, connected, as so much of Chaucer's mentality can be, with Italian developments. The most impressive handbook on arithmetic in the fourteenth century was by the Italian Fibonacci. His method is to use examples, frequently drawn from commerce, as quoted by Murray: ' 'The man who went to Constantinople to sell three pearls'; 'The two ships which sailed together'; 'Finding the equivalence of bad money and good'; 'The two men who formed a company in Constantinople'' (*op. cit.,* p. 190). Any of these might be the titles of stories by Chaucer. We are here at the origins of the salesman's repertoire of dirty jokes, and of many of Boccaccio's and Chaucer's more secular anecdotes: 'How to have your cake and eat it' (*The Reeve's Tale*); 'How to divide a fart into twelve equal portions' (*The Summoner's Tale*); 'How to turn good money into bad' (*The Canon's Yeoman's Tale*). It is quite significant that there are no extant literary analogues for the last two examples. Their origin perhaps lies in the arithmetical conditioning of the travelling salesman's purely oral repertoire. *The Cook's Tale,* about a London apprentice, would no doubt have had a similar base.

One of the further distinguishing elements of such stories is their naturalistic base: another is the implied relativism, or even abandonment, of accepted values. When these, and other rationalistic elements that cannot be further pursued here (like a powerful literalism) are taken into consideration, the contrast with traditional values, especially those of religion and love, which are so obvious elsewhere in Chaucer's work, can easily be appreciated. Chaucer appears, in his use of arithmetic, extremely rationalist and *avant-garde* in his time. His irony, even if nowadays often exaggerated, is so pervasive that its relativism is alarming. There is good reason to believe that it alarmed Chaucer himself. The *Retracciouns* to *The Canterbury Tales* unequivocally revoke, as sinful, all Chaucer's work that is secular, apparently only for that reason. The identification of sin with secularity, so strange and unnecessary to the modern reader, cannot be brushed aside. To consider the *Retracciouns* as ironic, or as spoken by some 'Narrator', is to apply totally anachronistic criteria and render the passage singularly pointless (which, as with the autobiographical passage in *The House of Fame* is not to claim that Chaucer might not have had different moods and other thoughts at other times, or even simultaneously with writing the patently and sincerely non-fictional *Retracciouns*). We recall the ending of the *Troilus,* often nowadays mistakenly attributed to a 'stupid' 'Narrator', who apparently, however, knew Gower and Strode. We must accept the differences of earlier times from our own. Because we are liberal humanist atheists does not mean that Chaucer must be.

Yet the reluctance to accept the narrow-minded ecclesiasticism which marks the *Retracciouns,* and is an element of the ending of the *Troilus,* has the justification that there is indeed a strong vein of modernistic rationalism in Chaucer, which is exemplified in and can be documented through his use of arithmetic. The solution is to accept that there is a deep internal tension in Chaucer's mind, as in the whole of medieval Gothic culture, which is caused by the co-existence of deeply incompatible elements. They may be variously described from different points of view, or summed up, as I have attempted to do elsewhere, as the co-existence of the traditional, or archaic, with the modern.[8] For Chaucer, arithmetic may well be seen as the leading edge of modern attitudes. It seems likely that the co-existence of such incompatibles is inherent in the human mind. Each culture, and each individual mind, will present its own characteristic complex structure, and it will be a worthwhile attempt to explore further Chaucer's own characteristic mentality.

---

8 See Derek Brewer, 'The Archaic and the Modern', in *Tradition and Innovation in Chaucer* (London, 1982); 'Malory: the Traditional Writer and the Archaic Mind', *Arthurian Literature I,* ed. Richard Barber (Cambridge, 1981); 'Gothic Chaucer', *Writers and their Background: Geoffrey Chaucer,* ed. Derek Brewer (London, 1974); *English Gothic Literature,* London (forthcoming).

PARENTS AND CHILDREN IN THE "CANTERBURY TALES"

JILL MANN

The aim of this essay is to show that the parent-child relationship is one of the central motifs of the Canterbury Tales.[1] It is a motif whose repetition and variation through the individual tales I shall discuss — those of the Monk, Man of Law, Physician, Prioress and Clerk — allows Chaucer to explore not only the relations of human beings to each other, but also (as I shall show) their relation to the universe in which they find themselves and to the forces governing it.[2] Although the discussion that follows first brings out the cruelty apparently inherent in the parent's right to exercise power over the child, and then tries to show how the cruelty is transmuted as it is subsumed into a larger vision, it is not intended to suggest that Chaucer propels his reader by ineluctable logic from 'problems' to 'answers'. Taken together, these tales do not suggest a debate with a formal resolution, but an extended and extendable meditation on different manifestations of a mystery — the mystery of the relation between power and love. This mystery is explored within the context of another — the mystery of kinship. Kinship not only binds human beings to each other, it also links them with the God who became kin to them in the Incarnation. To use the parent-child image to express man's relation to God is therefore to invoke more than the idea of dependence alone. Some comments made by Peter Dronke in a different context are also relevant here: 'Children not only depend on their parents for existence, they resemble their parents, and are a continuation of their parents in time'. The children of a divine father, therefore, are 'god-like'; 'they are theophanies'.[3] Chaucer's stories are founded on the assumption that such a revelation works in both directions: if these stories make manifest a god-like dimension within ordinary human existence, it is also true that in the story embodying the central Christian mystery — the Crucifixion — certain human potentialities find their fullest expression and most meaning-

---

1   For a more general treatment, see D.S. Brewer, 'Children in Chaucer', *Review of English Literature* 5.3 (1964) 52-60.
2   This essay represents a preliminary version of part of a larger study in which I am engaged, on structuring themes in the Canterbury Tales. I hope in this larger study to give a fuller account of the rich background to this motif in medieval literature, art, and religious writing, which constrictions of space make impossible here.
3   *Fabula: Explorations in the uses of Myth in Medieval Platonism* Leiden und Cologne, 1974), p. 113.

ful place. In stressing the divine resonances of these tales of Chaucer, there-fore, I am not in any way claiming that their 'real' subject is the divine, that they are mere vehicles for the rehearsal of Christian truths. Rather, they seek to penetrate a fundamental experience which generates both secular legend and Christian gospel, and which is common to both man and God.

Chaucer's most moving presentation of the father-child relationship is the story told in the *Monk's Tale* of Ugolino di Pisa ('Erl Hugelyn of Pize'), who was shut up with his children in a tower by his enemy, archbishop Ruggieri, and starved to death. As Chaucer himself indicates (2459-62), his authority for this story was Dante, who has Ugolino describe his cruel end in canto 33 of the *Inferno*. Dante's Ugolino tells how his children begged him for bread — echoing, as Piero Boitani has suggested, the prayer daily addressed by men to their heavenly father: 'give us this day our daily bread'.[4] Chaucer gives this prayer to one son in particular, a three year old child, and expands it to a whole stanza's length, increasing the pathos of the story through our sense of the father's helplessness in the face of this childish importunity. When the young child eventually dies, Ugolino gnaws his arms in the misery of his grief, and his children, misinterpreting this action as due to his hunger, beg him to eat their flesh rather than his own

> "Fader, do nat so, allas!
> But rather ete the flessh upon us two.
> Oure flessh thou yaf us, take oure flessh us fro,
> And ete ynogh," — right thus they to hym seyde,
> And after that, withinne a day or two,
> They leyde hem in his lappe adoun and deyde.   (2449-54)

The words of the children are based on those in Dante:

> . . . 'Padre, assai ci fia men doglia
> se tu mangi di noi: tu ne vestisti
> queste misere carni, e tu le spoglia.'   (61-3)

Behind these words (as Piero Boitani has likewise shown)[5] there lie the words of Job:

> Nudus egressus sum de utero matris meae, et nudus revertar illuc. Dominus dedit, Dominus abstulit; sicut Domino placuit, ita factum est. Sit nomen Domini benedictum.   (1:21)

It is significant that these words are Job's response to the death of his children; expressing his simple resignation to the will of God, he recognizes that not even his children can be claimed as possessions to which he has a

---

4   'The *Monk's Tale:* Dante and Boccaccio', *Medium Aevum* 45 (1976) 50-69, at p. 60.
5   Ibid., pp. 61-2.

right. Chaucer was evidently alive to the reminiscence of Job at this point, because he made it even clearer in his own text; the clothing image, which Dante does not use quite as in Job, is left out, and instead the focus is entirely on Job's contrast between giving and taking away. But the expression of Job's resignation undergoes a strange inversion when thus set in the Ugolino story: instead of the father's acceptance of the loss of his children, we have the children accepting their own re-absorption into their father. It seems to be suggested that they are so much a mere continuation of him that he may consume them. The religious resonances to the story, which prompt us to see the human father in this tale as analogous with the divine father who gives and takes away fleshly life, thus raise a silent disquiet. Beneath the tender poignancy of this scene in Chaucer, as in Dante, there lurks a potential horror: the suggestion that the power of a father over his children may extend to a right to devour them, and furthermore, that such power may belong to the God who is daily addressed as 'Our Father'. The Christian God threatens to transform himself into the pagan god Saturn, the god who devoured his own children.

Chaucer completely omits any suggestion that Ugolino did in fact eat the bodies of his children before he died, and even in Dante this suggestion is merely implicit.[6] The image of the cruel father lurks like a shadow behind the *Monk's Tale* story, but it is only a shadow. In the *Man of Law's Tale*, however, there is a quite unambiguous sense of the suffering that can attend the subordination of child to parent. Constance, the central figure of the tale, expresses with pitiable clarity her grief at having to leave her home and marry a stranger in obedience to her father's will. Weeping, she commends to her father's and mother's 'grace' their 'wrecched child Custance', who will, she believes, never see them again.

> "Allas! unto the Barbre nacioun
> I moste anoon, syn that it is youre wille;
> But Crist, that starf for our redempcioun
> So yeve me grace his heestes to fulfille!
> I, wrecche womman, no fors though I spille!
> Wommen are born to thraldom and penance,
> And to been under mannes governance."　　　　　　　　(281-7)

Constance's words on the destiny of women are based on God's decree that as a punishment for eating the apple, Eve and her daughters should suffer the enmity of the serpent, the pains of childbirth, and subjection to the domination of men (Gen. 3: 15-16). It is the prospect of being 'bounden'

6　For the pointers to this implication in Dante's version, see Piero Boitani's *lectura* of Inferno XXXIII, in *Cambridge Readings in Dante's Comedy*, ed. Kenelm Foster and Patrick Boyde (Cambridge, 1981), pp. 83-4.

under the 'subjeccioun' of her new husband that stimulates Constance's sorrow (267-71). The key words she chooses to articulate her experience of this 'subjeccioun' are 'thraldom' and 'governance'. To understand the implications of these terms, it is necessary to realize that it is not women alone who are under 'governance', or who experience bewilderment and misery at the forms it takes. In his translation of the *Consolation of Philosophy*, Chaucer consistently uses the verb 'govern', and its associates 'government', 'governor', and 'governance' to indicate the subordination of mankind to God. Boethius' initial outbursts against God are a passionate accusation of *mis*governance, as can be seen from the following example:

> "O thou governour, governynge alle thynges by certein ende, whi refusestow oonly to governe the werkes of men by duwe manere? Why suffrestow that slydynge Fortune turneth so grete enterchaungynges of thynges; so that anoyous peyne, that scholde duweliche punysche felons, punysscheth innocentz? . . . Thow governour, withdraugh and restreyne the ravysschynge flodes, and fastne and ferme thise erthes stable with thilke boonde by which thou governest the hevene that is so large."   (I m.5, 31-7, 54-8)

In answer to Boethius' complaint, Philosophy works to demonstrate that God 'governeth alle thinges by the keye of his goodnesse' (III pr. 12, 87-8), and that 'we foolis that reprehenden wikkidly the thinges that touchin Godis governance, we aughten ben asschamid of ourself' (ibid., 126-9). To show how Philosophy establishes the benign character of this 'governance' would mean summarizing the whole of the *Consolation*, but it is important in this context to note that in celebrating God's role as creator and regulator of the cosmos, she conceives this role as that of a father.

> "O thow Fadir, soowere and creatour of hevene and of erthes, that governest this world by perdurable resoun, that comaundest the tymes to gon from syn that age hadde bygynnynge; thow that duellest thiselve ay stedefast and stable, and yevest alle othere thynges to ben meved, ne foreyne causes necesseden the nevere to compoune werk of floterynge matere, but oonly the forme of sovereyn good iset within the withoute envye, that moevede the frely."   (III m.9, 1-11)

The word 'governance' thus constantly carries a Boethian colouring in Chaucer; even when it denotes human domination or power, it connotes the greater power of God over his creation. This connotation may be used seriously; it may lead us to see human authority as the copy, and the agent, of God's. Thus women attract attention because their subjection to male 'governance' is a model of the human subjection to God. It may, however, be used ironically, so that it leads us to reflect on the vain pretensions of men to be in control of their world. The same double possibility of seriousness or irony, applies to two other self-consciously Boethian words which

Chaucer frequently rhymes with 'governance': 'purveiance' and 'ordinance'. It is the ironic possibility that is realized, for example, in the lines describing the preparations made by Constance's father for her wedding:

> Now wolde som men waiten, as I gesse,
> That I sholde tellen all the purveiance
> That th'Emperour, of his grete noblesse,
> Hath shapen for his doghter, dame Custance,
> Wel may men knowen that so greet ordinance
> May no man tellen in a litel clause
> As was arrayed for so heigh a cause. (246-52)

The 'purveiance' and 'ordinance' with which God disposes the cosmos are here 'shrunk' so as to refer only to the provision of material comforts and a retinue, and the shrinking is a measure of the circumscribed area within which human, as opposed to divine, power can operate.

The word 'governance' in Constance's speech cannot, however, be interpreted in quite this way. Constance's utterance is an expression of resignation, so that her view of 'governance' cannot be explained away as stemming from the kind of impatience initially expressed by Boethius. But neither can it be aligned with the benign view of 'governance' in Philosophy's hymn. Constance's experience leads her to equate 'governance' with 'thraldom and penance'. The 'mannes governance' to whose 'subjeccioun' she is bound is not only that of her future husband, but also that of her father, as her words make clear ('Allas! unto the Barbre nacioun / I moste anoon, *syn that it is youre wille.* '). The use of the Boethian 'purveiance' and 'ordinance' presents the Emperor as a kind of mock-God, wielding power within his small domain; Constance's helplessness before her father's will follows the pattern of human helplessness before the will of the divine father. She is sent forth into 'hethenesse' as the soul is exiled on earth, separated from its true heavenly home — a conception that Chaucer would also have found in Boethius (I pr. 5; IV m.1). Through Constance's experience, the *Man of Law's Tale* invests the concept of 'subjeccioun' to a higher 'governance' with a sense of poignancy and bewilderment.

As a natural corollary of this, Philosophy's vision of the harmonious motions of the universe, expressed in her hymn to God as father and governor, gives way to an astonishing vision of the cosmos which presents an unnatural cruelty as fundamental to its structure and operation. It is a vision which arises from Chaucer's description of the malignant stellar influence blighting Constance's wedding.

> O firste moevyng! crueel firmament,
> With thy diurnal sweigh that crowdest ay
> And hurlest al from est til occident
> That naturelly wolde holde another way,

Thy crowdyng set the hevene in swich array
At the bigynnyng of this fiers viage,
That crueel Mars hath slayn this mariage.
Infortunat ascendent tortuous,
Of which the lord is helplees falle, allas,
Out of his angle into the derkeste hous!
O Mars, o atazir, as in this cas!
O fieble moone, unhappy been thy paas!
Thou knyttest thee ther thou art nat receyved;
Ther thou were weel, fro thennes artow weyved.
Imprudent Emperour of Rome, allas!
Was ther no philosophre in al thy toun?   (295-310)

These stanzas refer to the contradictory motions within the cosmos, as its
operations were conceived in the Middle Ages. Whereas the natural movement of the planets was from West to East, they were daily dragged from
East to West by the superior force of the Primum Mobile, the 'fyrste moev-
yng' sphere which lay beyond the planetary spheres. Consequently, the
planets managed to win back in the course of a year only a small degree of
advancement in the direction of their natural movement, which acted as
resistance to this 'crowdyng'. Although this cosmological model was developed to provide a quite neutral scientific explanation of physical phenomena, numerous medieval writers — including some known to Chaucer, such as
Alan of Lille and Dante — gave it a moral or emotional colouring. But in
doing so, they usually interpreted the subjection of the planets to the Primum Mobile as a *good* thing; Alan, for example, saw it as an analogue to the
subjection of the senses to reason. So far as I know, Chaucer is the *only*
medieval writer to use this cosmological model as an image of violence and
unnaturalness at the core of the universe's movement, or to call the Primum
Mobile 'cruel'.[7] A hint of the idea is there, perhaps, in Chaucer's translation

7   See Alan of Lille, *De Planctu Naturae*, prose 3 (ed. Nikolaus M. Häring, *Studi
    medievali* 3rd ser. 19.2 (1978) 797-879, at pp. 826-7; id., *Distinctiones Dictionum
    Theologicalium*, s.v. *Mundus*, PL 210, col. 866. Dante's clearest exposition of the
    function of the Primum Mobile is given in *Convivio* II.xv, where it is compared, in
    its ordering function, to the science of moral philosophy. For further references
    to the development of the tradition, see John Freccero, 'Dante's Pilgrim in a
    Gyre', *PMLA* 76.3 (1961) 168-81, and A.B. Chambers, 'Goodfriday, 1613. Riding
    Westward: The Poem and the Tradition', *ELH* 28 (1961) 31-53. The starting-point
    for the development of the idea of the dual motion in the medieval West was the
    passage in Plato's *Timaeus* on the Demiurge's creation of the world through the
    contrasting motions of the Same and the Different (see the Latin translation by
    Calcidius, ed. Raymond Klibansky [London and Leiden, 1962] 36-7, pp. 30-31) —
    and it is this Platonic idea that is reflected in Lady Philosphy's account of the
    'moevynge into two rowndes' by which the world-soul 'gooth to torne ayen to
    hymself' in her hymn (III . 9, 28-30).

of Boethius' complaint, which emphasizes the irresistible force to which the heavens are subject ('O thow makere of the wheel that bereth the sterres . . . and turnest the hevene with a *ravysschynge* sweigh, and *constreynest* the sterres to *suffren* thi lawe . . .'; I m.5, 1-5), but the complaint as a whole contrasts the order of the heavens with the disorder of human life, and does not link the anarchy of human existence with a cosmic derangement.

In both human and cosmological terms, then, the *Man of Law's Tale* raises in painful clarity the question of the nature of the 'subjeccioun' in which mankind finds itself bound. The question it poses is: are we God's children, or his thralls? Is his 'governance' the loving control of a father, or the arbitrary tyranny of a despot?

In answering this question, Chaucer has recourse to two principal motifs. The first is one that I would call the motif of the 'enthralled lord' — a motif which is apparent in the frequent use of images which suggest a *chain* of command. Two such images have already passed before us. The first is Constance's father, whose power, as it turns out, is subordinate to the influence of the planets, which make a mockery of his 'purveiance'. But what is strange about the stanzas describing this planetary influence is that they emphasize the impotence of the planets at the same time as they complain about their power. The lord of the ascendant — the dominant planet in any conjunction, as the very name suggests — 'is helplees falle'; the moon is 'fieble'. The planetary influence which blights Constance's wedding operates, as we have seen, under the greater influence of the Primum Mobile. Both the Emperor and the planets, then, at first look like figures of authority but turn out to be figures of subordination; they are 'enthralled lords'.

There are numerous other examples of such 'enthralled lords' in the tale; for example, Alla's constable, who exerts the authority of his office over Constance, sending her back out to sea, but who laments the fact that he is compelled to do so by a higher authority — and in doing so, significantly, echoes Boethius' central question about the just 'governance' of the universe.

> "O myghty God, if that it be thy wille,
> Sith thou art rightful juge, how may it be
> That thou wolt suffren innocentz to spille,
> And wikked folk regne in prosperitee?
> O goode Custance, allas! so wo is me
> That I moot be thy tormentour, or deye
> On shames deeth; ther is non oother weye." (813-19)

It might be objected that the tale offers examples of the untrammelled exercise of power, in the two mothers-in-law who usurp male 'governance' and insist on bending events to their own will. The mother of Constance's first husband, the Sultan, vigorously asserts her own will, rejecting 'thral-dom and penance' in words that are a deliberate echo of and contrast with

Constance's resignation (337-40). Yet her independence is a delusion; she too is subject to a greater power, which uses her as a mere instrument, as Chaucer's comment makes clear.

> O Sathan, envious syn thilke day
> That thou were chaced from oure heritage,
> Wel knowestow to wommen the olde way!
> Thoud madest Eva brynge us in servage;
> Thou wolt fordoon this Cristen mariage.
> Thyn instrument, so weylawey the while!
> Makestow of wommen, whan thou wolt bigile.   (365-71)

By the same token, Donegild's 'tirannye' leads to her own death, not Constance's; the extent of her 'ordinance' (805) is as circumscribed as the Emperor's.

If the figures of evil are instruments of Satan, Constance is the instrument of Christ. We can see this instrumentality in, for example, Chaucer's account of Hermengild's conversion to Christianity:

> This constable and dame Hermengyld, his wyf,
> Were payens, and that contree everywhere;
> But Hermengyld loved hire right as hir lyf,
> And Custance hath so longe sojourned there,
> In orisons, with many a bitter teere,
> Til Jhesu hath converted thurgh his grace
> Dame Hermengyld, constablesse of that place.   (533-9)

Almost imperceptibly, the subject of the sentence shifts from Constance to Jesus, so that her role, while essential, is felt as mediatory; Jesus works through her. The same pattern is repeated in the account of Hermengild's healing of the blind man:

> "In name of Crist", cride this blinde Britoun,
> "Dame Hermengyld, yif me my sighte agayn!"
> This lady weex affrayed of the soun,
> Lest that hir housbonde, shortly for to sayn,
> Wolde hire for Jhesu Cristes love han slayn,
> Til Custance made hire boold, and bad hire wirche
> The wyl of Crist, as doghter of his chirche.
>
> The constable weex abasshed of that sight,
> And seyde, "What amounteth al this fare?"
> Custance answerde, "Sire, it is Cristes myght,
> That helpeth folk out of the feendes snare."   (561-71)

The actual cure seems to take place between the stanzas, so that Chaucer need not commit himself to a sentence which presents Hermengild as the sole performer of the action. Her healing power is exerted in obedience to

Constance's command, and as a manifestation of Christ's will. But Christ's power is transmitted through a filial relation; it is as 'doghter of his chirche' that she can do His will. Equally significantly, it is as 'doghter of hooly chirche' that Constance is defended from false accusation by the divine voice (675).

This brings us to the second motif by which Chaucer explores the question of 'governance' — the motif of parenthood and childhood. It is a motif which can intertwine with the first: in Constance's prayer to Mary to save her from false condemnation —

> "... thou, merciful mayde,
> Marie I meene, doghter to Seint Anne,
> Bifore whos child angeles synge Osanne,
> If I be giltlees of this felonye,
> My socour be, for ellis shal I dye!"   (640-4)

— we can see in the dual presentation of Mary as mother and daughter a reminder that every parent is also a child, and can thus perceive one possible fusion of authority and subservience. But in order to understand the full intertwining of the two motifs, we need to explore further the nature of parental 'governance'. The cruel effect of the Emperor's 'governance' we have already noted, but there are far crueller images in the malevolent mothers of Constance's two husbands, the first of whom goes so far as to murder her own son. Satan, himself banished from the 'heritage' (366) which has been transferred to mankind, the 'sons of adoption', works through women, his instrument and traditional object of malice, to destroy the hereditary links of family love.[8] The cruel parent can create a cruel child; when Alla discovers his mother's treachery, he has her put to death. But Alla himself offers a more complicated and interesting image of parenthood, since he *appears* to be a cruel parent; the letter forged by his mother makes it appear that he has ordered his new-born son to be cast on to the mercy of the waves with Constance. Constance's lament to her little child, as she walks to the boat that is to take her out to sea, focusses on this paternal cruelty:

> "O litel child, allas! what is thy gilt,
> That nevere wroghtest synne as yet, pardee?
> Why wil thyn harde fader han thee spilt?
> O mercy, deere constable," quod she,
> "As lat my litel child dwelle heer with thee;
> And if thou darst nat saven hym, for blame,
> So kys hym ones in his fadres name!"

---

8   See Gal. 4: 5 for the link between sonship and inheritance, and the idea of man's 'adoption'.

> Therwith she looked bakward to the londe,
> And seyde, "Farewel, housbonde routheless!" (855-63)

Against this image of the cruel father, Constance's opening appeal to the Virgin, which aligns her suffering with Mary's, sets an image of maternal tenderness.

> "Mooder", quod she, "and mayde brigth, Marie,
> Sooth is that thurgh wommanes eggement

> Mankynde was lorn, and damned ay to dye,
> For which thy child was on a croys yrent.
> Thy blisful eyen sawe al his torment;
> Thanne is ther no comparison bitwene
> Thy wo and any wo man may sustene.

> "Thow sawe thy child yslayn bifore thyne yen,
> And yet now lyveth my litel child, parfay!
> Now, lady bright, to whom alle woful cryen,
> Thow glorie of wommanhede, thow faire may,
> Thow haven of refut, brighte sterre of day,
> Rewe on my child, that of thy gentillesse,
> Rewest on every reweful in distresse." (841-54)

Constance's words assume the identity of mother and child in suffering (they also provide the basis for generalizing this experience, by assuming a similar identity of pain between sufferer and beholder, founded on pity — the bond between 'every reweful' and those who 'rewe' being indicated by the verbal repetition itself).[9] Behind this assumption stirs memory of the words spoken to Mary by Simeon at the Presentation in the Temple: 'Yea, a sword shall pierce through thy own soul also' (Lc. 2: 35).

The parallel of Constance's experience with Mary's even greater suffering makes us aware of the disturbing fact that Constance's plaintive question to her child — 'Why wil thyn harde father han thee spilt?' — is one that could have been addressed to Jesus by Mary at the Crucifixion. Alla's cruelty is, as we know, only apparent; he has not, in fact, ordered his child's death. But what about God? Is he not a father who did slay his own son? This idea was by no means 'unthinkable' in fourteenth-century England: Langland speaks of laymen who presume to discuss theology, and 'telleth . . . of the trinite hou two slowen the thridde'.[10] But merely to pose this question is to realize its inevitable answer, and to realize the point to which the tale's exploration of 'governance' and 'subjeccioun' has led — a point at which the

---

9 Lack of space prevents me from commenting further on the important role of 'pitee' in these tales, and on the link between the notions of 'compassion' and 'family feeling' in the medieval Latin word 'pietas'.

10 *Piers Plowman: The A Version*, ed. George Kane (London, 1960), XI, 38-40.

two motifs we have been tracing make their most significant fusion. For God the Father *is* God the Son; he both ordains the suffering and suffers. The identity of parent and child in suffering takes on in him an utterly complete and utterly literal realization. As we move up through the 'chain of command' in the cosmos, to find that every exercise of power is subject to higher control, we increasingly come to feel that the final responsibility for the 'governance' of the world and its cruel consequences must rest with God — but when we reach the top of the chain of command we find that we are immediately returned to the bottom again. God is the last in the line of 'enthralled lords'. The God to whose 'governance' creation is subject enters his own creation and becomes subject to the 'governance' of his creatures.[11] To hark back to the *Monk's Tale,* and translate this perception into its terms, it is not God who eats the bodies of his children, but his children who in the Eucharist eat the body of their father and receive life from it.

The *Man of Law's Tale* ends, fittingly enough, with the moving reunion between Constance and her father — a reunion which is, significantly, prepared for by the revivification of the image of the lost daughter in her father, through sight of her son. But Chaucer has not finished with the theme of parents and children with this family reunion; this tale is only one of the possible narrative structures through which we can try to understand the mysterious relationship between suffering and a benevolent providence, the apparently cruel operations of omnipotent love. Another image of paternal cruelty is offered in *The Physician's Tale.* Again, however, the cruelty is apparent. Virginius kills his daughter because it is the only way to save her from the plots of Apius, who desires her sexually. The tale is briefly told, and its focal point is undoubtedly the poignant exchange between Virginius and Virginia in which he tells her she must die, and in which the tragic conflict between action and feeling is stressed by the insistent repetition of 'father' and 'doghter'. Virginius is another 'enthralled lord'; he expresses the agony of being compelled to be his daughter's executioner:

> "Doghter", quod he, "Virginia, by thy name,
> Ther been two weyes, outher deeth or shame,
> That thou most suffre; allas, that I was bore!
> For nevere thou deservedest wherfore
> To dyen with a swerd or with a knyf.
> O deere doghter, endere of my lyf,
> Which I have fostred up with swich plesaunce
> That thou were nevere out of my remembraunce!
> O doghter, which that art my laste wo,
> And in my lyf my laste joye also,

---

11 Cf. G.K. Chesterton's comments on Chaucer's entry into his own creation, the *Canterbury Tales* (*Chaucer* [London, 1932], pp. 21-2).

> O gemme of chastitee, in pacience
> Take thou thy deeth, for this is my sentence."   (213-24)

The tale shows us that the Marian experience expressed in the words 'a sword shall pierce through thy own soul also' is not an exclusively feminine one, by echoing those words in the description of Virginius 'With fadres pitee stikynge thurgh his herte' (211). The mother is absent from the scene, and cruelty and pity are lodged in the same parent. And this time, the cruelty is seen as an *expression* of the 'pitee':

> For love, and nat for hate, thou most be deed;
> My pitous hand moot smyten of thyn heed.   (225-6)

The tale also offers another variation on the theme of 'thraldom'. Apius bribes Claudius into claiming in his court that Virginia is a 'thral' of his who has been stolen away from him, hoping thus to win her away from her father's custody. Virginius thus kills his daughter to save her from 'thraldom'; the struggle over Virginia is precisely a struggle over whether she shall be daughter or thrall. Virginia herself chooses the authority of her father, even though it means her death, rather than the tyranny of Apius:

> She riseth up, and to hir fader sayde,
> "Blissed be God, that I shal dye a mayde!
> Yif me my deeth, er that I have a shame;
> Dooth with youre child youre wyl, a Goddes name!"   (247-50)

The *Physician's Tale* simplifies the family to father and daughter; the *Prioress's Tale* simplifies it to mother and son, since the mother of the little boy who is its central figure is a widow. The emphasis all the way through the tale is on motherhood. The Prologue is addressed to Mary as mother of Christ. The little boy learns to sing the antiphon *O alma redemptoris* because it celebrates 'Cristes mooder', and he sings it as he goes to and from school each day because 'On Cristes mooder set was his entente' (538, 550). After he has been murdered by the Jews, the anguish of his mother as she searches for him prompts her to appeal to Mary for help:

> With moodres pitee in hir brest enclosed:
> She gooth, as she were half out of hir mynde,
> To every place where she hath supposed
> By liklihede hir litel child to fynde:
> And evere on Cristes mooder meeke and kynde
> She cride, and atte laste thus she wroghte:
> Among the cursed Jues she hym soghte.   (593-9)

The mother's agony as she searches for her child is subtly reminiscent of the anxiety of Mary and Joseph, seeking for their lost son while he argues with the doctors in the Temple (Lc. 2: 48); and this raises, again like a shadow, the possibility of another variation in the parent-child theme — that the parent may be abandoned by the child (as God is by his children).[12] But the last line of the stanza brings the widow nearer to Mary's experience at the Crucifixion; it is 'the cursed Jues' who are responsible for the murder of her son as of Mary's. The image of the bereaved mother is multiplied in the tale; its constant echoes of the Mass for the Holy Innocents recall the grief of the mothers of the children slain for the sake of Mary's child.[13] Those mothers are themselves the fulfilment of Jeremiah's prophecy of the voice that is to be heard in Rama, 'Rachel weeping for her children' (1er. 31: 15; Mt. 2: 18), and the widow too is referred to as 'this newe Rachel' (627). The chorus of lamenting mothers stretches from the Old Testament through the New to the world of present experience, embracing human and divine in a single experience of pain.

The boy's body is eventually found because, miraculously, he continues to sing *O alma redemptoris* after death, and he explains to the abbot who questions him that Jesus allows this miracle 'for the worship of his Mooder deere' (654). Mary, he says, had come to him and laid a seed on his tongue, bidding him sing until it was removed.

> "And after that thus seyde she to me:
> 'My litel child, now wol I fecche thee,
> Whan that the greyn is from thy tonge ytake.
> Be nat agast, I wol thee nat forsake.' "   (667-9)

The death of the child is thus represented as the entry into relationship with a new mother — a mother, who, unlike the father to whom is addressed the cry 'My God, my God, why hast thou forsaken me?', will not forsake her child.[14] The absence of the father in this tale is in fact an important element in its structure. The world of the tale is a world of women and children. The absence of any father, human or divine, allows concentration on the tenderness that binds mother and son; the mother's tender protectiveness for the weakness of childhood is matched by the grown-up son's tender reverence for the relative weakness of womanhood — a reciprocity which is expressed in visual art by the balancing of Madonna and Child with the Coronation of the Virgin. But this isolation of mother and child raises also, I think, something like a yearning for the presence of a strong, protective father who might act as a powerful opponent of Satan and his human in-

---

12 I am grateful to Loretta Minghella, a student at Clare College, Cambridge, for this suggestion.

13 See Marie Padgett Hamilton, 'Echoes of Childermas in the Tale of the Prioress', first printed in *MLR* 34 (1939) 1-8; revised version in *Chaucer: Modern Essays in Criticism*, ed. Edward Wagenknecht (New York, 1959), pp. 88-97.

14 Mt. 27: 46; Mc. 15: 34. Cf. Piero Boitani's comments on Dante's evocation of this cry in the Ugolino episode (*Cambridge Readings*, pp. 82-3).

struments, the Jews. Transferred on to the divine level, we can see that this yearning could easily become a sense of indignation that the father had forsaken mother and child, had withdrawn his protective power; there exists here the possibility of the same questioning of God's cruelty as in the *Man of Law's Tale.* But here, as in the *Man of Law's Tale,* the counter to this indignation is the tale's demonstration of the *power* of helpless innocence. The comment on the miracle focusses on this:

> O grete God, that parfournest thy laude
> By mouth of innocentz, lo, heere thy myght! (607-8)

And in the *Prologue,* where the father is briefly introduced, it is as one subject to the compelling power of innocence, who is 'ravished' by Mary's humility (469).

The miraculous power of weakness and suffering is even more profoundly demonstrated in the *Clerk's Tale.* In the *Man of Law's Tale,* the cruelty of the father, Alla, turned out to be merely apparent. In the *Clerk's Tale,* Walter's behaviour to his children is also, in one sense, only apparently cruel, since he does not kill them, as Griselda believes, but sends them away to be brought up by his sister, and later returns them to her. Walter is not, however, innocent of cruelty in the same sense that Alla is; he really is cruel to his wife and children. He claims to be an 'enthralled lord', acting under compulsion, but his words are a hollow parody of the speeches of Alla's constable of Virginius, where both the compulsion and the grief are genuine. His claim that 'in greet lordship . . . /Ther is greet servitude', and that he 'may nat doon as every plowman may' (797-9) fits into the pattern established by other examples of the fusion of 'governance' and 'subjeccioun' only as a perverted mimicry of them, since it is not true that his people object to Griselda as their mistress, and it is the dictates of his own will to test her that he is following. Similarly, the servant who protests that he is acting under orders, when removing Griselda's children, is a debased parallel to Alla's constable. But in a different way, Walter really is an 'enthralled lord', as well as pretending to be one. He is a victim of his own obsessive desire, as Chaucer makes clear in describing it:

> But ther been folk of swich condicion
> That whan they have a certein purpos take,
> They kan nat stynte of hire entencion,
> But, right as they were bounden to a stake,
> They wol nat of that firste purpos slake.
> Right so this markys fulliche hath purposed
> To tempte his wyf as he was first disposed. (701-7)

There is nothing in Chaucer's source, the Latin tale of Petrarch, corresponding to the words 'as they were bounden to a stake'. Walter is 'bounden' to his cruel obsession; appearing to enjoy complete independence, he is in fact helplessly enslaved to his own will. Griselda, in contrast, turns 'subjeccioun' into 'governance' by the complete absorption of her vow to be obedient to Walter into her own will:

"This wyl is in myn herte, and ay shal be;
No lengthe of tyme or deeth may this deface,
Ne chaunge my corage to another place." (509-11)

And if Walter is bound by his own will, he is liberated from it by Griselda's patience. The miracle of the tale is that Walter's apparently endless desire to test Griselda does in fact come to an end, that her apparently helpless suffering inexorably breaks down his will to inflict torment.

In examining this suffering more closely, we should first note that for the first time in the tales we have been examining, we have an apparently cruel mother. The critics who complain of Griselda's 'unfeeling' relinquishment of her children are in fact focussing, albeit uncomprehendingly, on one of the problems that the tale exists to contemplate. Chaucer's awareness of this possible interpretation of Griselda's behaviour is made clear in the way he carefully points out that Walter would have thought this himself if he had not known of her love for her children (688-93). It is faith - the trust in the constants of characteristics, rather than external behaviour — that counteracts the outward image of cruelty. Walter's faith in Griselda's continuing love for her children convinces him that her obedience is not merely inertia, and enables him finally to abandon the test and restore her children. It is her own 'benignity' that, unconsciously, she meets and reaps in the joy of her reunion with her children:

"O tendre, o deere, o yonge children myne!
Youre woful mooder wende stedfastly
That crueel houndes or som foul vermyne
Hadde eten yow; but God, of his mercy,
And youre benyngne fader tendrely
Hath doon yow kept," — and in that same stounde
Al sodeynly she swapte adoun to grounde. (1093-9)

But Griselda's faith in Walter as "benyngne fader' is more difficult to maintain than his belief in her as benign mother. And the difficulty is again a measure of the difficulty in maintaining belief in the benign nature of God's 'governance'. The final stanzas of the tale parallel Griselda's position in relation to Walter with the human position in relation to God.

For, sith a womman was so pacient
Unto a mortal man, wel moore us oghte
Receyven al in gree that God us sent;
For greet skile is, he preeve that he wroghte.
But he ne tempteth no man that he boghte,

> As seith Seint Jame, if ye his pistel rede;
> He preeveth folk al day, it is no drede,
>
> And suffreth us, as for oure excercise,
> With sharpe scourges of adversitee
> Ful ofte to be bete in sondry wise;
> Nat for to knowe oure wyl, for certes he,
> Er we were born, knew al oure freletee;
> And for oure beste is al his governaunce.
> Lat us thanne lyve in vertuous suffraunce. (1149-62)

It would seem, once again, that the only role allowed to mankind is the patient 'suffraunce' of God's 'governaunce', whether its results are cruel or beneficent.

Yet, as I have already suggested, it is the power of 'suffraunce' that the tale exists to represent. It is a power which the Crucifixion evidences. And the words in which Griselda refers to the Crucifixion show how the problem of the apparent cruelty of the father is answered on a divine level, as in the *Man of Law's Tale,* by the identification of father and son; when bidding her daughter farewell 'in hire benygne voys', she says

> "Fareweel my child! I shal thee nevere see.
> But sith I thee have marked with the croys
> Of thilke Fader — blessed moote he be! —
> That for us deyde upon a croys of tree,
> Thy soule, litel child, I hym bitake,
> For this nyght shaltow dyen for my sake." (555-60)

She does not refer — as she most naturally might — to the Son who died for us, but to the Father who died for us.[15] The oddity of phrasing draws attention, once again, to the fact that God's role embraces that of both father and child; his cruelty is visited on himself. Like Chaucer's Ugolino, who gnaws his own arm, he eats himself rather than his children. The human follows the pattern of the divine; Griselda's 'this nyght shaltow dyen for my sake' places her own child's suffering in line with Christ's, as well as aligning her own parental sorrow with that of God the Father.

But Griselda's suffering is also Christ-like. The profundity of its resonances is established, first, by the linking of Griselda's resignation with Job's. The same speech of Job that lies behind the words of the children in the Ugolino story is echoed in her words to Walter:

> "Naked out of my fadres hous", quod she,
> "I cam, and naked moot I turne agayn.
> Al youre plesance wol I folwen fayn." (871-2)

---

15 I am grateful to Lars Engle, a former Cambridge student now preparing a PhD thesis at Yale University, for first drawing my attention to this.

And she is explicitly linked with Job by the stanzas claiming that even his 'humblesse' is outstripped by that of women. It is relevant here that the suffering of Job was interpreted in the middle ages as a type of the suffering of Christ. In late medieval art there appears a type-figure, known as the 'Christus im Elend', which represents Christ in the attitude of Job on his dunghill.[16] And Griselda too can be seen as a type of Christ. Pondering the apparent invitation at the end of the tale to equate God's role with Walter's, we can see that this is, in fact, appropriate only so far as the apparent cruelty of the divine father is concerned; if we plumb appearances, as the tale prompts us to do, we see that it is Griselda who offers a far truer and pro-founder image of the Christian God. It is her experience that gives depth of meaning of the Clerk's statement that God

> suffreth us, as for oure excercise,
> With sharpe scourges of adversitee
> Ful ofte to be bete in sondry wise.

The evocation of Christ's physical suffering which is made by Griselda's experience causes us to link the noun 'suffraunce' at the end of the last stanza back to the verb 'suffreth' at the beginning, and to give the latter a new meaning. God not only 'suffers' in the sense of 'allowing', he also suffers in the simplest sense, the experience of pain. And it is precisely the identity of father and child that leads to the fusion of the two kinds of 'suffering'. Chaucer must, we realize, have pondered the deeper implications of the word he chose to translate Boethius' questions in the passage I quoted earlier: 'Why *suffrestow* that slydynge Fortune turneth so grete enter-chaungynges of thynges . . .?' For God to 'allow' the world to be as it is, is for God to suffer, to endure its cruelties as their victim.

Julian of Norwich identifies the nature of the second Person of the Trinity with 'moderhede'. The identification is made, first, on the basis of mercy, the quality that characterizes both Christ and mothers. But it is also made on the basis of suffering, and in particular, the suffering undergone in child-birth, as Julian shows in a passage that exploits as Chaucer does the ambi-guity in the Middle English word 'suffer'. Its sharply physical sense is uppermost in the fusion of the Passion with the pains of childbirth:

> Thus he susteyneth vs with in hym in loue and traveyle, in to the full tyme þat he wolde suffer the sharpyst throwes and grevous paynes that evyr were or evyr shalle be, and dyed at the last. And whan he had done, and so borne vs to blysse, yett myght nott all thys make a seeth to his mervelous loue.[17]

16 See G. von der Osten, 'Job and Christ: The Development of a Devotional Image', *Journal of the Warburg and Courtauld Institutes* 16 (1953) 153-8.

17 *A Book of Showings to the Anchoress Julian of Norwich,* ed. Edmund Colledge and James Walsh (2 vols., Toronto, 1978), chapter 60, II, pp. 595-6. I have taken up the option offered by the editors of reading 'throwes' for 'thornes'.

And it is the testimony of love in this suffering which provides the assurance that the second kind of 'suffering' carries with it the first:

> The kynde lovyng moder that woot and knowyth the neyde of hyr chylde, she kepyth it full tenderly, as the kynde and condycion of moderhed wyll. Ande evyr as it waxith in age and in stature, she channgyth her werkes, but nott her loue. And when it is wexid of more age, she sufferyth it that it be chastised in brekyng downe of vicis, to make the chylde receyve vertues and grace.[18]

To speak of human beings as God's children is a cliché, but it is less usual to think of them as brought to birth in pain. For Chaucer, as for Julian, however, this idea is crucial. It is childbirth that determines the nature of the mother's role, and founds it in a different experience from that of the father — that is, the experience of pain. And Chaucer is like Julian too in seeing in childbirth a powerful image of 'suffraunce' in both its senses, 'suffering' and 'allowing'. One of his most hauntingly enigmatic alterations of Petrarch's Latin story is Griselda's response to the command that she relinquish her second child. In Petrarch, she adds to her acquiescence the comment: 'nor do I have any part in these children beyond the bearing of them' (neque . . . in hijs filijs quicquam habeo preter laborem').[19] In the *Clerk's Tale,* Griselda's words, though close, are subtly different:

> I have noght had no part of children tweyne
> But first siknesse, and after, wo and peyne.   (649-51)

Chaucer's addition — the reference to 'siknesse', 'wo and peyne' — is a deliberate reminder of the pain of childbirth. Brief though it is, the reminder gives a reality to the experience which enables us to link it with Griselda's 'suffraunce', and thus, through her, with God's.

There is a similarly brief but suggestive hint in the line describing Constance's pregnancy in the *Man of Law's Tale:*

> She halt hire chambre, abidyng Cristes wille.   (721)

— Christ's will, not her own or her husband's. The woman in childbirth is necessarily passive; she allows herself to become the instrument of a process, the vehicle of a power she cannot initiate and can control only by full acceptance of and identification with it. In Chaucer's tales, childbirth can thus become an image of the necessary surrender of the self to an external

---

18   Ibid., p. 599. On the tradition of 'Christ as mother', see Colledge and Walsh's Introduction, I, pp. 150-5.
19   *Sources and Analogues of Chaucer's Canterbury Tales,* ed. W.F. Bryan and Germaine Dempster (New York, 1941), p. 316.

will, to a larger 'governance', and in doing so it shows how the experience of child and parent can meet and become one, as they do in the God who is both Father and Son.

The childbirth which had seemed in Genesis merely punitive, a punishment for the sin in Paradise, thus finds a creative role — and by the same token, suggests one for human 'suffraunce'. And just as there can be no control over the process of birth, so there can be no control over its result. The child is not the property of the parent. Beside the Job-like resignation of the children in the *Monk's Tale,* therefore, we may set the Job-like resignation of the parent in the *Clerk's Tale:*

> I have noght had no part of children tweyne
> But first siknesse, and after, wo and peyne.

For Chaucer, the pains and resignation of childbirth are a model in which we can see and understand that an acknowledgement of powerlessness is a necessary accompaniment of the exercise of 'governance', and in which we can see also the necessity for God to allow to his children their independent existence, whatever the pain he — and they — must then suffer.

CHAUCERIAN AUTHORITY AND INHERITANCE

ANTHONY C. SPEARING

The title advertised for this lecture — 'Chaucerian Inheritance' — was composed last year; the lecture itself was composed only last week. The result is that the lecture and the title do not match perfectly, and I must begin by asking you kindly to imagine that the advertised title was 'Chaucerian Authority and Inheritance'. In what I have to say today, my purpose will be to sketch in and to relate to each other a certain cluster of ideas and attitudes in Chaucer and in his fifteenth-century successors that centre in the concepts of paternal authority and of the child's inheritance from the father. My lecture will not have the character of a single, unidirectional argument; it will rather be an attempt to suggest the existence of a significant topic. My theme is related in some ways to the work of two Cambridge colleagues, Dr. Derek Brewer and Dr. Jill Mann, both of whom will be known to some of you because they have been honoured, like myself, by the invitation to contribute to this series of J.A.W. Bennett Memorial Lectures. What is surprising is that we have all three been working and thinking independently, and yet along parallel or even converging lines. There is perhaps some infection, other than the common cold, borne on the chilly air of Cambridge, that has brought about this common interest.

Let me begin with some thought-provoking remarks made by Derek Brewer in his genially speculative book, *Chaucer and his World*. There he notes that 'Chaucer's poetry shows no sign of an imagination bothered by a dominating father-figure', and he comments especially on *Troilus and Criseyde* that Troilus 'is not in the least hampered by his father, King Priam, who is barely mentioned' and that in Criseyde's case it is indeed 'the absence, the *loss*, of a father-figure, of protective authority, which is so disturbing'.[1] If we look more widely, over the whole range of Chaucer's poetry, we shall find more cases in which the 'father-figure', the figure of 'protective authority', is disturbingly absent; and other cases again in which the father-figure is present, but presented in a most unfavourable light. What is rare indeed in Chaucer is the father who is present and good, possessor of the wisdom and benevolence that a patriarchal age might have expected. The only example I can call to mind of a Chaucerian father who seems unequivo-

---

1 Derek Brewer, *Chaucer and his World* (London, 1978), p. 43.

cally benevolent is the 'noble doughty kyng' (*Canterbury Tales* V 338)[2] Cambryuskan of *The Squire's Tale;* and in the extant part of this tale we learn nothing whatever of the relationship between him and his three children. Jill Mann, in the lecture on 'Fathers and Children in *The Canterbury Tales*' which she gave here last year, and which she has kindly allowed me to read, analysed in detail the equivocal portrayals of fathers in *The Man of Law's Tale*, in *The Physician's Tale*, and in the section of *The Monk's Tale* concerning Ugolino di Pisa — fathers who are kind and yet cruel, or authoritative and yet subservient, and whose equivocality she sees as a means by which Chaucer explores the mystery of divine providence. I shall say no more of these three tales, but for another example of an unfavourable portrayal of a father in *The Canterbury Tales* let me mention Symkyn the miller in *The Reeve's Tale*. He is a ludicrously arrogant and boastful image of husbandly and paternal authority, bristling with phallic weapons —

> Ay by his belt he baar a long panade,
> And of a swerd ful trenchant was the blade.
> A joly poppere baar he in his pouche;
> Ther was no man, for peril, dorste hym touche.
> A Sheffeld thwitel baar he in his hose. (I 3929-33)

— and always ready to counter any threat to his womenfolk 'With panade, or with knyf, or boidekyn' (3960). All his daughter inherits from him is his *camus,* or snub nose (3934, 3974), yet he is determined to protect her virginity and marry her in accordance with his own notions of social dignity. In the end he proves incapable of asserting his own authority or of preserving his daughter's maidenhood or indeed his wife's fidelity; tyrannous paternal authority is reduced to impotence by two young men from Cambridge.

Symkyn is a literal father; an interesting example of the father-figure is the authoritative informant who is encountered in the type of poetic dream called the *oraculum*. This is the kind of dream defined in Macrobius's commentary on the *Somnium Scipionis* as one in which 'a parent, or a pious or revered man, or a priest, or even a god' appears and gives information or advice.[3] The *Somnium Scipionis* itself belongs to this category; in it, the father-figure is Scipio Africanus the elder, who appears to his grandson in a dream and tells him of his future and of the other world. In *The Parliament of Fowls* Chaucer tells of how he read the *Somnium Scipionis,* and then had a dream influenced by it in which Africanus appeared to him. Africanus promises him a reward for his labour, shows him a gate which leads, according to the inscriptions above it, both to fulfilment and to frustration, pushes

---

2   Chaucer quotations are taken from *The Works of Geoffrey Chaucer*, ed. F.N. Robinson, 2nd edn (London, 1957).
3   Macrobius, *Commentary on the Dream of Scipio,* trans. William H. Stahl (New York, 1952), p. 90.

him firmly through it, comforts him in his indecision and fear by taking his hand — and then apparently vanishes, since he is mentioned no more in the whole poem. The paternal authority vanishes, and Chaucer is left to deal with the uncertainties of his dream by himself. Another of Chaucer's dream-poems that evidently belongs to the same category is *The House of Fame*. Here the eagle who carries Chaucer through the heavens and instructs him in the physics of sound might be seen as a kind of comic father-figure; but at the end of Book II he too abandons him: he says he will wait for him, but he is never seen again. In Book III, just as the dreamer seems on the verge of obtaining the 'love-tydynges' (2143) that he has been promised from one who 'semed for to be/A man of gret auctorite' (2157-58) — the authoritative informant expected in the *oraculum* — the poem breaks off. We do not of course know for certain why *The House of Fame* was not continued beyond this point, or why it was put into circulation in an unfinished form, but it is surely revealing about Chaucer's attitude towards paternal or quasi-paternal authority that it should break off at this precise point. I have suggested elsewhere that the dream in *The House of Fame* might best be seen not as an *oraculum*, but rather as an 'anti-*oraculum*'.[4] To some extent it was characteristic of Chaucer's age to question the patriarchal, authoritarian bent of the culture that it inherited. We have only to think of *Piers Plowman*, with its tearing of the pardon from Truth and its reduction of Holy Church from an awe-inspiring mother-figure to a crumbling barn, or of *Pearl*, with its reversal of expectation that makes the father the pupil and the child the teacher. But Chaucer goes further than most of his contemporaries in the persistence with which he presents paternal authority as absent or cruel.

Among the Canterbury pilgrims there are two whom we know to be fathers in the literal sense. One is the Knight, the father of the Squire; he may, for all we know, be a most benevolent parent, and certainly he exercises a quasi-paternal authority among the other pilgrims with benevolent and tactful firmness, as when he brings the Monk's dreary series of 'tragedies' to an end, or when he calls on the Pardoner and the Host to kiss and make up. But, surprisingly perhaps, we see nothing of his relations with his real son, and all we are told about them is that the son acted towards him in a way appropriate for a squire in the household of his lord: he 'carf biforn his fader at the table' (I 100). This act symbolizes the hierarchy of the social estates, without telling us anything about the warmth or otherwise of the family relationship between the two men. The other literal father is the Franklin, and he is evidently sharply at odds with his son, whom he compares most disadvantageously with the Squire. He cares for

---

4   A.C. Spearing, *Medieval Dream-Poetry* (Cambridge, 1976), p. 11.

nothing but gaming, he loses all his money (meaning, no doubt, his father's money) at dice, and he prefers low company to that which his father thinks suitable to his rank.

> I have my sone snybbed, and yet shal,
> For he to vertu listeth nat entende, (V 688-89)

says the father. The blame might seem to be differently distributed if seen from the son's point of view, but there can be no doubt that, with whatever justification, the Franklin judges and speaks harshly in relation to his son.

In the company of pilgrims there is another who is a father, not literally but metaphorically; I mean of course the Parson. The portrait of him in *The General Prologue* is unmistakeably favourable, but it is also unmistakeably negative. He is defined largely in terms of what he does *not* do — he does not 'cursen for his tithes' (I 486), or give up visiting his parishioners because of bad weather, or leave his flock to gain greater material rewards elsewhere, and so on. Towards any obstinate man in his flock he engages like the Franklin in the characteristic fatherly activity of 'snybbyng' or rebuke: 'Hym wolde he snybben sharply for the nonys' (I 523). His Christian virtue and his noble purpose remain unquestionable, but his role on the pilgrimage gives far less emphasis to attractive paternal qualities such as protectiveness, kindness, generosity, than to the negative aspects of fatherhood: his task is to forbid, to inhibit spontaneity and playfulness. In the Epilogue to *The Man of Law's Tale*, when the Host calls on him to tell the next tale, the Parson's response is to rebuke the Host for swearing, and thus to be classed as a 'Lollere' (II 1173), a Wycliffite. But his main appearance is of course in the Prologue to his own tale, the last of the collection as we have it. Here the Host once more calls on the Parson to tell a *fable* and thus 'knytte up wel a greet mateere' (X 28-29). Once more his answer has the effect of a rebuke: 'Thou getest fable noon ytoold for me' (31). He rejects fiction itself as mere *wrecchednesse,* mere *draf* (34-35), and he proceeds to offer instead the only tale of the collection that is not a tale, that has no element of narrative or fiction in it. It is indeed 'Moralitee and vertuous mateere' (38), and it makes an end, as he says, to the feast of tales (47), not just by being the last course, but by negating all that has gone before, substituting a systematic treatise on human sinfulness for the unpredictable and various life of the tales, reducing verse to prose, human voices to written discourse.[5] I do not imply that Chaucer means us to criticize the Parson for doing this, only that when the time at last comes for him to exercise his paternal authority over the other pilgrims, he does so — he has to do so — with an austerity that dampens the spirits, telling us that the way to eternal life is not through

---

5 For an excellent study of this aspect of *The Parson's Tale,* see Lee W. Patterson, 'The "Parson's Tale" and the Quitting of the "Canterbury Tales",' *Traditio* 34 (1978) 331-80.

a tale-telling competition which ends with a jolly supper at the Tabard Inn, but 'by deeth and mortificacioun of synne' (1080).

As a last example from *The Canterbury Tales* I choose *The Knight's Tale* because it ingeniously combines the two major Chaucerian images of paternal authority, the cruel father and the absent father. The supreme example of the father-figure in Chaucer's view of the world is of course God, and it is striking how many substantial passages there are in Chaucer's work that question the combination of benevolent wisdom with supreme power that is attributed to God in the Christian scheme of things. Jill Mann in her lecture discussed one such passage in *The Man of Law's Tale,* where what is questioned is not so much God himself as planetary influences. There are other passages which put the question more directly to the deity: if he is both loving and powerful, how can we explain the predominance of evil and suffering in human life? In *The Complaint of Mars* this question is asked in relation to human love. Why does 'the God that sit so hye' (218) cause men and women to love each other, when earthly love is either fleeting or unfortunate? —

> And that is wonder, that so juste a kyng
> Doth such hardnesse to his creature. (231-32)

It seems that God has enmity to lovers, and that he must be seen as a fisherman, dangling a bait before the fish in order to torment or destroy them. In the story of Philomela from *The Legend of Good Women* a similar question is put to God about the birth of the cruel rapist Tereus. God here is *dator formarum,* the 'yevere of the formes' (2228), the masculine principle that imposes shape on the shapeless feminine matter; and why, he is asked, having borne the whole created world in his thought before giving it substance, did he make or allow to be made such a poisonously evil man? There is no answer. In *The Franklin's Tale* a similar question is asked by Dorigen about the black rocks round the coast of Brittany,

> That semen rather a foul confusioun
> Of werk than any fair creacion
> Of swich a parfit wys God and a stable. (V 869-71)

Why did such a God make a part of the natural world of which the only conceivable purpose is destructive? Again there is no answer. In *The Knight's Tale,* finally, the questioning of God's paternal authority takes its most comprehensive form in Palamon's speech at the end of Part I. The gods are here described as cruel, and as treating men worse than beasts:

> What governance is in this prescience
> That giltelees tormenteth innocence? (I 1313-14)

We may note that in this case it is the gods, not strictly speaking God, about whom the question is put; and in the other three cases I have mentioned, too, the questioning is in some way associated with paganism. In *The Complaint of Mars* it is the pagan god himself who is speaking; in the legend of Philomela, the person about whom the question is asked is pagan, even though the questioning appears to come from the (presumably) Christian narrator; in *The Franklin's Tale* Dorigen is a pagan, even though she comes nearer than, say, Aurelius to a Christian conception of the deity; and in *The Knight's Tale* Palamon is a pagan speaking about the pagan gods. One could plausibly argue that Chaucer associated such questioning with paganism; the questions asked derive mainly from Boethius's *De Consolatione Philosophiae*, a work which Chaucer may have seen as (among other things) an illustration of the large overlap between philosophical paganism and Christianity; and it might be supposed that Chaucer took it for granted that Philosophy's answers to Boethius's questions were conclusive.

In *The Knight's Tale* some of those answers are indeed given by Theseus in the speech which concludes the poem's last Part, and which is clearly intended to match the questioning speech by Palamon that concludes its first Part. I set aside the question of the extent to which Theseus's speech is, or is meant to be, philosophically convincing.[6] For my purpose the crucial fact is that Theseus in that speech envisages a different heavenly father from the one we have seen exercising authority in the situation to which the speech is designed to respond. Venus and Mars as gods have granted the apparently conflicting prayers of Palamon to win Emelye and of Arcite to win the tournament which has been arranged to settle who should win her; which is to say that as planets Venus and Mars have predicted apparently conflicting futures. Jupiter attempts to bring to an end the strife in heaven between the two gods, but evidently without success, and it is 'the pale Saturnus the colde' (I 2443) who finds a means of doing so. The means is in accordance with his nature as the god of disasters, so fully and horrifyingly evoked in the speech (invented by Chaucer himself, not taken from the *Teseida*) in which he defines his own powers over sudden death, imprisonment, rebellion, 'the maladyes colde,/The derke tresons, and the castes olde' (2467-68). Saturn sends a 'furie infernal' (2684) to frighten Arcite's horse when he has gained victory in the tournament; Arcite dies a horrible death, described by Chaucer in clinical detail; and Theseus's final speech persuades Emelye to marry Palamon instead. In that final speech, Theseus refers to Jupiter as ruler and cause of all things, and urges that the survivors, instead of continuing to mourn, should 'thanken Juppiter of al his grace' (3069). Theseus

---

6 For discussion see Elizabeth Salter, *Chaucer: The Knight's Tale and the Clerk's Tale* (London, 1962), pp. 35-36 and *The Knight's Tale*, ed. A.C. Spearing (Cambridge, 1966), pp. 75-78.

thus comes as near as a virtuous pagan could to grasping a Christian conception of God and the universe; but, so far as what we have seen of the gods is concerned, he is wrong. Jupiter, the benevolent father of all things, is a mere idea; the reality, with whom he coexists in Chaucer's poem, is Saturn, the cruel father who does not hesitate to destroy his own children. One of the factors that place *The Knight's Tale* among the most powerful of all Chaucer's poems is surely that in it Chaucer has found a way of combining his two most compelling images of the father, as cruel and as absent.

I turn now from fathers to inheritance. I want to suggest that Chaucer's questioning of the role of the father should be associated with his questioning of the father's power to bequeath virtue to the son and the son's power to inherit virtue from the father. It is well known that this is a theme on which Chaucer touches rather prominently in several of his poems, though it is not of course original with him: he could have found it in Boethius, in Jean de Meun, in Dante, and doubtless in other sources too. Nevertheless, it was obviously a theme that greatly interested him, as is shown by the fact that he sometimes gives it an emphasis that seems disproportionate to its contextual relevance. In *The Wife of Bath's Tale,* for example, the Loathly Lady's lecture in bed to her reluctant husband includes a section of 78 lines on the nature of true *gentillesse* (III 1109-76). (Perhaps we should pause to remind ourselves that the word *gentil* is etymologically connected with familiy birth, fatherhood.) This seems an altogether excessive response to the husband's one-line complaint that she is of low birth; but Chaucer was obviously determined to set out in full the argument that our forefathers cannot 'biquethe . . ./To noon of us hir vertuous lyvyng' (1121-22); that if *gentillesse* were a natural inheritance, then those of *gentil* birth could 'nevere fyne/To doon of gentillesse the faire office' (1136-37); and that 'men may wel often fynde/A lordes sone do shame and vileynye' (1150-51); so that the true definition of *gentillesse* is that 'he is gentil that dooth gentil dedis' (1170). Regardless of its relevance to the tale, it is an argument appropriate to a self-made woman like the Wife of Bath, and perhaps equally appropriate to a man like Chaucer, of prosperous bourgeois family, who made his way by his own abilities to a place at court, a wife who was lady-in-waiting to the queen, a sister-in-law who was first John of Gaunt's mistress and then his wife, a son who was knighted, and a granddaughter who became Countess of Suffolk.

We have already seen how the Franklin, before beginning his tale, complains that his son does not possess the *vertu* that marks true *gentillesse.* We may surmise that the Franklin inwardly believes that he himself does possess that *vertu*, and that it is an understandable human weakness that leads him to feel aggrieved at his son's failure to inherit what cannot be inherited; but the burden of his tale is precisely that *gentillesse* is not derived from birth. By his deeds a squire can be as *gentil* as a knight, and a clerk can be as *gentil* as a squire; where moral virtue is concerned, inheritance from the father is of no significance. A very similar point is made in the ballade *Gentilesse,* but now in a way that contrasts God as father with human fathers. The 'fader of gentilesse' (1) is God alone, and the man who wishes to be *gentil* must address himself 'Vertu to sewe, and vyces for to flee' (4). The true heir to virtue is the man who loves virtue, whatever rank he may have inherited, for

> Vyce may wel be heir to old richesse;
> But ther may no man, as men may wel see,
> Byquethe his heir his vertuous noblesse.   (15-17)

Oddly enough, Chaucer's unfavourable attitude towards the power of the father goes so far that, while denying that good qualities can be bequeathed and inherited, he occasionally asserts that evil qualities can. An example that may spring to mind is that of Criseyde, the betrayer of Troilus whose father is a traitor to Troy — though that is not a point that Chaucer ever makes quite explicitly. Unmistakeably explicit is the statement at the beginning of the story of Phyllis in *The Legend of Good Women,* that the false lover Demophon was unmatched for falseness by any save 'his fader Theseus' (2400), a fact which demonstrates

> By preve as wel as by autorite,
> That wiked fruit cometh of a wiked tre.   (2394-95)

The same proverb is quoted by the Host, more jocularly, in *The Monk's Prologue,* with reference to the inheritance of sexual feebleness:

> Of fieble trees ther comen wrecched ympes.
> This maketh that oure heires been so sklendre
> And feble that they may nat wel engendre.   (VII 1956-58)

The proverb of course derives from Scripture — 'Sic omnis arbor bona fructus bonos facit: mala autem arbor malos fructus facit' (Matthew 7:17) — and it is surely significant that Chaucer alludes twice to the second clause, which is unfavourable to inheritance, but never to the first, which is favourable to it.

To take the discussion a stage further, I now need to introduce a different, metaphorical rather than literal, version of paternal authority — the authority of the literary precursor over his successors. There is justification for seeing this as analogous to the authority of the father, if only in the fact that writers before and after Chaucer have so often referred to their precursors in this way. Lucretius refers to Epicurus as father; Horace and Propertius both refer to Ennius as father; Cicero calls Isocrates the father of eloquence and Herodotus the father of history; and so on.[7] Among Chaucer's

---

7   *De Rerum Naturae* III 9; Horace, *Epistles* I xix; Propertius III iii 6; *De Oratore* II

successors, as we shall see, Hoccleve addresses Chaucer himself as 'reverend father', and Henryson in his *Moral Fables,* meeting Aesop as the father-figure in a dream of the *oraculum* type, addresses him as father and is in turn addressed by him as son.[8] As Dryden was to write in a later age, 'we [that is, the poets] have our lineal descents and clans as well as other families', so that Milton could be seen as 'the poetical son of Spenser', and Spenser in turn as a son 'begotten' by Chaucer 'two hundred years after his decease'.[9] Descent and inheritance from father to son provides a basic explanatory model for literary history; and the model retains its power, for example in Harold Bloom's view of the tensely Oedipal relation of son to father as char-acterizing the whole of English poetic history from Milton to the present.[10]

It is well known that by far the larger part of Chaucer's work is derived from existing literary sources, chiefly in Latin, French and Italian; yet Chaucer never refers to any of his predecessors as father. Indeed, there is something peculiar about Chaucer's attitude to literary authority. He has no objection at all to disclosing that he is indebted to other writers. Sometimes this is a matter of vague references to distant predecessors from whom the story as a whole is taken — 'Whilom, as olde stories tellen us' (*Knight's Tale,* I 859) or

> Thise olde gentil Britouns in hir dayes
> Of diverse aventures maden layes   (*Franklin's Tale,* V 709-10)

— while at other times it is a matter of giving references to specific sources for specific parts of a work:

> The remenant of the tale if ye wol heere,
> Reedeth Ovyde, and ther ye may it leere
>   (*Wife of Bath's Tale,* III 981-82)

or

> In Omer, or in Dares, or in Dite,
> Whoso that kan may rede hem as they write.
>   (*Troilus and Criseyde* I 146-47)

Like other medieval writers, Chaucer doubtless felt that his work gained prestige if it could claim to possess an ancestry, and that he himself gained prestige from references to authorities which would suggest that he was as

---

10; *De Legibus* I 5. I am greatly indebted to Dr. James Diggle for supplying me with these references.

8   *Moral Fables,* 11. 1363-69, in *The Works of Robert Henryson,* ed. Denton Fox (Oxford, 1981).

9   *Preface to Fables Ancient and Modern,* in John Dryden, *Of Dramatic Poesy and Other Critical Essays,* ed. George Watson (London, 1962), vol. II, p. 270.

10 E.g. *The Anxiety of Influence* (New York, 1973).

much a scholar as a poet.[11] Yet Chaucer's critical attitude towards paternal authority is also reflected in his approach to the authority of those precursors to whom he might refer as 'myn auctour' (e.g. *Troilus and Criseyde* II 18). It is rare for him to name a specific *auctour* as the authority for a complete work, as opposed to referring us to scholarly authorities for further information. One case where he does so, very straightforwardly, is *The Physician's Tale:*

> Ther was, as telleth Titus Livius,
> A knyght that called was Virginius (VI 1-2)

— and he proceeds to tell a story which does appear to have Livy as its ultimate source, though it is uncertain whether Chaucer's immediate source was that or the French version in the *Roman de la Rose*. But in two other cases his attitude is less straightforward. The story of Dido in *The Legend of Good Women* begins with a laudatory reference to Virgil (itself probably modelled on Dante's greeting of Virgil in the first canto of the *Inferno* and on Statius's praise of Virgil in the *Purgatorio* as a giver of light to those who follow);[12] and this is accompanied by a passing acknowledgement to Ovid too:

> Glorye and honour, Virgil Mantoan,
> Be to thy name! and I shal, as I can,
> Folwe thy lanterne, as thow gost byforn,
> How Eneas to Dido was forsworn.
> In Naso and Eneydos wol I take
> The tenor, and the grete effectes make. (924-29)

But the insistence that Chaucer will confine himself to the *tenor* or the *grete effectes,* the essential points, of Virgil's and Ovid's story is later developed into a sceptical and critical attitude towards his classical *auctours.* He will not repeat Virgil's explanation of how Dido came to *Libie* — 'It nedeth nat, it were but los of time' (997), and

> I coude folwe, word for word, Virgile,
> But it wolde lasten al to longe while. (1002-03)

When Aeneas visits the temple where Dido is praying Chaucer adds,

> I can nat seyn if that it be possible,
> But Venus hadde hym maked invysible —
> Thus seyth the bok, withouten any les. (1020-22)

---

11 For a valuable study of the medieval conceptions of *auctoritas* which form the background to Chaucer's attitude, see M.-D. Chenu, *Introduction à l'étude de saint Thomas d'Aquin* (Montreal and Paris, 1950), chapter IV.

12 *Inferno* I 82; *Purgatorio* XXII 67-69.

That phrase 'withouten any les' has an interesting function: it is no lie to say that Virgil asserts that Venus had made Aeneas invisible, but Chaucer evidently thinks it quite possible that Virgil is lying in making the assertion. Again, later, 'oure autour telleth us' (1139) that Cupid had taken on the form of Ascanius, 'but, as of that scripture,/Be as be may, I take of it no cure' (1144-45). The initial reverence for Virgil's paternal authority has been corroded by scepticism.

My other example of a questioning attitude towards a revered *auctour* is found in *The Clerk's Tale.* The Clerk begins with high praise of the 'worthy clerk' (IV 27) from whom he has taken his story of the patient Grisilde:

> Fraunceys Petrak, the lauriat poete,
> Highte this clerk, whos rethorike sweete
> Enlumyned al Ytaille of poetrie. (31-33)

But, just as in the legend of Dido, the narrator immediately proceeds to a declaration of independence from his *auctour:* Petrarch begins with a descriptive prologue,

> The which a long thyng were to devyse.
> And trewely, as to my juggement,
> Me thynketh it a thyng impertinent,
> Save that he wole conveyen his mateere. (52-55)

And he therefore omits it. And throughout the tale, the Clerk continues to apply his own *juggement* to his *auctour*'s work, and to protest vigorously against the cruelty of the tale, and especially against Walter's inexplicably harsh treatment of Grisilde.[13] In this case Chaucer has not even the excuse, as he has with Virgil, that the *auctour* is pagan and therefore open to doubt. *The Clerk's Tale* indeed provides a particularly interesting example of the parallel questioning of two kinds of authority — the authorial authority of Petrarch and the husbandly and paternal authority of Walter.

Chaucer, then, seems concerned to be, or at least to present himself as being, something other than a passive inheritor of material bequeathed by his literary forefathers. It is in keeping with this that he should sometimes mystify us about his sources. The most notorious case is that of *Troilus and Criseyde.* There indeed Chaucer claims to be no more than a translator (and that is the defence of *Troilus and Criseyde* proposed in *The Prologue to the Legend of Good Women* against the God of Love's objection to it as heresy); but his claim is to be translating 'out of Latyn' (II 14) from 'myn auctour called Lollius' (I 394), not, as was in fact the case, from the Italian of Boccaccio. There are perhaps two reasons why Chaucer should attempt to

---

13   For more detailed discussion, see my *Criticism and Medieval Poetry,* 2nd edn (London, 1972), chapter 4.

deceive us in this way. One is that the claim to have a Latin source adds to the work's appearance of historical authenticity; for Chaucer is really aiming to create the illusion of a classical past, while at the same time conveying a sense of the difficulty of any such reconstruction of antiquity. The other reason I wish to suggest — admittedly a more speculative one — is that the supposed Lollius, like other classical authors, belongs to a remote past and constitutes no threat to Chaucer's independence; whereas Boccaccio, a vernacular author of his own century, and one indeed from whom he may have learned of the very possibility of reconstructing the pagan past in a modern language, is dangerously close, a father rather than a remote ancestor. Nowhere in his work does Chaucer name Boccaccio, the *auctour* from whom he derives the three 'classical romances' that constitute his own highest claim to poetic dignity (*Troilus and Criseyde, The Knight's Tale, The Franklin's Tale*), and, of all his sources, the one who might best be called his literary father. The name of the father is too dangerous to be mentioned. The other two Italian writers who, with Boccaccio, enabled Chaucer to be a poet of major importance — it is no exaggeration to say that — were less dangerous because Chaucer derived less from them. Petrarch could be mentioned as a Latin author, as the source of *The Clerk's Tale,* but there his death is so strongly emphasized that it is as if Chaucer, Oedipus-like, had killed him himself — 'He is now deed and nayled in his cheste' (IV 29). The death is much to be regretted, and we shall all die in our turn, but how reassuring those nails are that keep Petrarch in his coffin! On the other hand, when Chaucer borrows from Petrarch's vernacular work, for Troilus's song in Book I of *Troilus and Criseyde,* his name must be suppressed and that of Lollius substituted. The influence of Dante on Chaucer is almost beyond assessment, but he was not the father of any single one of Chaucer's works (not even *The House of Fame*), and his name could therefore be mentioned several times without danger.

My discourse has been somewhat rambling, and it may be helpful if I now summarize my findings so far. First, Chaucer in his work nearly always presents the father unfavourably, either as absent or as cruel. Second, he does not allow that good qualities can be inherited by sons from their fathers, though he occasionally concedes that bad qualities can. Third, he is unwilling to concede authority to his major poetic ancestors, and especially to the most important of all — Boccaccio, who was of the right generation really to have been Chaucer's father, and who was truly his poetic father as a writer of vernacular narratives which aimed at an imaginative reconstruction of pagan antiquity. I now turn to a further aspect of my subject: the authority of Chaucer as author and father of his own work. Chaucer is the first secular writer in English to be known by name as the author of a body of work. (In the field of religious writing, Richard Rolle may perhaps have preceded him.) Chaucer indeed takes care to establish his name as an author, by including in his writings several lists of his own works (the first such lists by any English author) — one in *The Prologue to the Legend of Good Women,* another in *The Man of Law's Prologue,* and a third, paradoxically enough, in the *Retractions* to *The Canterbury Tales,* where the very words in which he expresses regret at having composed nearly all his poems also act as a final Chaucer checklist. Yet within his work Chaucer is most unwilling to assume paternal authority. It has often been noted how modest are the roles he plays as narrator throughout his career: first a mere dreamer, a channel through which fantasy or truth is conveyed, perpetually surprised and puzzled by the events of his dreams; then a clerkly but incompetent historian, who is constantly finding that his sources (on which he is totally dependent for his knowledge of love) fail to tell him crucial things such as his heroine's age, and whether she had any children, and whether or not she really gave her heart to Diomede; last the naive reporter of the Canterbury pilgrimage, whose own powers of poetic composition are confined to 'rym dogerel' (VII 925). And it surely cannot be quite by chance that two of his most important unfinished works break off just *before* some authoritative pronouncement of meaning is to be made: *The House of Fame,* as we have seen, at the very moment when the dreamer glimpses the 'man of greet auctorite', and *The Legend of Good Women,* almost at the end of the account of Hypermnestra, with the tantalizing line, 'This tale is seyd for this conclusioun —' (2723). Robinson comments that 'It is a little surprising that the legend should have been left incomplete, when the story is finished and a very few lines would have sufficed to make the application'.[14] It is not surprising when we take into account Chaucer's pervasive unwillingness to state definitively the meaning and purpose of his writing.

It is in *The Canterbury Tales* that that unwillingness, that rejection of fatherhood, reaches its culmination. There every tale but two (the two told by the pilgrim Chaucer, one in 'rym dogerel' and the other an exceptionally long 'Litel thyng in prose' [VII 937]) is attributed to someone other than Chaucer himself; and the mere fact of its attribution to a specific pilgrim-teller guarantees that Chaucer has no responsibility for it. The principle is stated explicitly in *The Miller's Prologue:* The 'cherles tale' (I 3169) that follows is included only because the drunken Miller insisted on thrusting himself forward to tell it, much to Chaucer's regret:

> And therefore every gentil wight I preye,
> For Goddes love, demeth nat that I seye
> Of yvel entente, but for I moot reherce
> Hir tales alle, be they bettre or werse,
> Or elles falsen som of my mateere. (I 3171-75)

---

14   F.N. Robinson, ed. cit., p. 854.

The responsibility for the selection of tales then becomes not Chaucer's but the reader's: 'Blameth nat me if that ye chese amys!' (3181). The same applies to the establishment of a tale's meaning. The teller may have a particular meaning in mind (though even that is not necessarily Chaucer's), and may direct us to it by some such remark as 'Therfore I rede yow this conseil take' (*Physician's Tale*, VI 285), or 'Taketh the moralite, goode men' (*Nun's Priest's Tale*, VII 3440) or 'Lordynges, by this ensample I yow preye,/ Beth war . . .' (*Manciple's Tale*, IX 309-10), but it is for us to decide whether that is what the tale *really* means. The pilgrim-Chaucer's second tale, the tale of Melibeus, is a prose allegory which for him is evidently meant to show how a ruler can gain good counsel and learn to be merciful. But when it is finished the Host's comments make it clear that for him it was about marriage and how wives ought to behave: he wishes his own virago of a wife could be as patient as the allegorical figure of Prudence in the tale. There is no-one to tell us authoritatively which is the right way to interpret the tale: Harry Bailly is not a very subtle literary critic, but then the tale is not a very coherent moral allegory, and the pilgrim-Chaucer is not a very intelligent tale-teller. We are left with a variety of possible interpretations, a variety summed up in a line which in differing forms is repeated several times in *The Canterbury Tales:* 'Diverse folk diversely they seyde' (I 3857); 'Diverse men diverse thynges seyden' (II 211); 'Diverse men diversely hym tolde' (VI 1469); 'Diverse folk diversely they demed' (V 202). Different people judge differently; and Chaucer's acknowledgment of that fact, his withdrawal of authority both from the tales and from their interpretations, amounts to what might be called a de-authorization of the whole work, or, in the terms used by some more recent theorists, of the conscious transformation of the *Tales* from a 'work' to a 'text'.

What I have in mind may be exemplified by two of the most penetrating essays of Roland Barthes, 'The Death of the Author' (1968) and 'From Work to Text' (1971). Here we may find the 'work' defined as writing governed and limited by the purposes of its author, while the 'text' is an anonymous, fatherless space in which an irreducible plurality of meanings play against each other. 'The author', writes Barthes, 'is reputed the father and owner of his work', while 'As for the Text, it reads without the inscription of the Father'. Again, 'The Author is thought to *nourish* the book, which is to say that he exists before it, thinks, suffers, lives for it, is in the same relation of antecedence to his work as a father to his child'. Thus it may be said that 'a text is not a line of words releasing a single "theological" meaning (the "message" of the Author-God) but a multi-dimensional space in which a variety of writings, none of them original, blend and clash'. To quote Barthes once more, 'It is not that the Author may not "come back" in the Text, in his text, but he then does so as a "guest". If he is a novelist, he is inscribed in the novel like one of his characters, figured in the carpet;

no longer privileged, paternal . . . '.[15] The phrases that I have been quoting offer an extraordinarily accurate description of what Chaucer would seem to have been consciously trying to do in *The Canterbury Tales:* to relinquish his own paternal authority, and to enter the text thereby produced, that 'tissue of quotations',[16] only as a guest. The Host indeed is someone else, and each tale is literally a 'quotation', set in quotation-marks, not as the message of the Author-God, but as the potentially prejudiced statement of one of a large various group of all-too-human pilgrims. We, looking back on Chaucer, thus confront an acute paradox. He is the first English poet to exist as an 'author', the first to be known by name as the father of a body of work; and yet throughout his career he seems to be striving towards the culmination achieved in *The Canterbury Tales,* the relinquishment of his own fatherhood, the transformation of his work into a text.

The final stage of my discussion is to suggest that that paradox was already a source of embarrassment to Chaucer's immediate successors, his fifteenth-century poetic sons. Chaucer was of course widely admired and praised by the poets of the following century precisely as what Dryden was later to call him, 'the Father of English Poetry'.[17] For them that meant above all that he was the first creator of a rhetorical high style which raised the language to a level at which real poetry could be written: as Lydgate put it in his *Troy Book:*

> Noble Galfride, poete of Breteyne,
> Amonge oure englisch þat made first to reyne
> Þe gold dewe-dropis of rethorik so fyne,
> Oure rude langage only tenlwmyne.[18]

That perception of Chaucer, to which many parallels could be quoted from fifteenth-century poets, naturally led to a wish to imitate his achievement, and it was there that the difficulty lay. It was seen clearly enough by Hoccleve, author of what is perhaps the earliest fifteenth-century eulogy of Chaucer:

> O mayster dere and fadir reuerent,
> My mayster Chaucer, flour of eloquence,
> Mirrour of fructuous entendement,
> O vniuersal fader in science,
> Allas, that thou thyn excellent prudence
> In thy bed mortal mightyst noȝt byqethe.[19]

15 Roland Barthes, *Image-Music-Text,* trans. Stephen Heath (London, 1977), pp. 160, 161, 145, 146, 161.
16 Ibid., p. 146.
17 Dryden, ed. cit., p. 280.
18 Ed. H. Bergen, vol. I, EETS ES 97 (London, 1906), II 4697-700.
19 *The Regement of Princes,* 11. 1961–66, in *Selections from Hoccleve,* ed. M. C. Seymour (Oxford, 1981).

In the following stanza of *The Regement of Princes* Hoccleve refers to
Chaucer's 'hye vertu'; the impossibility of the father's bequeathing his virtue
to the son is undoubtedly a theme borrowed by Hoccleve from one of the
passages in Chaucer quoted above.[20] The son wishes to inherit the authority
of a father who has denied that any such inheritance is possible, and has in any
case denied his own fatherhood. Chaucer seemed already to have done everything: he was truly a 'universal father', whose achievement was coextensive
with the whole range of possibilities for poetry in English; what territory,
what 'imaginative space' (to use Harold Bloom's formulation),[21] did this
leave for would-be sons? As late as the 1470s, just this point was being made
in the anonymous *Book of Curtesye* about Chaucer, the 'fader and founder
of ornate eloquence', and Gower, the 'auncyent fader of memorye', now
seen as joint originators of the English poetic tradition:

> Loo my childe / these faders auncynte
> Repen the feldes fresshe of fulsomnes
> The flours fresh they gadred vp & hente
> Of siluer langage / the grete riches.
> Who wil it haue my lityl childe doutles
> Muste of hem begge / ther is no more to saye
> For of oure tunge / they were both lok & kaye.[22]

And even this acknowledgment of indebtedness could not be made without
incurring a further debt, for the image of precursors as reapers who have
already gathered the harvest of poetry is itself borrowed from Chaucer's
Prologue to the Legend of Good Women.[23]

A consequence of this attitude towards Chaucer seems to have been a
widespread anxiety among his poetic descendants about the impossibility
of the task they were undertaking. In many passages scattered throughout
his voluminous works, Chaucer's most prominent disciple, John Lydgate,
expresses his sense of inferiority as a mere star beside the sun, 'compared
ageyn the bemys briht / Off this poete'.[24] He sees himself and other descendants of Chaucer as mere imitators, who cannot hope to match their
model:

> Whan we wolde his stile counterfet,
> We may al day oure colour grynde & bete,

---

20 Henry Scogan also recalls this theme from Chaucer's *Gentilesse* in his *Moral
    Balade*, ed. W.W. Skeat, *Chaucerian and Other Pieces* (Oxford, 1897), 11. 65-104.
21 Op. cit., p. 3.
22 *Caxton's Book of Curtesye*, ed. F.J. Furnivall, EETS ES 3 (London, 1868),
    11. 330, 324, 400-06.
23 F 73-77.
24 *Lydgate's Fall of Princes*, ed. H. Bergen, Part I (Washington, 1923), II 999-1000.

Tempre our aʒour and vermyloun:
But al I holde but presumpcioun –
It folweþ nat, þerfore I lette be.[25]

That is from Lydgate's *Troy Book;* earlier, using the same terminology of 'counterfeiting' Chaucer's style, he had written in *The Flour of Curtesye:*

We may assaye for to counterfete
His gaye style, but it wil not be.[26]

A less well-known disciple of Chaucer is John Walton, composer of a verse translation of Boethius, in the preface to which he expresses a similar anxiety:

To chaucer þat is floure of rethoryk
In englisshe tong & excellent poete
This wot I wel no þing may I do lyk
Þogh so þat I of makynge entyrmete.[27]

There is a passage in one of Petrarch's letters in which he takes up this characteristically Renaissance issue of stylistic imitation, and distinguishes between two kinds of similarity:

He who imitates must have a care that what he writes be similar, not identical, and that the similarity should not be of that kind that exists between a portrait and a sitter, where the artist earns the more praise the greater the likeness, but rather of the kind that obtains between a son and his father . . . We should therefore make use of another man's inner quality and tone, but avoid his words. For the one kind of similarity is hidden and the other protrudes; the one creates poets, and the other apes.[28]

Lydgate's use of the language of painting in the lines quoted above from the *Troy Book* strongly suggests that for him the ideal goal of Chaucerian imitation was identicality, literal counterfeiting. He may have seen Chaucer as father, but he did not really want to be his son; he simply wanted to be Chaucer. It is perhaps significant that in Lydgate's addition to *The Canterbury Tales, The Siege of Thebes,* when he describes himself as meeting the Canterbury pilgrims, there is no mention of Chaucer among them. It is as if Lydgate, in his wishes at least, has *become* Chaucer; and the nearer *The*

---

25 *Troy Book*, ed. cit., II 4715-19.
26 *Chaucerian and Other Pieces*, 11. 239-40.
27 Ed. Eleanor P. Hammond, *English Verse between Chaucer and Surrey* (Durham, N. C., 1927), p. 42; II. 33-36.
28 *Le familiari* XXIII 19, 78-94, as cited by E.H. Gombrich, *Norm and Form* (London, 1966), p. 122.

Siege of Thebes gets to *The Knight's Tale*, of which it is a kind of backward continuation, the more of Chaucer's actual words Lydgate uses.[29]

In a way, it might have been easier for Chaucer's poetic descendants to follow him if he had been more willing to play the role of father that they thrust upon him. Lydgate in particular, when he is striving hardest to be Chaucerian, tends to impose on his work a didacticism — 'the "message" of the Author-God' — very different from Chaucer's indeterminacy of ultimate meaning. D.H. Lawrence wrote in a letter to Edward Garnett, 'We have to hate our immediate predecessors, to get free from their authority'.[30] Who could possibly have hated the Chaucer who appears only as a guest in his own work, the Chaucer rightly described by Lydgate as 'gronde of wel-seying'? —

> Hym liste nat pinche nor gruche at every blot,
> Nor meue hym silf to parturbe his reste
> (I haue herde telle), but seide alweie the best,
> Suffring goodly of his gentilnes
> Ful many þing enbracid with rudnes.[31]

A Chaucer who had insisted more sternly on his parental authority might have provoked a healthy rebelliousness in his sons. Whatever the reason, it was not until nearly a century after his death that Chaucer's descendents were able to free themselves from the gentle bond of their universal father, his 'repressive tolerance'. Then John Skelton was able to make radically new use of the Chaucerian inheritance, for example by his comparative assessment of Chaucer and of Lydgate in *Philip Sparrow*, and later by suggesting in *The Garland of Laurel* that the true purpose of the English poetic tradition that sprang from Chaucer was that it should culminate in the crowning with laurel of John Skelton. And in Scotland Robert Henryson, even while praising 'worthie Chaucer glorious', dared to ask, 'Quha wait gif all that Chauceir wrait was trew?',[32] and proceeded to write an alternative ending to *Troilus and Criseyde;* and a little later Gavin Douglas was to judge, boldly but justly, that Chaucer 'standis beneth Virgill in gre' and that his legend of Dido quite misrepresents the account given by that 'prynce of poetis' in the *Aeneid.*[33] Skelton, Henryson and Douglas were truly the sons of Chaucer in daring to be themselves, to adopt a sceptical independence of judgment that is genuinely Chaucerian but that could not be passively inherited from father Chaucer.

---

29 For a more detailed study of Lydgate's attitude to Chaucer in *The Siege of Thebes*, see my article, 'Lydgate's Canterbury Tale: *The Siege of Thebes* and Fifteenth-Century Chaucerianism', forthcoming in *The Fifteenth Century: Recent Essays*, ed. R.F. Yeager.

30 *The Letters of D.H. Lawrence*, vol. I, ed. James T. Boulton (Cambridge, 1979).

31 *Troy Book*, ed. cit., vol. III, EETS ES 106 (London, 1910), V 3519-26.

32 Henryson, ed. cit., *The Testament of Cresseid*, 11. 41, 64.

33 *The Proloug of the First Buke of Eneados*, 11. 407, 418, in *Virgil's Aeneid*, ed. David F.C. Coldwell, vol. II (Edinburgh, 1957).

KING LEAR AND VOLPONE

JOHN NORTON-SMITH

In the old days at the college of the Impenitent Magdalen at Oxford, there were few of the strict demarcations of tutorial duty which we find so prevalent nowadays. Jack Bennett, Emrys Jones and myself regularly taught 'periods' of literature and language which, according to modern lights, might be thought to lie outside one's sphere of specialization. In common with Jack Bennett, I often found myself teaching Shakespeare and the seventeenth century as a natural continuation of earlier, medieval interests. It never occurred to us that any strict boundary should be seen to separate great movements of cultural activity. The doctrine had been preached earlier by another tutor of the college, C. S. Lewis. It seemed only natural that he should have been elected the founding Professor of the Chair of Medieval and Renaissance English Literature at Cambridge ('Cambridge' alone seemed the strange part of it), and that he (in turn) should have been succeeded by Jack Bennett. So, lest it should be imagined that the proper subjects of the J.A.W. Bennett Memorial Lectures at Perugia should concern themselves exclusively with the great Ages of Faith, I stand before you (however imperfectly) as an image or shadow of the Renaissance concerns and interests of those far-off Oxford days.

The argument of this lecture is simple – some of you may be tempted to say 'absurdly' simple – namely, that the dramatic imaginations, the shaping poetic powers of Shakespeare and Ben Jonson, are, *au fond*, utterly distinct. Shakespeare's dramatic imagination is to be characterized by its scenic power, its vitality at imagining physical and symbolic arrangements which take their dramatic shape from pre-verbal or even non-verbal material. This scenic capacity has been admirably defined, described and analysized by Emrys Jones in his two great books, *Scenic Form in Shakespeare* and *The Origins of Shakespeare*. Ben Jonson's dramatic invention, on the other hand, is abstract, verbal and rhetorical. Of the pre-verbal or non-verbal he has little appreciation. If one were to draw an analogy with the Roman drama which both poets read and sometimes imitated, we should say that Shakespeare's scenic imagination worked more like that of Plautus whilst Jonson's *inventio* more resembled that of Terence.

In this lecture, the yoking together of Shakespeare's great, mature tragedy, *King Lear* and Ben Jonson's most polished satiric comedy, *Volpone,* must seem at first sight *bizarre* — or perhaps a pedantic *marriage de convenance* contrived to illustrate the distinctness of the two dramatic imaginations. But what I want to argue this morning is not quite as quaint or school-masterly as may be thought at first sight. My thesis will be that each play contains a vivid double scene, a scene characteristic of Shakespeare's dramatic invention, but not characteristic of Ben Jonson. Further, that Jonson consciously borrowed that double scene from Shakespeare's *King Lear* and grafted it into the verbal and rhetorical dramatic formulation of his own play, *Volpone*. Jonson's debt to Shakespeare's imagination has never been seen to have been acknowledged in this pragmatic way, though, of course, Jonson's laudatory poem addressed to Shakespeare's genius (printed in the First Folio) acknowledges Shakespeare's dramatic powers in a conventional formal expression. My argument stands or falls according to the priority of the writing of the texts of the plays and I regret that I must begin a little dryly with some account of the dating of the two plays.

Ben Jonson's great modern editors, Herford and Simpson, wisely instruct us to ignore the putative 1605 date on the title-page of the 1607 Quarto. Straightforward internal references indicate that the play was written almost certainly during the first few months of 1606. *Volpone's* first recorded stage production was by the King's Men at the Globe sometime before 24 March, 1606. These dates associate the composition and stage production of *Volpone* with the period when Shakespeare had finished the writing of *King Lear*. The earliest date advanced for the writing of *Lear* has been March, 1603, but Professor Kenneth Muir more sensibly suggests the winter of 1604—5 — and this dating has been generally accepted. An entry in the Stationer's Register for 1606 notes that *Lear* 'was played before the King's Majesty at Whitehall, St. Stephen's Night'. That is, it was played on Boxing Day, the 26 December by the same company though not at the same venue. This evidence suggests that *Volpone* may have been performed earlier than *Lear* but that Shakespeare's play had been composed first by at least a twelve month. The possibility is, then, that Jonson could have seen *Lear* in written copy well before his own work on *Volpone* began in January-February of 1606. That is the generally accepted explanation and I think it squares with the aesthetic, internal, evidence which I will put before you in this lecture. I will not rehearse the scenic structure of *Lear,* since this has already been done by Emrys Jones in his *Scenic Form in Shakespeare.* But a detailed account of Ben Jonson's scenic structure in *Volpone* is needed, and there I begin.

There is no single model for Jonson's dramatic conception for *Volpone,* although most modern criticism tries to link the play with one predominant tradition — the current favourite, I must tell you, is the Aristophanic 'Old Comedy' — which it is not in the least like, even given Renaissance distortions of the text and comic purpose of Aristophanes. Jonson, unlike most of his modern critics, had enough Greek to have grasped that. Some strands of the play are non-dramatic, descending mainly from Roman satire, some strands borrowed from Plautine and Terentian comedy, some strands taken from the most widely disseminated inventions of Italian popular comedy. All of these traits had already passed into English comedy before Shakespeare, but Jonson's imaginative contribution was the *concentration* of these elements: mainly by the sheer velocity of pace in constructing a Terentian plot generated by a series of what Roman dramatists called *involutiones*, 'complications' which depend on a single range of psychological motivation: material self-interest pursued without a trace of humanity or allowance for human frailty, together with an identifiable force of constant authorial satiric exposure conducted largely through including passages taken from Horace, Juvenal and the Greek satiric writer, Lucian. A moderately educated Elizabethan would have been familiar with the Roman material, a well-educated Elizabethan could probably have identified the Lucian, since Latin translations (in Greek and Latin facing texts) had been appearing on the continent from the 1580s.

The non-dramatic material, Horace, Juvenal, Lucian and Petronius, was identified years ago by Herford and Simpson, and in this play centres on the Roman criticism of legacy-hunting or *captatio*. The long-established view that this was a public institution lacking to England in the Renaissance is only partially true. *Captatio* had passed into Roman drama as a long reference in Plautus's *Miles Gloriosus* (III.i. 705ff.) — a school curriculum text and popular with English dramatists. It had passed into Italian popular comedy, most obviously in *Il Vecchio Avaro*, also known to English writers. Further, there is an obvious parallel in the popular early sixteenth-century comedy *Il Negromante* where we find a bustling character, *Astrologo*, who is a mountebank, a fortune-hunting archdeceiver, whose purpose in the plot is to generate the complex operation of a series of mounting complications or *involutiones:* legacies are part of his trade of deception. Thus, Plautine comedy knows of this area of human weakness and so does the Italian popular comedy of the sixteenth century.

Although the Roman system of the appointment of heirs was not a feature of the English social landscape, the disinheriting of heirs and substitution of legatees nominated by lawyers was a feature of English sixteenth-century life. It is mentioned in *Volpone* (*en passant*), and forms many passages in the satiric verse of Hall, Marston and Donne. The tradition of disinheritance extends well into the nineteenth century, as a famous passage which ends Cowper's *Task* book III attests — not to mention the stock-in-trade of Ivy Compton-Burnett or P.G. Wodehouse. Thus, the English audience would have had ample experience in literature and in reality of the basic situation of Jonson's comedy. The author sets his play in Venice, one of the great mercantile republics of the western world, thereby exploiting all the audience's shared knowledge of 'liquid capital' and the life of anxious bargaining of Shakespeare's *Merchant of Venice* which had seen the stage since 1598. Venice, both remote and familiar, makes an ideal blend of *milieux* for comedy and satire. Unlike Shakespeare, who provided a perfect foil for Venice's daylight bustle of 'getting and spending' in the closing and reconciling night-piece of the settled County wealth of Belmont, Jonson provides the main-plot of *Volpone* (the hectic, climactic, crescendo of deceptions) with a series of parallel and contrasting 'interlude' scenes which centre on the English observers, Sir Politic and Lady Would-Be and the nearly innocent Peregrine, a gentleman traveller on the English continental 'grand tour'.

The second element has been called a 'double plot', but however anxious the author may be to attempt to include the characters of these scenes in the main plot, the Sir Politic Would-Be scenes are not properly integrated with the main, climactic, crescendoing sequences of *involutiones*. The only point of intercalated relation with the main plot occurs in the person of Lady Politic Would-Be, who figures as a preseduction curtain-raiser for Volpone's sexual desire for Celia. Thus, the whole of Act III, scene iv, although preparing the way for Volpone's later sexual fantasies and fatal passion, consists of a set-piece satire on Ladies of Learning. Lady Politic is an early English Blue-stocking, a Lady Mary Wortley-Montague before her time. Her physical appearance and some of her accidental comments stimulate Volpone to a fever-pitch of physical cupidity but her incessant, learned chatter talk the poor old pedophile into the ground. She literally detumifies him before our eyes. In the end, he will do anything to be rid of her: all passion not so much spent as 'annoyed away'. In many of the eighteenth-century stage versions where the interlude scenes have been totally cut, this scene with Lady Politic was retained, out of respect for the sheer comic brilliance of the writing — for the sharp exposure of a prototype of a *femme savante*.

Sir Politic Would-Be is a parody of wise, statesmanlike English Grandee — the stage impersonation is reminiscent of an actual English traveller, Sir Anthony Shirley. What Jonson invents is a chatterbox, a 'Pol', a 'polly-parrot', endlessly caught-up in stratagems of his own devising: in short, a cautious, oversubtle fool. He is, ostensibly, an anti-type of Volpone, parallels abound. His final exposure, trapped within a gigantic tortoise-shell, disguised as the animal itself, slowly crawling off-stage only to be opened and prized out, the object of ridicule, of course, foreshadows the 'uncasing' of Volpone in the final scene, 'the mortifying of a fox'. Professor Donaldson has shown that the visual 'emblem' Jonson had in mind for this scene was that used in Wilson's *Three Ladies of London* (a play of 1594) where the symbol of 'Policy', 'Pol', was a tortoise. Thus, Sir Politic is found out inside the animal appropriate to his idea of himself. Yet in terms of construction, the scene is not an integral part of the action. It represents a symbolic parallel, and nothing more. The scene ought to be amusing, but even the seventeenth-century found it feeble. It is not so much unimaginative in its own right, as much as it is left high-and-dry by the galloping, cresting intensity of the main-plot. The two scenic rhythms are incompatible. At this late stage of the dramatic development of the complication of the plot, the last interlude type scene comes as an anti-climax, an unwelcome digression which diverts the audience's attention away from the monomanatic duping, counter-duping and ferocious intensity of the struggle for self-survival of the principal action.

The central plot and main sequence of scenes derives its dramatic coherence and force from the stage-mechanics of Plautine and Terentian Roman comedy. It is a simple, linear, additive structure built out of a montage of 'complications', what the Romans called *involutio*. The inevitable end of the play comes with a *devolutio*, an untying of the action in which reversal, recognition scene and denouement are almost simultaneous. Jonson's sequence of comic action is further based on a rapid compounding of 'deceptions'. The Romans called such a sequence in comedy *frustrationes*, duping-scenes. The technical sense is not recorded in Latin dictionaries, but Plautus uses the noun in this sense in Act V, scene i of the *Mostellaria*, 'The Haunted House': *Optimas frustrationes dederis in comoediis*. ('You'll have furnished them with the best duping-scenes on the comic stage) (1150). Now, this famous play of Plautus not only provided an excellent model for a parasite's paroxysm of *frustrationes* or crescendo of duping-scenes. From Act III onwards in the *Mostellaria*, Tranio the parasite is forced to engage on a breath-taking series of deceitful inventions, of multiple deceptions, intrigues and lies: each invention more dazzling and more precariously close to being uncovered than the last. Like Mosca, he confesses to the audience that he is nearly at the end of power of invention — he is almost doomed to exposure. Where will his next idea come from?

In *Volpone*, like the *Mostellaria*, the playwright constructs a contradictory aesthetic morality whereby the audience wishes both 'truth' and the lying 'fictions' to survive each other. There is considerable moral and aesthetic pleasure created in delaying for as long as possible the *devolutio*, or exposure of the sequence of duping-scenes. The underlying moral impulse is the primitive desire for 'reality-as-it-is' to eventually triumph over deception. Thus, in *Volpone*, the deceiving legacy-hunters are duped by Volpone as assisted by the arch-villain Mosca. This sequence hastens on until Act III when Mosca, recognizing his own supremacy of self-interest, begins to dupe Volpone as well. The audience's fascination with this fantastic rodomontage of deceit, cruelty, and naked predatory greed lies in an instinctive sympathy for 'constructions', its association of the inventions of the characters, the fictions of the deceivers with the 'invention', the total invention, of the artistic mind, the activity of the playwright; — and with the dangerous delight in seeing virtuous truth tested and almost overwhelmed by the forces of immorality. Instinctively, we wish for both aesthetic and moral triumph. If we seldom or never get it in 'real life', drama provides the 'ought-to-be'.

Although the playwright in his prologue to the play insists upon the piece's classical purity, its scrupulous avoidance of the irrelevancies, and loosenesses and vulgarities of the common Elizabethan and Jacobean stage amusements, the author is only partially to be believed. Professor Donaldson has shown in his article in *Essays in Criticism* (Volume 21, 1971) that the neo-humanist 'rules' of time and place are observed but the anarchic energy of the playwright's invention derives from his duping his audience into believing that he does not break the rules. Like Goethe, in the Prologue to *Faust*, Jonson takes a Mosca-like delight in producing the very extraneous vulgar elements which he pretends to castigate in his contemporary stage-authors. The artistic pleasure lies in knowing that the audience will probably not get the joke. Jonson's modern critics take the bait every time. Elaborate parallels, analogues and symbolic usages are invented for every detail of the Sir Politic Would-Be scenes. 'It is all intensely sad', as the modern poet puts it — for part of the Jonsonian invention lies in a kind of insulting superiority over his audience's mentality: the poet's pride of inventive place in the vulgar theatre of life. Hence, the hectic concentration of dupings, cross-dupings and counter-dupings is interrupted and eased in intensity by the trivializing interlude scenes of English foolishness. So, too, the delightful songs, often skilled adaptations of More or Catullus. There is no room for innocent beauty or gracious humanity in Volpone's Venice. Instead, the author provides the easeful vistas, those delightful irrelevancies which the contemporary audience so much enjoyed.

The analogue for this relation of alternative moments of pleasure to the intense sequences of trickery and deception is early established in Volpone's deformed household's 'performance' in Act I, scene ii of the 'interlude' of the Transformation of the Soul according to Pythagoras. It is given out as Mosca's invention, but is, of course, Ben Jonson's and is not as innocent as we may imagine. The interlude is followed by a song, partially a translation of phrases from More's *Encomium Moriae* in praise of folly. Pythagoras's theory of the transmigration of the soul was known popularly as 'the Fool's Doctrine' and was especially offensive to conscientious Christians. We know this from the famous imprisoning scene of Malvolio in Shakespeare's *Twelfth Night*. The Pythagorean theory degrades the soul into a mechanical, bestial force and it amuses Volpone who can take no offence since his whole *modus vivendi* is characterized by bestiality and a morbid fascination in degrading those who surround him. His closest associates in his household are creatures of potential derision: a dwarf, an eunuch, an hermaphrodite, a parasite. It is they who sing the praises of Fools. But you will notice it is not Erasmus's Praise of Folly, not wise-folly in the tradition of St. Paul or Shakespeare, it is the cunning of those who survive by the appearance of being beneath notice and who by their ludicrousness amuse and flatter the superior 'wisdom' of their predatory masters. Scenes i and ii of Act I define the essential halves of Jonson's Venetian society; those who are successful in the exercise of a cruel and rapacious reason, and those who are their habitual victims. If you cannot bear to be one or the other, it is best to be accounted a mere fool, and so escape being devoured, 'Free from care or sorrow-taking', as the song puts it. In an after-thought the song also asserts 'And he speaks truth, free from slaughter' — but there is precious little concern for truth in this degraded and revolting company.

As you will have gathered from these remarks, the play abounds in animal references and imagery. The main moral concern is that embodied in the late antique myth of Comus, well-known to the Renaissance. When human reason is contaminated by the material concerns of the appetites, when the mind is turned to a concern for sensual gratification and descends to appetitive self-consumation, the face is degraded into an animal equivalent of its ruling passion. Volpone, a fox; Mosca, a fly; Corvino, a crow; Corbaccio, a great raven; Voltore, a Vulture. The tradition was wide-spread in classical antiquity. There are references in Aristotle, in Theophrastus's *Characters*, in Plautus's comedies, in the Aesopic writings in Greek and in Phaedrus's *Fables* in Latin. The mentally-destructive exercise of self-interest in these characters is nowhere illuminated by a glimmer of human sensitivity or ordinary sympathy. There are no recognized bonds of human love or affection. The natural victims of the hunt for wealth and power are members of families — the eldest son of Corbaccio whom the father is willing to disinherit; and Celia, the very young wife of Corvino, whom the husband is willing to loan to Volpone to be dishonoured — if only because he has been assured that Volpone is impotent. Human ties of affection and personal dignity have no definable existence in this familiar arrangement.

If Jonson's grasp of the plot-mechanics of Roman comedy or popular Italian comedy is strong and secure, his originality in inventing scenic moments and sequences must be accounted weak in comparison with Shakespeare. Jonson's realization of scenes is based largely on the language and rhetoric appropriate to the advancement of action through conversation and dialogue, embellished from time to time by set-pieces of a satirical nature or displays of psychological fantasy. Vividness of place, memorableness of non-verbal occasions or larger symbolic arrangements of ideas, characters and stage space do not come naturally to Jonson's mind. For all of Jonson's classical education, Greek and Latin dramatic writings seem to have left very little impression on him in terms of scenic invention. The complex insights into Senecan scenic organisation and imagery of the order of Shakespeare's reworking of the *Troades*, as reflected in *King John,* seem not to have been a part of Ben Jonson's creative power. Occasionally he attempts a broad and striking *mise-en-scène,* usually at the very beginning of a dramatic sequence but the scene quickly develops into a purely verbal exposition of moral attitudes and character exposé.

For example, Act I, scene i opens in Volpone's bedchamber which is being prepared by Mosca for the morning *levée* or *salutatio* of his patron. From the opening speeches and imagery it is easy to reconstruct the visual scene: Volpone lying in his great state bed gazes at two similar areas which are curtained. Mosca draws the curtains on the window allowing in the sunlight; then, he draws the curtains on the alcove containing Volpone's treasure, money and gold-plate. The light which gleams from the treasure must seem to be more intensely bright than the natural sunlight. In antiphonic speeches between Mosca and Volpone the natural light of day is compared unfavourably with the unnatural luminosity of gold. A simple moral contrast is being made. Visually, at least, the scene has a memorable physical and moral setting. For the rest of the play, the physical sense of space, stage articulation and mimetic forms of scenes tend to evaporate. The close plotting of the play through dialogue and speeches prevails as its dominant dramatic texture. Scenic structure in the Shakespearean sense is thrust towards the margins, towards the 'interlude' scenes with their broad symbolic parallelism. The mountebank's scene (Act II, scenes ii and iii) amounts to an enormous rhetorical prose pomp: an inflated display of sophistic logic and egocentricity, a comic opera version of continental contemporary customs — a fleshing out of John Florio's English account of mountebankery. It has very little to do with the progress of the action. Similarly, the later tortoise scene (Act V, scene iv) amounts to a symbolic digression which mechanically eliminates the Would-Bes from the main action and denouement.

Yet one scene, at least, has struck nearly all the critics and commentators of the play as 'the most remarkable' in the whole play. That is, Act III, scene i, Mosca's soliloquy, his discourse on the discovery of his own nature as supremo of parasites. It is easy to see why the scene should stand out from the rest of the play. For one thing, it is the only extended soliloquy in the piece; and it is the only exposé of character which indulges in introspective analysis. But Mosca's exultation in vice, his open pleasure taken in contemplating the future exercise of villany should not be separated from the very next scene which is an extension of his new confidence of personality. Immediately Mosca has determined on unlimited self-expression of evil, he chances on the innocent Bonario, deceives him into thinking he is 'honest', then cruelly reveals Bonario's father's completed design of dis-inheriting him, of making him a bastard. As we later learn, the object of this confession is not moral honesty. Mosca hopes that Bonario will kill his own father, thereby making Volpone's claim to Corvino's legacy certain. Beyond this design, the critics of the play are not slow to point out, lurk any number of further sinister possibilities which may arise from Bonario's being hidden in Volpone's house, possibly the injuring of Volpone, or his murder. Various wills, including a blank will, are within the calculating parasite's reach.

The gulling of Bonario is a strongly written scene and naturally engages our attention, for, unlike the legacy-hunters, Bonario (as his name suggests) engages our moral sympathy and Mosca's deceiving of him should outrage the audience's sensibility. Nevertheless, I think the scenic energy of these two related dramatic moments derives from Jonson's conscious modelling of the Mosca soliloquy and deception scene on a double scene which Shakespeare had recently written the winter before Jonson had begun his 'five weeks' labour' on *Volpone*. I mean Act I, scene ii of *King Lear*. Shakespeare's scene is divided into two major units: the soliloquy of Edmund, wherein he exults in his own evil, 'natural' disposition. Mosca's speech is in recognition of parasites, Edmund's on the universal supremacy of bastards. Edmund's declamatory soliloquy is immediately followed by his cruel gulling of his father and his own brother, effectively putting into operation his intention of bastardizing Edgar and causing him to be disinherited.

Both Edmund's and Mosca's speeches are characterized by imagery of swelling, enlargement and a physical sensation of growing, of increasing in confidence and self-love. Shakespeare's soliloquy is better constructed in that the justification for recognition of Edmund's concept of 'Nature' precedes the declaration of physical sensation. Shakespeare's imagery of growing is not generically related to animal sensation (as in Jonson). It is purposely left initially abstract and then connected directly to a physical gesture of Edmund: his gradual rising from a sitting position to full erection. Heilman and other critics are right here in seeing an explicit sexual gesture: an enactment of the rebellious principle of the Illegitimate's right to whatever he wants, his new moral law of entitlement: rude natural instinct divorced from any moral limitations. What is 'base' rises to new 'heights'. There is something disturbingly obscene in Edmund's manifesto:

> Why brand they vs
> With Base? with basenes Ba[s]tardie? Base, Base?
> Who in the lusty stealth of Nature, take
> More composition, and fierce qualitie,
> Then doth within a dull stale tyred bed
> Goe to th'creating a whole tribe of Fops
> Got 'tweene a sleep and wake? Well then,
> Legitimate Edgar, I must haue your land,
> Our Fathers loue, is to the bastard Edmund
> As to th'legitimate: fine word: legitimate:
> Well, my legitimate, if this Letter speed,
> And my inuention thriue, Edmund the base

> Shall to' th'Legitimate: I grow, I prosper:
> Now, Gods, stand vp for Bastards!

The thriving of invention, the physical sensation of prospering and growing, has a natural climactic force, culminating in the physical gesture, the enactment of erection. Jonson's scene reverses the physical and verbal activity. Mosca begins with his declaration of physical sensation and afterwards falls to the exultation of his tribe. There is no correlation of word-imagery and stage action. But Mosca's scene still owes much of its power to Shakespeare's better invention:

> I fear I shall begin to grow in love
> With my dear self, and my most prosp'rous parts,
> They do spring and burgeon, I can feel
> A whimsie in my blood: (I know not how),
> Success hath made we wanton. I could skip
> Out of my skin, now, like as subtle snake,
> I am so limber!

The delicate, sycophantic, nimble energy of this passage owes a great deal to Jonson's verbal resourcefulness. The use of nouns and verbs associated with erotic activity ('parts', 'burgeon', 'wanton', 'limber') though here severely qualified by another set of concerns, go some way to creating in the audience's mind an inclination to accept that 'self-love' here is not only *amour propre* but in some sense auto-eroticism. Words obviously used in figurative application still remain very close to their primary, concrete origins, *e.g.*, 'prosp'rous parts', 'whimsie', 'skip out of my skin'. The noun 'whimsie' does not mean the *Oxford English Dictionary*'s 'whim', 'a fantasy' (so understood by all editors) but 'dizziness', the physical sensation of vertigo in the animal spirits generated by the blood. 'Whimsie' was a symptom of states of high erotic excitement. Compare Troilus's speech as he waits for a meeting with Cressid in Shakspeare (Act III, scene ii):

> I am giddy; expectation whirles me round,
> Th'imaginary relish is so sweete,
> That it inchants my sence . . .

Mosca, not in love with any one outside himself does not lose command of his sense of understanding. His reason is only ignorant of 'how' the sensation has come about. Had he ever been truly in love, his reason would have understood that.

There are other compelling reasons for accepting Jonson's reliance on Shakespeare's scenic imagination. Although Mosca's soliloquy marks the emergence of Mosca the prime duper, the signal moment when he seizes the initiative from his master, it is not aesthetically necessary to the development of Mosca's character or the specific direction of the plot. We already know he is capable of managing Volpone, not only because of his superior guile and cunning, but because we know Volpone has one weakness: sexual appetite. But Shakespeare, on the other hand, requires aesthetically that we early discover the true 'nature' of Edmund – and that concept of Nature can only be revealed in a soliloquy when no other living person can discover the hidden source of his evil and its almost carnal enjoyment of its recognition of self-hood. The sub-plot of *Lear* develops *ab initio* out of the main-plot – its natural family progenitor is Edmund. The main-plot and the sub-plot bifurcate along two parallel paths: the old being made to relinquish their vital power, to undergo deprivation and enfeeblement; the calculating young to spring and blossom in the acquisition of power. The one to be made more human, more feeling by the tragic action of decline and deprivation; the other to be dehumanized by the acquisition of the power which is being resigned to them.

Did Jonson simply stumble across the Edmund double scene of *Lear*, grasp its dramatic potential and just appropriate it for his own play, or was there some other connection which drew him to it? I think there is another broad resemblance between Shakespeare's *Lear* and Jonson's *Volpone* which attracted Ben Jonson's attention. Emrys Jones, commenting on the overall structure of *King Lear*, remarks on the 'static nature' of much of the play's construction. He remarks:

> [Lear] is as a whole less exciting, certainly less *entertaining*, than *Hamlet* or *Othello:* it has less than either of the element of melodrama. One might put it another way by saying that *Lear* is more exacting, more painful and exhausting to experience; it gives less immediate pleasure. And this can in part be explained in terms of structure; for despite its scenes of episodic heightening, the over-all action lacks, or appears to lack, a clear *terminus ad quem* – we are given nothing specific to *wait for.* Nothing, that is, except perhaps something which cannot be brought about by any foreseeable move in the plot: the death of the old man who is the hero. In his first speech Lear declares that
>
>   'tis our fast intent
> To shake all cares and burdens from our age,
> Conferring them on younger strengths, while we
> Unburden'd crawl toward death.
>
> And 'crawl toward death' is, in a sense, what the play does. Its movement of sinking spasmodically into final lethargy and dissolution is what can make it seem, to reader and playgoer, so powerfully oppressive, powerful, it goes without saying, but also laying a burdensome weight on the feelings.
>
> (*Scenic Form in Shakespeare*, p. 156)

The mainspring of Jonson's comedy is the superabundant, 'entertaining' energy derived from an old man who only pretends that he is dying. He has everything to *wait for.* The duped ones are going to be the friends who will finally have nothing to wait for — not only no will made in their favour, but little of their own resources for these have been made over to an old man who has no intention of dying. Jonson must have seen the ironic parallel between *Lear* (where there is a genuine deprivation of power accompanied by the slow relinquishment of life and reason for living) and *Volpone* where pretended dying generates an opposite, satiric rhythm of criminal expectation.

But however clever of Jonson to see what he could gain by imitating Shakespeare's scenic invention, his talent remains almost exclusively verbal — scenic imaginings of a vivid and original energy are characteristic of Shakespeare's dramatic genius. In *Volpone* we have a brilliant, if flawed, example of a university-trained dramatist's blending together of Roman, Italian, and English comic topoi and elements. In its innermost heart it is a deeply satirizing talent, playful and somewhat cruel. The repulsive poetic justice which concludes the play shows that the ranging minds of Mosca and Jonson are not far from each other's ability to imagine themselves. As the dramatist and friend John Fletcher noticed in 1607:

> Faith, for thy FOXES sake, forgive then those
> Who are not worthy to be friends, nor foes.
> Or, for their owne braue sake, let them bee still
> Fooles at thy mercy, and like what they will.

INDEX

Weitere Bände dieser Reihe: